Fighting the Flying Circus

Captain Edward V. Rickenbacker

𝕿𝖍𝖊 𝕷𝖆𝖐𝖊𝖘𝖎𝖉𝖊 𝕮𝖑𝖆𝖘𝖘𝖎𝖈𝖘

FIGHTING THE FLYING CIRCUS

By
Capt. Edward V. Rickenbacker
Commanding Officer 94th Pursuit Squadron
U.S. Air Service

With a Foreword by
Laurence La Tourette Driggs

EDITED BY
W. DAVID LEWIS

𝕿𝖍𝖊 𝕷𝖆𝖐𝖊𝖘𝖎𝖉𝖊 𝕻𝖗𝖊𝖘𝖘

R.R. DONNELLEY & SONS COMPANY

CHICAGO

December, 1997

PUBLISHERS' PREFACE

With the publication of this volume, The Lakeside Classics shifts its focus into the twentieth century and World War I, one of this country's and this century's defining events. When the war began, America was but fifty years removed from its own Civil War. Its leadership tried to maintain a policy of neutrality until acts of aggression demanded a response. By war's end, the country was becoming a world power, and President Woodrow Wilson's Fourteen Points laid the groundwork for the long-sought Armistice.

Fighting the Flying Circus is a first-person account of aerial combat during this Great War. Written by the American Ace of Aces, Captain Edward V. Rickenbacker, the book captures the danger, the triumphs, and the tragedy of the young men of the first American air service.

Although America did not declare war until late in 1917, the entire country had been mobilizing for some time. From the printing shop floor to the executive offices, R.R. Donnelley contributed to the war effort. More than 200 employees of R.R. Donnelley & Sons Company served; four employees died in the conflict. T.E. Donnelley's active membership on America's War Industries Board secured for him the thanks of his country and a token payment of one dollar. The check is signed by both President Woodrow Wilson and Bernard M. Baruch, who served as chairman of the

War Industries Board. One of our company's most cherished and personal historical documents, the check is on display in the Gaylord Donnelley Library at our Chicago, Illinois, offices.

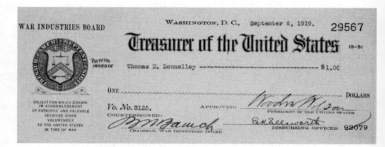

Token payment acknowledges T.E. Donnelley's service on the War Industries Board during World War I

R.R. Donnelley & Sons Company Archives

Fighting the Flying Circus is the ninety-fifth book in The Lakeside Classics series, which was conceived by Thomas E. Donnelley, son of the company's founder, in 1903. T.E. believed that a simple, dignified, and well-designed book using advanced manufacturing methods would be an appropriate holiday gift from a company that prided itself on the quality of its printing and binding. This, we believe, is still true today.

* * * *

As is our custom with The Classics, we looked to experts in the field for help in editing and annotating the text, writing the Introduction, and selecting photography and illustrations. W. David Lewis, Distinguished University Professor at Auburn University, Alabama, served as editor. Among his honors are the da Vinci Medal, the highest honor of the Society for the History of Technology; and appointment in 1993-94 as Charles A. Lindbergh Professor, National Air and Space Museum. He has been a National Humanities Fellow at the University of Chicago and a Mellon Fellow at the Virginia Historical Society. In 1992, at Lucerne, Switzerland, he directed the first international conference on the history of civil and commercial aviation. He is currently writing a biography of Rickenbacker.

This edition represents a version of *Fighting the Flying Circus* that is as faithful as possible to the diary and original text prepared by Rickenbacker in 1918. But it also preserves the eloquent prose added by Laurence La Tourette Driggs, the ghost writer. The editor compared Rickenbacker's typewritten manuscript with the published 1919 version and eliminated many passages that were not based on the original manuscript.

Also eliminated were passages that Driggs added to promote sales among readers who were still inflamed with war-time prejudices in 1919. For this reason, pejorative expressions have been deleted unless they appear in direct quotations. To preserve some of the more evocative passages in the book, embellishments with no counterparts in the original text have been allowed to stand, but have been so annotated. At least one of the episodes, the celebration that took place on Armistice night, is based on what Driggs, not Rickenbacker, experienced. But to have eliminated Driggs's prose would have done damage to the eloquent way in which the book ends.

Preparing a new edition of an important historical work requires the help of many organizations and individuals. Our thanks to the following: University of Chicago Library; Auburn University Archives and the Ralph Brown Draughon Library, Auburn University; the Library of Congress; National Air and Space Museum at Smithsonian Institution; the National Archives; U.S. Air Force Museum; U.S. Air Force Historical Research Center, Maxwell Air Force Base; 1st Fighter Wing History Office, U.S. Air Force; and, finally, to Patricia L. Lewis, Mrs. Laurence La Tourette Driggs, and Tom D. Crouch, Chairman of the Aeronautics Department at the National Air and Space Museum.

* * * *

"It seemed to all of us that, the war being over, we would drop back quickly in our accustomed ways of daily living. But we had forgotten our history, which tells us that the recovery from the destruction and license of war to the ways of orderly and ample production leads through a period of . . . difficult readjustment," wrote the company in the Preface to the 1919 edition of The Lakeside Classics. Today, our company is undergoing another readjustment.

This reevaluation began late last year with our search for a new chairman. In March 1997, we announced the election of William L. Davis, formerly of Emerson Electric, as the eighth chairman in our 135-year history. Within six months, Bill Davis formulated a new strategic vision. Our first commitment is to our core businesses: the printing and binding of books, magazines, catalogs, directories, and financial documents for our customers in the United States and around the world.

Our long-term commitment is to grow profitably and offer greater value to our customers. We will build upon our advantages as the industry leader, including our strong relationships with magazine publishers; our unmatched list of catalog customers; our long-term directory printing contracts; our continuing strengths in book publishing; the depth of our financial printing capabilities.

Our challenge: We will learn how to take advantage of our size and scale so we can deliver superior value at the best cost to our customers. Our tactic: We will emphasize the things that no one else can do as well, and then we will work on doing those things better and better, again and again.

Our printing operations are doing well. We continue to lead our industry in size, in the strength of our customer relationships, the quality of our services, and our ability to deliver solutions to strategic business issues. To that end, we divested ourselves this year of marginal businesses and technologies that did not contribute to the core business, restructured our international operations, and consolidated a number of other functions and operations into our core businesses.

We are developing services such as logistics management, where we, as the largest user of the U.S. Postal Service, can offer our customers immediate cost savings based on volume. We are tapping into our marketing expertise to build steady, reliable, orderly growth for our core businesses. We are adopting technology that creates decided advantages for our customers, either by lowering our costs, reducing their inventories, or shortening the time it takes to get products to market.

Our new $62-million book plant in Roanoke, Virginia, offers Title Life Management^{SM} (TLM), which embodies all those advantages. Using a completely digital workflow, TLM redefines the book-publishing business model. Publishers can move away from costly *physical* inventories of books printed and stored in warehouses, to *virtual* inventories stored in databases, with books printed and distributed on a just-in-time basis. TLM represents the most cost- and time-efficient way to produce every stage in the life of a book title—from market test and review copies, to launch of the title and reprints. Publishers accustomed to waiting weeks for books can now get product into stores in as little as ten days. Books with short runs, previously dismissed as uneconomical, can now be brought to market profitably.

Technology like that used at Roanoke can drive down costs, as well as create value for our customers. Other examples include our introduction of four-color printing to our yellow-pages customers and economical personalized communications for customers who sell mutual funds.

We will become better business partners with our customers. During 1997, we made a sound beginning toward that goal.

* * * *

The company would like to thank John M. Richman, who served as acting chairman and CEO from November 1996 through March 1997. Under his direction, the company made progress on important projects and completed its search for a new chairman. Mr. Richman retired in December after ten years on the Board of Directors. We also say thank you and farewell to Blair White, who retired in September with eighteen years of service on the Board.

As the end of the year approaches, we wish all of you and your families good health and good luck in the new year.

THE PUBLISHERS

December 1997

CONTENTS

List of Illustrations & Maps xvii
Historical Introduction xix
Glossary of Aviation Expressions 5
Foreword 7
   I. Introducing "Archy" 11
   II. The Aerodrome 23
   III. Our First Sorties 37
   IV. Downing My First Enemy 53
   V. Jimmy Meissner Strips His Wings . 61
   VI. Jimmy Hall's Last Fight 71
   VII. New Responsibilities 81
  VIII. A Victory and a Narrow Escape . . 91
   IX. Down in Flames 103
   X. Lufbery is Killed 113
   XI. Squadron Activities 121
   XII. Jimmy Meissner Again 131
   XIII. America's First Ace 143
   XIV. Rumpler No. 16 159
   XV. Campbell's Last Fight 173
   XVI. Becoming an Ace 183
   XVII. A Perplexing Bank of Fog 191
  XVIII. Strafing the *Drachen*. 203
   XIX. The Château-Thierry Salient . . . 215
   XX. The Death of Quentin Roosevelt . . 223
   XXI. The Flying Circus Scores Heavily . 237
   XXII. Our Spads Arrive 241
  XXIII. Back Close to Verdun 251
  XXIV. The St. Mihiel Drive. 257

xv

XXV.	American Ace of Aces	27c
XXVI.	Captain of the Hat-in-the-Ring Squadron	28c
XXVII.	An Eventful "D" Day	30c
XXVIII.	Frank Luke Strafes His Last Balloon	31c
XXIX.	A Night Mission	32c
XXX.	A Day's Work—Six Victories	33c
XXXI.	"Seeing the War"	34c
XXXII.	A Regular Dogfight	35c
XXXIII.	An Aeroplane Movie Show	36c
XXXIV.	An Overzealous Ally	37c
XXXV.	The End Draws Near	38c
XXXVI.	Last Victory of the Great War	401
Epilogue		411
Additional Reading		41c
Index		421
List of The Lakeside Classics		42c

ILLUSTRATIONS & MAPS

Captain Edward V. Rickenbacker . . *Frontispiece*
Token payment from the
    War Industries Board viii
Captain Rickenbacker xxi
Baron Manfred von Richthofen xxi
Elizabeth Basler Rickenbacher xxv
William Rickenbacher xxv
Rickenbacker's childhood home xxv
Rickenbacker, ca. 1908 xxxi
Rickenbacker and riding mechanic in
    racing car xxxvii
The "Hat in the Ring" Squadron lvii
Laurence La Tourette Driggs lxv
Illustration of aerial maneuvers 3
Major Raoul Lufbery 13
Captain James Norman Hall 13
Aerodrome hangar, France 25
1st Pursuit Squadron 39
Lieutenant Hamilton Coolidge 65
Lieutenant James A. Meissner 65
Major Reed Chambers 93
No-Man's-Land 139
Lieutenant Douglas Campbell 145
Trench warfare 155
Major Bert Atkinson 193
Rickenbacker in a Spad XIII 219
Lieutenant Quentin Roosevelt 225
Roosevelt's Grave 225

Rickenbacker in his Spad   245

Forward America!   265

Map: European Theatre of Operations . . .   266

Map: American Aerial Operations Area . . .   267

The Air War   268

And You? Subscribe to the War Loan   269

Good books, good comrades   270

Books Wanted   271

Keep Him Free   272

Captain Edward Vernon Rickenbacker . . .   273

Emblem of Hat-in-the-Ring Squadron . . .   274

Captain Edward V. Rickenbacker   299

Rickenbacker in a Nieuport 28   299

Rickenbacker with captured Hannover . . .   367

Rickenbacker after sea rescue   413

Rickenbacker during tenure at
     Eastern Airlines   413

HISTORICAL INTRODUCTION

WHEN A MAJOR European war broke out in August 1914, no one imagined that it would become an interminable defensive stalemate. Millions of men were killed and maimed while attacking trenches defended by barbed wire, machine guns, and poison gas. Public enthusiasm, high at the outset, disappeared as the war became a catastrophic nightmare.

Political and military leaders looked for ways to boost public morale. One tactic they seized upon was to glamorize a new and unanticipated aspect of the war. High above the trenches, where infantrymen sometimes stood up to their knees in ground water, courageous young pilots flying frail planes made of fabric, wood, and wire fought aerial duels that resembled medieval jousts. Chivalrous encounters in the clouds seemed far more exciting, yet somehow more civilized, than the butchery taking place at ground level.[1]

Thus was created the Cult of the Ace, a heroic flyer who became one of the few shining symbols of a horrendous war. Even today, eight decades later, memories linger of winged warriors such as Manfred von Richthofen, Germany's "Red Baron," and Eddie Rickenbacker, America's "Ace of Aces."

[1]Dominick A. Pisano et al, *Legend, Memory and the Great War in the Air* (Seattle: University of Washington Press, 1992), 30-41.

The romantic aspects of the aerial combat waged in World War I lie "mainly in the minds of fiction writers and film-makers," as one account states. "The idea that the air battles were fought under the rules of chivalry is in the main a myth."[2] Rickenbacker himself admitted that "fighting in the air is not a sport. It is scientific murder."[3] Still, the Cult of the Ace remains alive.

The criteria for achieving recognition as an Ace—the term was coined by the French, after the top cards in a deck—varied from nation to nation. Winning this distinction demanded an impressive number of victories—at least five, in Germany's case ten—subject to carefully stipulated methods of verification. Whatever standards were used, the heroic flyers who met them were showered with adulation and medals.

In America, Rickenbacker epitomized the Cult of the Ace. In only a few months of combat flying in 1918, he won twenty-five confirmed victories over German aircraft, more than any other American pilot.[4] After

[2]Terry C. Treadwell and Alan C. Wood, *The First Air War: A Pictorial History, 1914-1919* (London and Washington: Brassey's, 1996), vi.

[3]"Eddie Rickenbacker Discusses Flying," newspaper clipping in Rickenbacker Scrapbooks, Auburn University Archives (hereafter cited as AUA), Scrapbook I (1913-1922). AUA's collection includes twenty-six scrapbooks documenting every phase of Rickenbacker's life.

[4]He was later credited with twenty-six, a figure that had been well documented by the time *Fighting the Flying Circus* was published in 1919. The misplacement of a confirming document prevented one of his victories from being awarded until 1960.

Captain Rickenbacker,
after World War I

Courtesy Auburn
University Archives

Baron
Manfred von Richthofen

Courtesy National Air and
Space Museum,
Smithsonian Institution

coming home in January 1919, he received a tumultuous welcome. Not until Charles A. Lindbergh returned from his nonstop flight from New York to Paris in May 1927 did a hero receive comparable adulation.

Soon after his triumphal homecoming, Rickenbacker published a book that became a classic. Its name, *Fighting the Flying Circus*, was derived from combat waged by Allied flyers against units of gaudily painted German pursuit planes that were kept in tents, like caged animals, and then dispatched rapidly to the sectors where they were needed to engage numerically superior Allied aircraft.

The perennial appeal of Rickenbacker's book stems partly from the dramatic story it tells. But it is also notable for the high quality of its prose. Passages about the death of flyers like Raoul Lufbery and Quentin Roosevelt and evocations of artillery barrages seen from aloft are a notable part of the literary legacy left by the world's first war in the air. These passages, and the smooth-flowing style of the book, are the work of Laurence La Tourette Driggs, a gifted ghostwriter who transformed a much shorter preliminary text into a well-crafted narrative.

* * * *

A hero's journey began in Columbus, Ohio, when on 8 October 1890, Elizabeth Rickenbacher presented her husband, Wilhelm, a construction worker, with their third child, a boy whom they named Edward. The Rickenbachers had come to America in the 1870s

from the Swiss canton of Baselland, joining a flood of
Germanic immigrants who settled in the Midwest because of its rich soil and diversified industries.[5]

Buying a lot on the outskirts of Columbus, they
built a small cottage at 1334 East Livingston Avenue
and raised a family of eight children. To them, America was a land of opportunity. Because of their gratitude to their adopted country, they had inculcated
patriotism, individualism, and religious faith in the
boy who would become famous as Eddie Rickenbacker. (He changed the "h" to a "k" in 1918 at a time
of anti-German sentiment in the United States.)

Edward was an unruly youth who fought for
parental attention by getting involved in dangerous
stunts and escapades from which he barely escaped
alive. In one of many boyhood adventures, he tried to

[5]The account of Rickenbacker's early life in this essay is derived
largely from Edward V. Rickenbacker, *Rickenbacker: An Autobiography* (Englewood Cliffs, N.J.: Prentice-Hall, 1967). Some details,
however, are taken from "Life Story of Captain Edward V. Rickenbacker," a typewritten document compiled in 1943 for "Captain
Eddie," a film about his life, and from an even larger collection of
transcripts of taped interviews with Rickenbacker conducted in
1965 by Booten Herndon, the ghostwriter of his autobiography.
Copies of these materials from the Ohio State University Library
and the United States Air Force Museum are in my possession.
Rickenbacker has not received the recognition he deserves in published biographies. The only biographies that exist, by Hans Chris-
tian Adamson, *Eddie Rickenbacker* (New York: Macmillan, 1946),
and Finis Farr, *Rickenbacker's Luck: An American Life* (Boston:
Houghton Mifflin, 1979), are inadequate. On Rickenbacker's life,
see also my essay, "Edward V. Rickenbacker," in William M. Leary,
ed., *The Airline Industry* (New York: Facts on File, 1992), 398-415.
I am currently writing a biography of Rickenbacker.

Elizabeth Basler Rickenbacher   *William Rickenbacher*

Rickenbacker's childhood home, Columbus, Ohio

Courtesy Auburn University Archives

fly by plunging off the roof of a barn while sitting on a bicycle to which he had attached an umbrella. He escaped serious injury only by landing in a sand pile.

Rickenbacker remained a thrill-seeker throughout his life. Nothing gave him a greater feeling of elation than cheating death. After he had matured from an impetuous youth to one of the best combat pilots of World War I, however, he did not court danger recklessly. "The experienced fighting pilot does not take unnecessary risks," he told a reporter after returning home in 1919. "His business is to shoot down enemy planes, not to get shot down. His trained eye and hand and judgment are as much a part of his armament as the machine gun and a 50-50 chance is the worst he will take or should take."[6]

Born in an era that put Teddy Roosevelt in the White House and equated masculinity with physical toughness, Rickenbacker started smoking cigarettes when he was five, hated school, bullied his fellow students, became a gang leader, and used his fists at the slightest provocation. His parents worried lest he be sent to a reformatory. Inwardly, however, he was warm, tender-hearted, and compassionate. His command of English was poor and he read with difficulty, but he had artistic talent and hoped to become a great painter or sculptor. His strong visual orientation, acute depth perception, and manual dexterity contributed to his success as a combat pilot.

[6]"Eddie Rickenbacker Discusses Flying," previously cited.

Rickenbacker's youthful misbehavior stopped in 1904 when his father was killed by an assailant. Dropping out of school in the seventh grade, Edward, who idolized his mother, took a series of low-paying jobs to support her. But he continued to crave thrills.

Exhilarated by a ride in a Ford runabout, Rickenbacker decided to look for a job in the automobile industry. Ohio's capital city was at that time a leading center of motor vehicle manufacturing. Starting work at a small garage that repaired cars and bicycles, he moved on to the Oscar Lear Company, which made gasoline-powered vehicles featuring an ingenious air-cooled engine designed by Lee Frayer, a mechanical engineer who was a partner in the firm. Noticing Rickenbacker's technological abilities, Frayer became a surrogate father to him.

Frayer became chief designer in 1906 for the Columbus Buggy Company, which at that time was a major automobile manufacturer. It was making a transition from electric to gasoline-powered cars. Frayer took Rickenbacker with him and put him in charge of its testing department at the age of sixteen.

Rickenbacker had an instinctive feeling for technology. He could diagnose mechanical malfunctions merely by listening to a sputtering engine or sensing the peculiar vibrations caused by a faulty component. His problem-solving ability brought him to the attention of Clinton D. Firestone, the principal owner of the Columbus Buggy Company. In 1909, Firestone sent Rickenbacker to Texas and Arizona to help wealthy

ranchers cope with mechanical problems they encountered after buying the company's Firestone-
Columbus automobiles and driving them on bad
roads. By 1910, after being transferred to Omaha, Ne-
braska, he was the Buggy Company's branch manager for five midwestern states and had six salesmen
working under him.

Like Henry Ford and many other automobile designers at the time, Frayer was a racing driver. In 1906,
while he was still with the Oscar Lear Company, he
entered a car featuring his air-cooled engine in the
Vanderbilt Cup Race on Long Island and took Rickenbacker along as his riding mechanic. This job required steady nerves, quick judgment, and intense
concentration. Sitting beside the driver in the cramped
seat of a racing car, a riding mechanic hand-pumped
gas and oil, checked fuel consumption, monitored tire
wear, and signaled the driver to warn him about impending hazards or other drivers attempting to pass.
Because a riding mechanic could not brace himself
against the steering wheel, he was much more likely
than a driver to be thrown from a car and killed if it
crashed or turned over.

Bored by merely selling motor vehicles for the
Columbus Buggy Company in Omaha, Rickenbacker
followed a common practice among dealers by strip-
ping down a Firestone-Columbus car and racing in it
at county fairs. In a race in Iowa, despite taking practice runs to calculate the maximum speed at which he
could take unbanked turns on a track designed for

horse racing, he put too much strain on his right rear wheel, hurtled across a ditch, and crashed through a fence. He came out of the accident unscathed.

Drawn irresistibly by the prospect of experiencing greater thrills, Rickenbacker entered as many races as possible. He won so often and attracted so much attention that Frayer invited him to come home and take part in a 100-mile event at Columbus's Driving Park with famous drivers like America's reigning speed king, Barney Oldfield. Frayer and Rickenbacker devised a clever strategy to take advantage of Oldfield's ego by tempting him to take turns at a speed that would wear down the tires of his heavy six-cylinder Knox. The plan succeeded so well that Rickenbacker almost won the race before being forced out in the final laps with a broken connecting rod. Long before he became a combat pilot, he learned the value of strategic and tactical planning.

In 1911, Frayer invited him to be his relief driver on Memorial Day at the first running of the Indianapolis 500. Selling cars was stultifying to Rickenbacker, but Frayer again came to his rescue in 1912 by retiring from racing and allowing Rickenbacker to drive his "Red Wing Special" at the second Indy 500. Despite being forced off the track by a burned camshaft in the fourth lap, he could no longer resist the lure of a racing career.

Rickenbacker resigned from his position with the Columbus Buggy Company very soon after the Indianapolis race and then secured a professional driving

Eighteen-year-old Edward Rickenbacker, ca. 1908

Courtesy Auburn University Archives

license from the American Automobile Association (AAA) Contest Board, which regulated motor sport at the time. Lacking the financial backing to take part in major events, he signed on with a Chicago promoter. During the 1912 racing season, he competed at county fairs only to find that the events were not sanctioned by the AAA. When the Contest Board discovered that he was racing in the unauthorized circuit, it suspended his license.

Rickenbacker, however, still had his two greatest assets—his mechanical ability and determination to succeed. Going to Des Moines, Iowa, he found a job with two German immigrants, Frederick and August Duesenberg, who had designed a new racing car. Rickenbacker worked for the Duesenbergs as a mechanic throughout the winter of 1912-1913.

Soon afterward, with the help of influential friends in Ohio, Rickenbacker was reinstated by the AAA and drove as a member of the Duesenberg team in a 200-mile race at Columbus. During the summer of 1913, he continued to drive for the Duesenbergs and became one of the most exciting newcomers on the AAA tour. In a race at St. Paul, Minnesota, he endeared himself to the fans by showing his coolness after a serious accident. Losing control of his car while trying to pass another racer, he did a triple somersault, crashed through a fence, and turned upside down. Falling out of his car as it gyrated in the air, he landed heavily on the track, unhurt but badly shaken. Struggling to his feet, he nonchalantly picked up some nail-studded boards from the fence, lest they puncture the tires of other drivers, and then limped around the track to the pit. The crowd gave him a standing ovation.

Rickenbacker scored an impressive triumph in a 100-mile contest at Cincinnati, and placed fourth in the Elgin Road Race, a major attraction in the Chicago area. Famous drivers praised his gritty style.

Rickenbacker's immaturity was quite evident at this early stage of his career. Along with rational planning, he also was extremely superstitious. After returning to the racing tour for the 1914 season, he took a black cat named "Lady Luck" to the Indy 500 and let it ride with him in a box behind the seat of his car. He finished tenth and won a share of the purse but was determined to do better in a 300-mile race at Sioux City on the Fourth of July. Following the advice of his mother, who had a deep knowledge of Swiss folklore, he killed a bat on the eve of the race and tied its heart around one of his fingers with a silk thread. But he also displayed the rational part of his makeup by fashioning a metal screen that he attached to the cowl of his racer to protect him from loose stones, known among racers as "gumbo," that lay under the dirt track. He conceived a strategy to outperform racers with more powerful cars by taking the turns at a blistering speed, realizing he could not keep up on the straightaways.

The screen proved useless; indeed, Rickenbacker's riding mechanic was temporarily knocked unconscious when a piece of gumbo hit him in the head. The bat's heart was also a dubious asset. But Rickenbacker's strategy of taking near-suicidal chances on the turns to compensate for his lack of power in the straightaways paid off as he won the first major victory of his career. He finished a scant forty seconds ahead of Spencer Wishart, a wealthy sportsman who drove a big Mercer that had purportedly cost the staggering sum of $63,000. Rickenbacker won $10,000. More important, he became an established star in racing.

Ambitious to achieve ever greater success, Rickenbacker left the Duesenbergs to drive for a more prestigious sponsor, Peugeot. But he did not yet have the patience he needed to sustain him in the inevitable reverses that even a champion must undergo. Early in the 1915 season he lost several races, got discouraged, and sold the car that Peugeot had supplied. This was a mistake; Dario Resta, who drove the vehicle for the rest of the season, won the national championship.

After quitting Peugeot, Rickenbacker signed with the makers of an American automobile, the Maxwell, and suffered several more setbacks. At this point, he hired Harry van Hoven, an Iowan who excelled in the study of time and motion. Inspired by Frederick Winslow Taylor, the father of scientific management, van Hoven drilled Rickenbacker's pit crew in rapid tire-changing and other time-saving operations. A series of first-place finishes resulted, placing Rickenbacker sixth among all money winners on the 1915 tour. He had ranked twenty-seventh the previous year.

Rickenbacker was now a racing superstar. But he received a setback when the makers of Maxwell decided to withdraw from motor sport. Resourcefully, he capitalized on his fame by negotiating a lucrative agreement with two partners including Carl Fisher, the principal owner of the Indianapolis Speedway. Fisher, who manufactured Prest-o-Lite headlamps, bought Maxwell's fleet of race cars and made Rickenbacker manager of the "Prest-o-Lite Racing Team," with a guaranteed share of its winnings.

Rickenbacker had learned a lesson from being too impatient with the Peugeot auto. Realizing that the Maxwells were fundamentally sound, he redesigned them, drew up a detailed list of rules that he imposed upon his drivers and pit crews to maximize their efficiency, and streamlined operations so that two separate teams of drivers could enter as many races as possible on the 1916 tour. He also dispensed with good luck charms. He was now functioning as a business manager who ran a profitable enterprise. During 1916, he won six events, vaulting into third place among money-winners on the tour.

Rickenbacker was determined to win the national racing championship in 1917. Backed by William Weightman III, a wealthy sportsman, he went to Europe at the end of the 1916 season to visit automobile plants in England, France, and Italy and study mechanical innovations taking place under the spur of wartime conditions. He especially wanted to learn as much as possible about a new racer being developed for the Sunbeam Motor Company by one of England's leading designers, Louis Coatalen.

Rickenbacker and riding mechanic in Maxwell racing car, ca. 1915

Courtesy National Air and Space Museum, Smithsonian Institution

After arriving at Liverpool, however, Rickenbacker was arrested on suspicion of being a German spy. American sports reporters embellished his public image by writing stories that his father was a Prussian nobleman. Taking this misinformation at face value, detectives from Scotland Yard held him incommunicado and grilled him until Coatalen arranged for his release. Rickenbacker remained under surveillance throughout his visit to England. Working on weekdays with the design staff of the Sunbeam plant at Wolverhampton, he visited London on weekends, where he reported to the Bow Street police station and stayed at the Savoy Hotel as Coatalen's guest.

From his window at the Savoy, Rickenbacker noticed airplanes flying up and down the Thames and learned that they were flown by Royal Air Service recruits stationed at the nearby Brooklands motor speedway. Brooklands had been the world's first facility designed specifically for automobile racing. The grassy infield was a natural place for takeoffs and landings. After Great Britain declared war on Germany in 1914, it became a training facility for combat pilots.[7]

Rickenbacker's imagination was aroused. When he visited Brooklands, flying instructors told him about their experiences in the air war raging in France. Rickenbacker envied these men. Shortly before sailing for Europe, he had met two important figures in American aviation: Glenn Martin, a noted aircraft designer

[7]Howard Johnson, *Wings over Brooklands* (London: Whittet Books, Ltd., 1981).

and manufacturer who had taken him on his first plane ride; and Major Townsend F. Dodd, a rising officer in the Army Air Service, whom Rickenbacker had helped when Dodd's car broke down. Newspaper accounts of the European war also inspired Rickenbacker, especially publicity given to the Lafayette Escadrille, a unit of the French air force composed of young American volunteers.

The idea of becoming a fighter pilot, therefore, was already germinating in Rickenbacker's mind even before he went to Europe. Before he could leave England to proceed to France and Italy as he had planned, the German high command decided to wage unrestricted submarine warfare, and the United States responded by severing diplomatic relations with Berlin. Rickenbacker abruptly returned home and traveled throughout the country advocating that America declare war on Germany. During his journeys he talked to racing drivers about becoming pilots and forming a volunteer unit similar to the Lafayette Escadrille.

After the United States declared war on Germany in 1917, Rickenbacker went to Washington to persuade the Signal Corps, which was in charge of the army's woefully inadequate aviation program, to authorize formation of the volunteer squadron he had in mind. Military officials denied his request. Rickenbacker made a poor impression on the Signal Corps officers to whom he talked. Having passed his twenty-fifth birthday, he was already too old for aerial service. Even more important, however, he did not have a college degree or its equivalent, which the Signal Corps looked upon as a *sine qua non* for military flying. Early American aviation was an elite activity largely confined to wealthy sporting enthusiasts and college students from prominent families. No matter how famous he had become in the sports world, he did not have the education and bearing to become an officer in the armed forces. He lacked polish, his speech was laced with slang, his grammar was faulty, and his manners were unrefined.

Humiliated by being rejected, Rickenbacker prepared to enter an automobile race at Cincinnati, Ohio. But just before the event took place, he received a telephone call from Burgess Lewis, a high-ranking military officer and a racing enthusiast. If Rickenbacker would go immediately to New York City, Lewis told him, he could become an automobile driver on the staff of the supreme commander of the American Expeditionary Force, General John J. Pershing. Pershing and his entourage were about to sail to England on the *Baltic*, an ocean liner that had been converted to a troopship. If Rickenbacker arrived in New York quickly enough, he could accompany them.

Leaving Cincinnati in great haste, stopping only briefly at Columbus for what he thought might be the last time he would ever see his mother, Rickenbacker caught an overnight train to New York and enlisted as a sergeant on the following day. By nightfall he was on his way to England. Major Dodd, whose car he had fixed the previous year, was now Pershing's chief aviation officer. Dodd, too, was a passenger on the *Baltic*.

Rickenbacker had no intention of remaining a driver any longer than was necessary. Upon reaching
France after a short stay in London, he told reporters
he was going to become a fighter pilot. Meanwhile,
Dodd made frequent use of his services as a chauffeur.
Dodd, however, did not remain Pershing's top aviation
officer; a far more resourceful person, William ("Billy")
Mitchell, soon took his place. Mitchell was an ambi-
tious career officer who had been promoted in 1913 to
the General Staff in Washington, where he made pow-
erful contacts and became deputy to the head of the
Signal Corps' Aviation Section. After learning to fly, he
was sent to Europe as an aeronautical observer. He
reached Paris in April 1917, only four days after the
United States declared war on Germany. By the time
Pershing and his staff arrived in the French capital,
Mitchell had been promoted to Lieutenant Colonel.
He replaced Dodd as Pershing's aviation officer.

Mitchell took command of the Army Air Service's
operations on the Western Front and was posted to
Pershing's headquarters at Chaumont. Soon thereafter, he accompanied Dodd on an inspection tour of
the Toul sector, a relatively quiet area that had been assigned to the United States as a good place to station
inexperienced pilots and their ground crews before
they were exposed to combat in more dangerous
places. Mitchell and Dodd rode in two Packards that
had been assigned to them. Rickenbacker drove
Dodd's car. After spending a night near Nancy, where
they witnessed an attack by German bombers, they

headed for Neufchatel. Before they arrived there, Mitchell's automobile broke down and his driver could not fix the problem. "Dodd suggested that his driver see what he could do," Mitchell recalled. "So the tall, lithe young man dived into the engine and in a moment he had removed the whole carburetor assembly . . . . He found that the needle valve had bent, and in less time than it takes to tell he cleaned it, put it back, and had the engine going. I had never seen a man do anything so quickly with a gasoline engine, or who knew more about what he was doing."[8]

Learning from Dodd that Rickenbacker was a championship racing driver, Mitchell commandeered his services. "I drove him all over the French countryside," Rickenbacker remembered. At one point he drove Mitchell to a village called Issoudun, where Mitchell chose a site in a wheatfield for what became the main training facility of the Army Air Service. On another trip, when a bearing burned in an automobile that Mitchell was using, Rickenbacker managed to get the car to a nearby village and found a garage. "I heated some babbitt metal in a pot with a blowtorch, made a mold from sand and water, and poured the babbitt into it," he said. "Then I filed it down and made it fit. We had a bearing. By 6:00 that night we were on the road again. Mitchell could hardly believe it."

Rickenbacker's knack for being in the right place at

[8]William Mitchell, "Rickenbacker — The Ace of the American Expeditionary Force," in Frank C. Platt, *Great Battles of World War I* (New York: Weathervane Books, 1966), 90.

the right time also served him well one day when he was strolling the Champs Elysées and met James Miller, a New York banker and sports fan with whom he had become friends during his racing days. Miller had become an officer in the Air Service and was about to be put in charge of the flying school at Issoudun. He needed an engineering officer, and he offered Rickenbacker the job. Mitchell hated to lose a superb driver but did not want to hold Rickenbacker back, and agreed to let him go. Because pilot training was required for his new post, Rickenbacker had to take a physical examination. It was administered by a doctor from Chicago who was also a racing fan. After pronouncing Rickenbacker physically fit for flying, he certified that he was twenty-five years old instead of his actual twenty-seven, two years over the age limit.

Rickenbacker was posted to the French aviation school at Tours for pilot training because America's badly understaffed and ill-equipped Army Air Service had neither the instructors nor planes to teach cadets how to fly. Under French training methods, novices were taught by first having them roll around an airfield in Penguins—"low-powered machines with clipped wings, which are not capable of leaving the ground," as a member of the Lafayette Escadrille described them.[9] After learning to taxi without actually taking off, fledglings went through further stages involving short hops of two or three meters, longer hops

[9]James Norman Hall, *High Adventure* (Boston: Houghton Mifflin, 1918), 25-26.

of up to fifty meters, landings made without the use of engines, actual flights around the aerodrome, progressively longer flights made only under the safest weather conditions, and, finally, cross-country trips over a triangular route involving two distant airfields.

Starting with a Morane-Saulnier, "a funny little monoplane with a 3-cylinder engine" that reminded him of a grasshopper as he bumped along the field, Rickenbacker advanced to a Caudron biplane with a "tremendous wingspread" and nine-cylinder engine. His first flights were harrowing, but he eventually made smoother ones during a seventeen-day period out of which he emerged as a duly qualified pilot in the U. S. Signal Corps, with the rank of First Lieutenant.

Posted to Issoudun in September as chief engineer, Rickenbacker put his technical background and his managerial experience to good use by organizing the new facility and requisitioning millions of dollars' worth of equipment. The flying school lacked even the most basic amenities. The first pilot-trainees, young men from social and educational backgrounds superior to that of Rickenbacker, dug latrines and did other menial jobs under his direction.

After work on the base was completed, the recruits, who had received only ground training in the United States, began to take flying lessons. Rickenbacker, who was already far ahead of them by virtue of his training at Tours, did not intend to stay any longer than necessary in a logistical position. "The only way to improve my own flying was to take a few minutes here and a half hour there," he recalled. "I would duck into the lecture sessions when I could. To apply what I learned, I would have to sneak an airplane out and take it up."

Rickenbacker tried constantly to persuade his immediate superior, Carl Spaatz,[10] to post him to one of the combat squadrons that were about to go to the front, but Spaatz told him that his engineering services were too valuable to let him go. When the first group of trainees was sent to gunnery school and Rickenbacker's name was not on the list, he took action. Being sick with a severe cold, he prevailed upon the head surgeon to put him in the base hospital for two weeks while a substitute performed his engineering duties. When things went satisfactorily without Rickenbacker's help, Spaatz relented and sent him for gunnery training at Cazeau, an isolated spot on the Bay of Biscay where fledgling combat pilots could shoot without hitting anything of value. After learning how to hit moving targets with machine-gun fire from boats and planes, Rickenbacker was sent to Paris on leave, pending assignment to the 94th Pursuit Squadron at an aerodrome at Villeneuve-les-Vertus in the Toul sector. At last he was a combat pilot.

* * * *

Because Rickenbacker's achievements in aerial warfare are discussed at some length in *Fighting the Flying Circus*, it would be superfluous to cover them again

---

[10]Spaatz then spelled his name with only one "a."

here. To understand how and why his story unfolded as it did, however, it is pertinent to take a brief glance at the early development of American military aviation and aircraft.

When the United States declared war on Germany in April 1917, every branch of its armed services was woefully ill-prepared. Particularly unimpressive was the state of American air power. The Aviation Section of the Signal Corps had only 65 officers and 1,120 enlisted men.[11] To meet the demands of war, its ranks had to be swiftly expanded, giving men like Rickenbacker opportunities for advancement not normally available.

The Aviation Section had about 200 aircraft, of which only a few were even marginally fit for wartime service. Acting on French advice, the army and navy asked for funding to create a combat force of 12,000 planes, composed of observation aircraft, fighters, and bombers. Congress voted an unprecedentedly large appropriation, $640 million, for this purpose. Because there was great confidence in America's ability to mass-produce planes, it was predicted that the skies of Europe would be darkened by aircraft made in the United States. By April 1918, however, total production was only fifteen De Havilland DH-4 bombers, made under British license. They were obsolete as soon as they reached the front. Most of the planes

[11]The account of American unpreparedness that follows is based on Irving B. Holley, *Ideas and Weapons: Exploitation of the Aerial Weapon by the United States During World War I* (New Haven: Yale University Press, 1953).

flown by American pilots in the war were made in France or Great Britain.

The fighter plane itself did not exist as an air weapon when the war began in 1914.[12] The consensus among European military officers was that, to the extent that airplanes were used at all, they would observe and report on enemy troop movements, a task traditionally assigned to the cavalry. In the early stages of the war, pilots of observation planes did not attempt to interfere with reconnaissance operations conducted by their opponents. As the value of the information that aircraft could provide became increasingly obvious, the men who flew such planes tried to bring each other down with hand-thrown objects and firearms. Because these tactics were generally futile, flyers took machine guns aloft and used them with much greater success. Quickly, therefore, specialized planes evolved that were flying platforms for machine guns. Various types of guns were developed capable of firing increasing numbers of bullets. The weight of such guns and their ammunition required more and more powerful engines, both to take the planes to greater altitudes and enable them to execute difficult maneuvers at higher and higher speeds. Thus the fighter plane was born.

Because it was difficult to maneuver a plane and aim

[12]The following account of the development of pursuit planes in World War I is based on Richard P. Hallion, *Rise of the Fighter Aircraft, 1914-1918* (Baltimore, Md.: Nautical & Aviation Publishing Company of America, Inc., 1984).

a machine gun at the same time, the guns were attached to the aircraft so that a pilot could draw a bead on an opponent simply by pointing the plane directly at him. The best way to mount a gun was to have it fire straight forward. This was not hard to do when the engine was of the pusher type, impelling the plane from behind the pilot. If the aircraft were of the tractor type, however, in which the engine and propeller were in front of the pilot and pulled the craft through the air, a machine gun could not fire directly forward without damaging or destroying the propeller.

In April of 1915, a French pilot, Roland Garros, mounted wedge-shaped steel deflector plates on the propeller of a tractor-type plane so that bullets fired from a gun mounted behind the propeller would bounce off the blades if they did not go through the spaces between them. Garros shot down five German planes in eighteen days before making a forced landing behind enemy lines. Because he could not destroy his plane before being captured, the Germans learned the secret behind his recent victories and greatly improved upon his rudimentary device. A team of technicians led by a gifted aircraft designer, Anthony Fokker, devised a cam-actuated interrupter gear that operated off the propeller shaft in such a way as to prevent a machine gun from firing if its barrel was in line with one of the blades. Despite having a slow airspeed, a low ceiling, and limited range, the Fokker E-III *Eindecker* (German for monoplane), armed with such equipment, became the first truly successful fighter plane and inflicted heavy losses on the Allied aircraft.

Because the Allied nations were slow in developing a satisfactory interrupter gear, they had to employ other means of countering what came to be called the "Fokker Scourge," either by building better pusher-type planes or by mounting machine guns on the top wings of tractor-type models. Improved aircraft like the British Bristol and French Nieuport types wrested control of the skies from the Germans in 1916, forcing the latter to develop a new generation of pursuit planes. The most notable of these fighters was the Albatros D-III, a sturdy biplane introduced late in 1916. It temporarily turned the tables on Allied opponents because of its clean aerodynamic design and superior armament. Sheathed in plywood, it was armed with two air-cooled machine guns that used a belt drive to feed bullets into the firing chambers. Rickenbacker fought against an improved model, the Albatros D-Va.

In 1916 the Allies finally developed a synchronizing mechanism that permitted a machine gun to fire through the propeller arc. It was used in a new generation of British and French pursuit planes, including the Sopwith Pup, the Nieuport 17, and the Spad VII. Technological leapfrogging continued throughout the final two years of the war as both sides tried to gain the upper hand. A French machine, the Nieuport 28, had clean, graceful lines that made it perhaps the most aesthetically pleasing aircraft developed by either side. This was the type of plane Rickenbacker flew during his first months of combat. Another French plane, which was more rugged and had greater power than the Nieuport 28, was the Spad XIII, which Rickenbacker flew in the war's closing months. Against such planes the Germans pitted machines like the Fokker D-VII, which many experts regard as the best fighter used by either side.

Many types of machine guns were developed on both sides in a search for more effective cooling, more convenient loading, and greater firepower.[13] The most vexing problem encountered in using these guns was their tendency to jam because of overheating or minute differences in the size and shape of mass-produced bullets. No theme appears more frequently in *Fighting the Flying Circus* than the frustration Rickenbacker felt when a machine gun jammed at the worst possible time in a duel with the enemy. One of Rickenbacker's greatest assets as a combat pilot was his skill in analyzing problems affecting his machine guns and teaching ground crews how to keep them in good repair. He also took great care in inspecting his bullets and would file them down with carborundum to eliminate irregularities.

Because Rickenbacker flew the Nieuport 28 and Spad XIII, both planes play prominent roles in *Fighting the Flying Circus*. It is therefore pertinent to review their advantages and shortcomings. Despite being frequently maligned, by the many pilots who used it and

[13]The account that follows is based on Harry Woodman, *Early Aircraft Armament: The Aeroplane and the Gun up to 1918* (Washington: Smithsonian Institution Press, 1989).

later historians, the Nieuport 28 was an excellent plane whose extraordinary buoyancy and favorable horse-power-to-weight ratio enabled it to take off in a remarkably short time, climb rapidly, respond quickly to the movements of a pilot's hands and feet, and perform intricate maneuvers that the larger and heavier Spad XIII could not match.

The most unfortunate feature of the Nieuport 28 was its tendency to shed its upper wing fabric during a rapid dive, resulting in a spin from which it was extremely hard to escape. Numerous explanations have been given for this problem, which is frequently mentioned in *Fighting the Flying Circus,* but it was probably caused by some weakness in the stitching that attached the fabric to the wing.[14]

One of the most prominent features of the Nieuport 28 was its Gnome *monosoupape* (single-valve) engine.[15] This noisy power plant, whose distinctive sound was instantly recognizable even from a distance, was of the rotary type: the entire engine, which had up to nine cylinders, revolved on a stationary crankshaft. The reason for this feature was the intense heat produced by the engine; the spinning of its cylinders in the ambient air made it self-cooling. Because its heat was dissipated by fins that were integral parts of its nickel-steel

[14]I am indebted to Edward S. Chapman of the curatorial staff of the United States Air Force Museum for reviewing evidence with me on this point.

[15]The discussion of engines that follows is based on Herschel Smith, *A History of Aircraft Piston Engines*, repr. ed. (Manhattan, Kan.: Sunflower University Press, 1986).

cylinders, it needed no radiator, giving the plane its favorable horsepower-to-weight ratio. Because a rotary engine needed no warm-up, a Nieuport 28 could take off in an extremely short time.

Like any plane with a rotary engine, the Nieuport 28 had many idiosyncrasies. Its airspeed could be controlled only by using a switch that varied the number of cylinders firing at a particular time. Because of the size of the engine, a pilot had no forward visibility on his takeoff roll and had to sideslip the plane toward a runway while landing so that he could look over the side to see where he was going to touch down. One of the greatest drawbacks of a rotary engine, from which Rickenbacker and every other pilot who used it suffered, was that castor oil was the only lubricant capable of withstanding the heat that it generated. Even though the engine was enclosed in a protective cowling, the pilot of a plane with a rotary engine inhaled a constant vapor spray of castor oil that produced nausea and diarrhea.

The simplicity of the Gnome *monosoupape* motor was itself a virtue, helping explain why some American units were reluctant to stop using the Nieuport 28 when it was ultimately replaced by the Spad XIII, which had a complicated Hispano-Suiza engine of the water-cooled, in-line type. Although this engine required frequent overhauls, the Spad was much more dependable than the Nieuport in a dive and had the power and speed to outrun German fighters. It was well liked by French units that used it, and it is now regarded by many historians as the best Allied fighter plane of the war. Rickenbacker, who was not intimidated by the Spad's mechanical complexities, greatly favored it over the Nieuport.

The basic rules of aerial combat were established midway through the war by Oswald Boelcke, the most significant figure in making the German air service the superb fighting force that it became.[16] Boelcke, who was an excellent teacher and organizer as well as a skilled aerial duelist, taught recruits the necessity of surprising an adversary by seeing him from a distance, gaining altitude on him, coming at him from behind, and waiting patiently until he was close enough to have the best possible shot. Boelcke also drilled his pupils in one of the most fundamental principles of aerial combat: coming at an opponent with the sun at one's back so that he would be blinded by its glare. "Beware of the Hun in the Sun" became an adage among Allied pilots.

By 1916, Boelcke also realized that the early individual style of combat, in which pilots flew alone and won dramatic victories in one-on-one encounters, was no longer effective because of the number and quality of airplanes and pilots now active in the war. It was simply too hard for a flyer to see in all directions so that he would not be taken by surprise by a sudden attack from an unanticipated quarter. Boelcke, therefore,

[16]The discussion of tactics that follows is based on Edward H. Sims, *Fighter Tactics and Strategy 1914-1970,* 2nd ed. (Fallbrook, Calif.: Aero Publishers, Inc., 1980).

stressed the necessity of flying in formations whose members would watch out for one another. One basic formation was a "V" shape in which the lead pilot flew ahead of the rest at a lower altitude, flanked by pilots flying at progressively higher levels to make sure that the men in front of them could not be unsuspectingly attacked from above or from the rear.

The tactics that Boelcke taught became standard among combat pilots of all the nations involved in the war. But tactical skill was not enough; pilots who survived developed a high degree of "situational awareness"—knowing what was going on at all times and in all places in the thick of combat. Rickenbacker had to practice constantly in the early weeks of his training at the front before he mastered this highly demanding art. Continually turning his head up and down, forward and backward, and from side to side while his plane was buffeted by air currents or the shock waves of exploding antiaircraft shells caused him great physical strain. It also nauseated him, particularly because he was continually inhaling castor oil vapor.

Just as German recruits developed situational awareness under teachers like Boelcke, Rickenbacker learned this skill under Raoul Lufbery, who played the same mentoring role in his military career that Lee Frayer had provided earlier in his life. Lufbery, who was born in France but had become an American citizen during a fascinating career that took him around the world, was a veteran of the Lafayette Escadrille. His flying skills were legendary; as one account states, "he flew as a bird flies, without any thought of how it was done." He had won seventeen victories with the Escadrille, and newspapers in America were full of stories about his exploits. After the United States declared war on Germany he was transferred to the Army Air Service. Commissioned as a major and posted to Issoudun, he was given an office job that made him miserable. As a result, he was sent to the front to prepare pilots like Rickenbacker for combat.[17]

The first chapter of *Fighting the Flying Circus* begins by telling how Lufbery led two members of the 94th Pursuit Squadron, of whom Rickenbacker was one, on a patrol across the German lines. The fact that the sortie *crossed* the enemy lines is also significant. Throughout the war, partly because the Germans had fewer pilots and planes than the Allies, and also because they had to conserve fuel, they practiced a defensive mode of aerial warfare, waiting for Allied planes to enter their territory before taking off to attack them.

By contrast, British, French, and American squadrons pursued a policy of attrition, with large numbers of aircraft sent into German-held areas to seek targets. These contrasting strategies explain why most of the action in *Fighting the Flying Circus* takes place behind the German lines.

[17]James Norman Hall and Charles B. Nordhoff, *The Lafayette Flying Corps* (Boston and New York: Houghton Mifflin Company, 1920), 328-338. It should be noted that Lufbery did not command the 94th, as some writers have supposed. He was a flight leader.

The "Hat in the Ring" Squadron (all are lieutenants at the time, except as noted).
Left to right—first row: L. Prinz, H.H. Tittman, F. Ordway, W.W. Smyth. Second row:
W.G. Loomis, C.A. Snow, M.E. Green, A.F. Winslow, Capt. K. Marr, E.V. Rickenbacker,
J.A. Meissner, T.C. Taylor, G.W. Zacharias. Third row: H. Coolidge, A.L. Cunningham,
W.W. Chalmers, J.H. Eastman, A.B. Sherry, J. Wentworth, R.Z. Cates, E. Clark, J.N. Jeffers.

Courtesy United States Air Force, 1st Fighter Wing History Office

lvii

As Rickenbacker and his comrades gained experience and self-confidence under the tutelage of flyers like Lufbery, they fought with great skill and distinction. The 94th had the best record of any American squadron in the war. It won the first and last victories scored by an American unit, shot down more German planes, and had more Aces on its roster. It also had the first officially recognized American Ace, Douglas Campbell, and the American Ace of Aces, Rickenbacker. Its Hat-in-the-Ring emblem, with which Rickenbacker proudly identified himself throughout his life, became one of the most honored insignias to come out of the war.

But the 94th had a far less enviable record before Rickenbacker finally took command of the unit on 25 September 1918. The reason behind his promotion shows how war could catapult a person with little formal education but much ability into a leadership position he could not have attained in peacetime.

Jean W. F. M. Huffer, an American who had been born in Paris and spoke French as his native language, had led the 94th when it started operations at Villeneuve in March 1918. Highly personable, he was a popular commander. In June, however, he was given a new post and was succeeded by Kenneth Marr, veteran of the Lafayette Escadrille whom the members of the unit disliked. Morale dwindled and the number of victories won by the squadron declined sharply. Mechanics who had been accustomed to the Gnome *monosoupape* had difficulty with the complexity of the

Hispano-Suiza engine after the Nieuport 28s were replaced by Spad XIIIs. Often, the 94th did not have
enough flyable aircraft to conduct assigned operations. Harold E. Hartney, a Canadian-born colonel
who headed the 1st Pursuit Group, of which the 94th
squadron was a part, became frustrated. Late in September he relieved Marr of his command.[18]

Acting against the advice of his own superiors on
the staff of Pershing's headquarters at Chaumont,
Hartney replaced Marr with Rickenbacker. "In the
first place he was older and more mature," Hartney explained later. "The average age of our war flyers was
around 19 and 20. They were reckless, daring, brilliant
and often foolhardy. When Rickenbacker started to
fly he was 28 and remarkably mature even for that age.
He was daring, fearless, often brilliant but never reckless and never foolhardy. An army of Rickenbackers in
the sky would be invincible."[19]

The most important reason why Hartney chose
Rickenbacker, however, was that he needed his help
in solving the mechanical problems plaguing the 94th
after the Nieuports, which Hartney admired, were replaced by the Spads, which he detested. Hartney was

---

[18]For a history of the 1st Pursuit Group containing references
to the internal politics mentioned here, see James J. Sloan, Jr.,
Wings of Honor: American Airmen in World War I (Atglen, Pa.:
Schiffer Publishing Ltd., 1994), 101-135.
[19]Harold E. Hartney, *Up And At 'Em* (Harrisburg, Pa.: Stack-
pole Sons, 1940), 290. Chapter 16 of Hartney's book explains in
detail the circumstances under which Rickenbacker replaced
Marr.

much concerned about the morale of his mechanics. He knew that Rickenbacker could communicate better with the men who repaired and serviced the Spads than any officer in the unit. In particular, Hartney knew that Rickenbacker understood the Spad's Hispano-Suiza engines.

Hartney encountered much skepticism at Pershing's headquarters about Rickenbacker's fitness to command the 94th. But there was no opposition to the move on the base at Rembercourt where the unit was now stationed. Before making his decision, Hartney spoke privately to every pilot in the squadron who outranked Rickenbacker in terms of seniority, receiving their unanimous support. Meanwhile, at Chaumont, Mitchell's knowledge of Rickenbacker's abilities stood his former driver in good stead. Much to Rickenbacker's surprise, for he knew nothing about the discussions that were taking place, Hartney gave him control of the 94th and he was promoted to the rank of captain. Had he been the type of person held suitable for a leadership post by Pershing's staff, he would have become a major, which was the usual rank for the chief officer of a squadron.

The mostly college-trained pilots who served under Rickenbacker did not question his qualifications. "His officers respected him greatly and he not only led them always but ruled them with a rather firm hand and they liked it," Hartney stated. Rickenbacker's rough edges were apparent to well-educated pilots who winced at his faulty grammar during briefings, but what really counted was the quality of his leadership skills. "It has been said that in no other Allied squadron in France," stated one study of Ace combat pilots, "was there so much fraternalism, and such subordination of the individual to the organization."[20]

Rickenbacker stressed the importance of unselfishness and ordered his pilots to subordinate their egos to the greater good of the squadron as a whole. He believed strongly in formation flying and instructed his men to "look after each other." He also stated that it was no disgrace for a pilot to get out of a combat situation in which the odds were heavily stacked against him. His policy of avoiding casualties by practicing prudence at all times later became known as "Calculated Risk Management," and he is regarded as one of its pioneers.

The bedrock of Rickenbacker's leadership style was that he asked nothing of his pilots that he was unwilling to do himself. On the day of his promotion he took on seven enemy planes single-handedly, shooting down two and scattering the rest of the formation. He belatedly received the Medal of Honor in 1930 for his conduct in this engagement. Nevertheless, he did not try to aggrandize his victory total, high as it became. When accompanying younger pilots on instructional flights, he let them go for the final kill rather than inflate his personal score.

Rickenbacker had good reason to be proud of his

[20]Quoted in Tony Kern, *Redefining Airmanship* (New York: McGraw-Hill, 1997), 16.

accomplishments. He had decided to publish a book about his experiences. His only problem was that he lacked the requisite writing skills. As usual, this was an obstacle that he would overcome.

* * * *

Rickenbacker decided to publish his book during the summer of 1918, when he was hospitalized in Paris. His motives then were consistent with the American Dream. He had heard that Lufbery had been offered $50,000 for his memoirs. Rickenbacker's winnings on the racetrack, which he had given to his mother, would not last indefinitely; he needed to make provision for his return to civilian life. First, however, he needed a ghostwriter. Fortunately, an excellent choice became available to him.

Laurence La Tourette Driggs came from a social and economic background far superior to that of Rickenbacker.[21] He was born in 1876 in Saginaw, Michigan, where his grandfather, John Fletcher Driggs, had prospered in the lumber and salt industries and been active in Republican politics. During the 1860s, he represented Michigan's upper peninsula in Congress for three terms before being defeated in a race for the United States Senate.

Laroy Channing Driggs, Laurence's father, was also

[21]I am grateful to Mrs. Laurence La Tourette Driggs II, of Easton, Md., for granting access to an unpublished typewritten autobiography, on which the discussion that follows is based, that Driggs wrote for a genealogy.

a person of substance. While John Fletcher Driggs
was in Congress, Laroy was his personal secretary. He
then pursued banking and the lumber business in
Michigan, New Jersey, and Arkansas before moving to
Oregon. There, he went into partnership in the same
fields of enterprise with relatives of his wife, Mary La
Tourette, from whom Laurence derived his distinctive
middle name.

Laurence La Tourette Driggs was raised in afflu-
ence in Willamette, Oregon. After graduating from
high school, he went to the University of Michigan,
whose president had been a close friend of his grandfather. He managed a student newspaper in Ann Arbor
while working toward an undergraduate degree to
qualify for admission to the university law school.
When his father was swindled by some business associates, he financed the rest of his college education
by working at a publishing house in Chicago.

After he had completed a year of law school at the
University of Michigan, Driggs went to New York City
to visit his brother Edmund, who was a lawyer, and decided to stay there to complete his legal training. Living on Washington Square, he clerked for his brother
while going to classes at New York Law School. He
completed his studies in one year through furious
cramming, passed his bar examinations, and became
an accident investigator. He also argued cases in superior court.

As his reputation grew, Driggs prospered. He
opened a law office on Nassau Street in New York

Laurence La Tourette Driggs

Courtesy W. David Lewis

City and earned increasingly large fees for his professional services. Becoming active in Republican politics, he ran for Congress in a Democratic district and lost by 30,000 votes. He traveled abroad, became an officer in a militia unit, joined prestigious clubs, and patronized the arts.

Driggs, however, had a restless streak that impelled him in new directions. In 1911 he bought a 20,000-acre ranch in the Texas Panhandle and ran it for two years. In 1915 he bought a copper mine in Colorado. Returning to New York, he joined one of his cousins, who headed an ordnance firm, in developing a gun for use in airplanes. Going to England, he took seaplane trips down the Thames, demonstrating the gun to military officials. He secured an order from the Royal Air Service and familiarized himself with the British aviation program by visiting various factories and training schools.

Aviation had fascinated Driggs since 1909, when he joined the Aero Club of America. He learned to fly in 1913 by taking lessons at Mineola on Long Island. During the next few years, he became well known among aviation enthusiasts. After coming home from England in 1917 he went to Washington and spent two days reporting to Billy Mitchell and other officers in the Signal Corps about what he had seen.

Unlike Rickenbacker, who got a cold shoulder from the military establishment because he lacked social and educational credentials, Driggs was told by the Signal Corps he would be commissioned as an officer if the United States entered the war. On going back to New York, he published an article in *Outlook* on the role of aviation in warfare.[22] It caught the attention of Theodore Roosevelt, who was trying to form a volunteer unit to fight for the Allied cause. Encouraged by Roosevelt and General Leonard Wood, Driggs recruited a group of aviators that he was slated to command with the rank of colonel (he was known as "Colonel Driggs" for the rest of his life). But the unit was never approved by Woodrow Wilson, who was hostile to Roosevelt and Wood.

After the United States declared war on Germany, Driggs went to Washington to claim the commission the Signal Corps had promised him. But the War Department vetoed the appointment because of his Republican ties. Frustrated and resentful, Driggs returned to New York, where he wrote articles about the role of aviation in the war for several magazines. He also created a fictional Ace named Arnold Adair and wrote stories about him.[23] Driggs thus became one of the chief American exponents of the Cult of the Ace.

Eager to play a more active role in the war, Driggs finally got his wish when Lord Northcliffe, owner of the *London Times* and British minister of information, visited the United States and happened to play golf with him. After Northcliffe returned to England he invited Driggs to visit as a guest of the British gov-

[22]"Fourth Arm in Warfare," published in the March 21 issue.
[23]"Air Scout: The Adventures of Arnold Adair," serialized in *Outlook*, 17, 31 October, 7, 21 November, and 5, 16 December 1917.

ernment, to be an official observer of military operations. Jumping at the chance, Driggs sailed from New York in July 1918 on a troop transport.

Driggs became a member of the Royal Air Force Club and met prominent British aviation officials. He helped Northcliffe's staff prepare propaganda leaflets to be dropped inside the German lines, visited aircraft factories, inspected captured enemy planes, and met prominent figures in the British aviation industry.

In June 1918, Driggs went to France as an official observer of British air operations. Landing at Boulogne, he was lodged in a chateau reserved for important guests and given tours of Ypres, Vimy Ridge, Arras, Bapaume, and Amiens. No courtesy was withheld from him. He visited forty squadrons and gathered large amounts of information for future books and articles. Billy Mitchell invited him to lunch and gave him permission to inspect American aerodromes.

Driggs met Rickenbacker while visiting Hartney's pursuit group. He could not help but be impressed with the tall young pilot who had achieved so much in such a short time. Rickenbacker quickly recognized that Driggs was the person he needed to write his book. On 9 November 1918, two days before the war ended, he asked Driggs to be his ghostwriter. Driggs agreed, and the two men worked out the details of a contract signed on 16 November. In exchange for 25 percent of the gross receipts from all sales, Driggs would "edit and revamp the experiences of [Rickenbacker's] aerial career on the Western Front for the

purpose of serial stories for magazines and composition of book." The contract also specified that the
book and stories would appear only under the name
of Rickenbacker, and that Rickenbacker would own
the copyright.[24]

Rickenbacker provided Driggs with a diary he had
kept, and later gave him a preliminary account of his
experiences.[25] The latter has 122 typewritten pages,
most of which are single-spaced. It is composed of
short segments, sometimes only three pages long.
Rickenbacker began preparing it on 13 November
1918. The writing style of the document, which is now
in the Library of Congress, is not polished. The typewritten format suggests that Rickenbacker dictated
oral reminiscences to someone on his clerical staff—
perhaps the squadron's information officer—who took
handwritten notes and would presumably type them
up at the end of each day.

Because of its outstanding combat record, the 94th
was given the honor of being the only squadron to accompany Pershing and his staff into Germany, where
the Americans would be headquartered at Coblenz.
Before the move took place, Driggs went to Coblenz
with Rickenbacker and two of his comrades, Douglas
Campbell and James A. Meissner, to find a suitable

[24]A copy of the contract is in the Rickenbacker Collection,
AUA.
[25]The diary is now at the United States Air Force Museum; the
preliminary text is in Box 91 of the Edward V. Rickenbacker Papers at the Library of Congress.

aerodrome for the squadron's planes for the duration.

"We spent three days touring the Rhine country, visiting the Saar and Luxembourg, seeing the first American troops marching over the bridge to occupy the Rhine," Driggs wrote. When the 94th occupied its new quarters, Driggs went along.

Just before Christmas, Driggs left Coblenz to spend the holidays in Paris and London. A week after he reached London, Rickenbacker, Campbell, and Meissner arrived and took him to a theater. Shortly thereafter, Driggs sailed for America on the *Aquitania*. While waiting at Liverpool for the ship to depart, and "all the way over," he "worked steadily on Rick's book, finally naming it *Fighting the Flying Circus*."

After Driggs reached the United States and completed the manuscript, Driggs and Rickenbacker accepted $25,000 from the McClure Syndicate for serial rights. While Rickenbacker was swept up in celebrations held in his honor all across America, Driggs negotiated a contract with the Frederick A. Stokes Company of New York City to publish the manuscript in book form. It came out within a few months, and Driggs and Rickenbacker jointly earned approximately $25,000 in royalties.

The reviews were good; one that appeared in a trade publication, *Bookseller*, stated that it would "make an American leap with patriotic joy."[26] Stokes continued to reprint *Fighting the Flying Circus* into the

[26]Clipping in Scrapbook I, Rickenbacker Collection, AUA.

1930s. Rickenbacker also distributed a large number of copies in the mid-1920s, when he manufactured an automobile bearing his own name. Every customer who bought a Rickenbacker received the book as a gift.

* * * *

A word of caution is in order before proceeding to the vivid and entertaining narrative that follows. In addition to finding an appreciative audience among general readers, *Fighting the Flying Circus* has been used by scholars as a source of information about World War I. Most of the events that it recounts can be verified from dependable sources. It is well to remember, however, that the book was conceived as a collection of stories, and that neither Driggs nor Rickenbacker intended everything it contains to be taken literally. Driggs was free to embellish the details that Rickenbacker gave him, and he sometimes did so. Thus, in the end, *Fighting the Flying Circus* should be judged as an absorbing tale of adventure and human courage, for that is what it is and always will be as long as readers savor the eternal delights of a good tale, well told.

W. DAVID LEWIS

Auburn University
June 1997

Fighting the Flying Circus

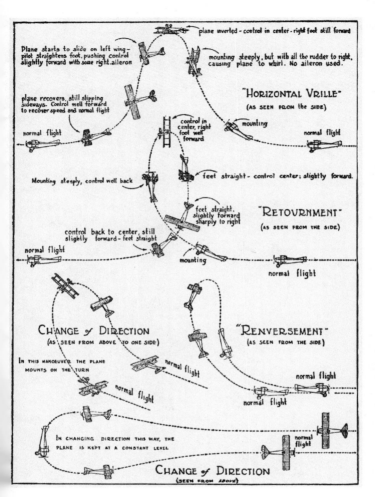

Illustration of aerial maneuvers, from the original edition of Fighting the Flying Circus

GLOSSARY OF
AVIATION EXPRESSIONS

ACE. A fighting pilot who has brought down five enemy machines.

ARCHY. Antiaircraft shells.

AERODROME. Field where aeroplanes land and are housed.

BANK. To tilt an aeroplane sideways in rounding a corner.

BARREL. Rolling the aeroplane over and over in the air, like a barrel.

BIPLACE. Two places or seats, a two-seater aeroplane. A monoplace has but one seat. A triplace has three.

CEILING. Topmost level an aeroplane can reach.

CHANDELLE. To make an upward corkscrew climb.

CONTACT. To put on the spark.

COUPEZ. Cut off the spark.

DUD. Dead, or bad.

HANGAR. Garage for housing aeroplanes.

JAGDSTAFFEL. German term for fighting squadron.

JOYSTICK. The aeroplane's steering and control lever.

OFFICE. The cockpit of an aeroplane, where the pilot sits.

PANNE. A forced landing caused by engine failure.

PIQUÉ. To dive vertically downward, with engine either open or shut.

RENVERSEMENT. A sudden reversal of direction of flight. This is not to be confused with "bank," as the latter is a slow movement. A renversement is usually executed by suddenly zooming up, then throwing the aeroplane over onto one wing and kicking the tail around to the rear.

SAUCE. Petrol or gasoline.

5

STRAFING. Assailing an enemy with bullets or bombs.

VIRAGE. A bank or circle in the air.

VOLUNTARY PATROL. A voluntary flight by a pilot over the lines.

VRILLE. A tailspin. The aeroplane falls earthward, with tail above always swinging around the nose of the machine, which acts as a pivot. The motion is similar to the rotation of a match in a whirlpool.

WIND UP. Scared, having the wind go up one's spine, causing the hair to stand on end with fear.

ZOOM. To pitch the aeroplane suddenly upward at great speed. Usually accomplished after a dive has given the aeroplane additional momentum.

FOREWORD

EDDIE RICKENBACKER's stories of his air battles in France are of exciting interest, both in the narration of the thrilling adventures with enemy airmen and in the revealment to the reader of his intimate thoughts and feelings, as he went out day after day to attack the boasted champions of the German Air Service.

Eddie Rickenbacker was the idol of the automobile racing world at the moment when America entered the war. He was then in England, engaged in the production of a racing car with which to win further laurels in his profession.[1] Burning with the desire to enter war aviation and convinced of the advantages that his racing experiences would give him in this exciting sport of the air, he returned to New York where he sought to enlist all the automobile racing men into one squadron of fighting pilots. But official enthusiasm could not be aroused in Washington for this project, and necessary funds were lacking.

Mindful of the delays that the consummation of his plan might occasion, Eddie Rickenbacker suddenly accepted General Pershing's invitation to sail with him the next day. He enlisted in the infantry and became the driver of the general's automobile at the front, where he wisely foresaw that he would find a quicker opportunity for entering the flying service.

[1]This statement is in error; EVR was back in America by the time the United States declared war on Germany.

7

In eighteen months he returned, the American Ace of Aces!

Captain Rickenbacker deserves the gratitude of the American people—not only because he is the American Ace of Aces —not only because he destroyed twenty-six German aircraft in combat —but more especially because the extraordinary inspiration of his examples at the front and his ability as a squadron leader brought very remarkable success to many other American air fighters who were under his leadership.

After having visited some sixty-odd British flying squadrons at the front, many of the French escadrilles and all of the American squadrons, I was given the pleasure of entering Germany, after the Armistice was signed, as the guest of the Hat-in-the-Ring Squadron, of which Captain Rickenbacker was the commanding officer. In no other organization in France did I find so great a loyalty to a leader, such true squadron fraternalism, such subordination of the individual to the organization. In other words, the commander of Squadron 94 had perfected the finest flying corps I have ever seen.

This recognition of the author's character is essential to an adequate appreciation of his story. Between the lines one is impressed with the constant desire of perfecting himself that permeates his every combat. Rickenbacker is full of the feeling of responsibility that every true leader must know. He is frankly scared over the additional risks that leadership must force upon him. Yet he carries on, assuming these additional risks, which in truth not only limit his private successes but constantly threaten to sacrifice his life for a companion.

If he had been a free lance, Eddie Rickenbacker might easily have doubled his score of victories even in the short period of America's service in the war. Without the duty of directing the movements and guarding the safety of his less competent pilots, he would have had both the time and the opportunity for brilliant successes innumerable.

Never once in all his fighting career did Captain Rickenbacker permit an enemy pilot to injure him!

This remarkable fact at once forces the conclusion that our American Ace of Aces was not only superior to the enemy airmen he vanquished, but by saving himself for the continued service of his country, he was superior to all those rival expert duelists who, despite their extraordinary ability as pilots and sharp-shooters, unfortunately lacked the judgment to save from wounds their valuable persons for further encounters with the enemy.

The Hat-in-the-Ring Squadron ended the war with the greatest number of victories won by an American squadron. It was the first to go over the enemy's lines—it was the first to destroy an enemy machine—it brought down the last German aeroplane to fall in this war.

It contained the first American Ace, Douglas Campbell, of California, and the greatest American Ace, Eddie Rickenbacker, of Ohio. It totaled more hours of flying over enemy lines than any other American squadron can claim. And finally, Squadron 94 was given the distinction it so richly deserved when it was selected as the only fighting squadron in all our forces to move into Germany with our Army of Occupation.

To the leadership of Captain Rickenbacker this crack squadron of American pilots owes its proud position. It will go down in history as the greatest fighting squadron America sent to the war.

Popular as Eddie Rickenbacker is at home, that popularity does not equal the esteem in which he is held by airmen in France. Perhaps no soldier today holds quite so high a position in the hearts of the American aviators and the American public as does Captain Eddie Rickenbacker. I am sure it is due him to say, none could deserve it more.

LAURENCE LA TOURETTE DRIGGS

I

Introducing "Archy"

Aftre days of schooling and nights of anticipation, I woke up one morning to find my dreams come true. Major Raoul Lufbery, the most famous of our American flyers, and the commanding officer of our group, announced that a flight would take off after breakfast for a look at the war across the German lines. He, himself, was to lead the flight. The patrol was to be over enemy territory in the Champagne sector.

"Who is to go?" was the thought in every pilot's mind as we all stood by in more or less unconcealed eagerness. None of us had as yet caught a glimpse of our future arenas. We all had vague ideas of the several kinds of surprises in store for us over enemy lines and every one of us was keen to get into it.

Major Lufbery looked us over without saying much. Luf was very quiet in manner and very droll when he wanted to be. He had seen four years of service with the French Air Service and the Lafayette Escadrille,[1] and had shot down seventeen aeroplanes before the

[1] Escadrille refers to a squadron. After the French organized an American aerial volunteer unit on 16 April 1916, it was known as the "Escadrille Americaine." German objections to having the name of a neutral country used in this manner caused it to be re-named the "Escadrille Lafayette" on 9 December 1916.

American Air Service began active work at the front. Every one of us idolized Lufbery.

"Rick!" said the major casually, "you and Campbell be ready to leave at 8:15."

I tried to appear nonchalant as I replied, "Yes, sir."

Douglas Campbell put up a much better face than I did. The other boys crowded around and presented us with good advice, such as "Look out for Archy, mind," and one thoughtful fellow kindly cautioned me to crash in our lines if the enemy got me, so that he could personally put a cross over my grave.

That most memorable morning was 6 March 1918.[2] I had joined the Hat-in-the-Ring Squadron just two days before at Villeneuve.[3] We were then some twenty miles behind the lines and were well installed on an old aerodrome that had been used previously by several French aero squadrons. This expedition was to be the first essay over the lines by a made-in-America squadron.

Sharp upon eight o'clock I walked into the Squadron 94 hangar and called my mechanics. We were flying the French single-seater Nieuport with a rotary motor, and every machine was kept in the pink of condition at all times. Nevertheless I wanted to make doubly sure that everything was right on this occa-

[2]According to Rickenbacker's diary, 28 March 1918. The opening page of the original text of *Fighting the Flying Circus* (see Edward Vernon Rickenbacker Papers, Library of Congress, Washington, D.C., Box 91) is badly organized, explaining several errors made by Driggs in the first chapter of the published book.

[3]EVR arrived at Villeneuve-les-Vertus 6 March 1918.

Major Raoul Lufbery   *Captain James Norman Hall*

Courtesy Auburn University Archives

sion, for Major Lufbery had a well-known reputation for punctuality.

I left the hangar and looked down the road for the major. Campbell was already in his flying clothes. I wanted to be ready on the exact minute, but not too soon. So I lit a cigarette and kept an eye on the major's door. All the boys came sauntering up, trying to look as though they were not half mad with envy over my chance to get my head blown off first. They wished me well, they said, but they would like to know what to do with my personal effects.

When Major Lufbery entered the hangar he found us ready for him. It takes about ten seconds to step into your Teddy-Bear suit, slip a flying helmet over your head, and snap on the glasses.[4] Campbell and I climbed into our Nieuports. The major gave a few instructions to Lieutenant Campbell, then came over to me. I felt like a man in the chair when the dentist approaches. Of course I listened very politely to his parting words, but the only things that appealed to me in his discourse were the orders to stick close to him and keep formation. He did not have to repeat that order. Never before did I realize how seductively cold death beckons a pilot toward his first trip over enemy lines.

Lufbery ran up his motor for a moment, then took

[4]"Teddy-Bear suit": the fur-lined coat and helmet worn to protect pilots from extreme cold at high altitudes. "Glasses": EVR would have used the term "goggles" had he actually written this passage.

off. Campbell followed on his heels and then I opened up my throttle. I cast a last, longing glance at the familiar flying field as I felt my tail go up; the wheels began to skim the ground, and, with the wind in my teeth, I pulled her up and headed after Campbell. What a devil of a hurry they were in! I knew I should never catch up with them.

The beautiful ruins of Reims soon spread beneath my right wing.[5] My machine was certainly not as fast as either Lufbery's or Campbell's. I continued to hang back far behind my formation. The lines of the enemy were approaching and Lufbery, my only salvation, as it appeared to me, was at least a mile ahead of me.

I shall believe to my dying day that Major Lufbery knew my thoughts at that moment. For just as I felt that he had forgotten all about me, he suddenly made a *virage* and took up a position a few hundred feet from me, as much as to say, "Don't worry, my boy, I have an eye on you." Again and again this occurred.

It was with great difficulty that I tried to perform the same maneuvers that Major Lufbery executed with such great ease. I grew somewhat interested with my attempts to imitate his example in preserving our little flight formation, and this occupation of keeping within shouting distance of my companions made me forget entirely that old Mother Earth was some 15,000 feet underneath me and the trenches about the same

[5]Reims was hit repeatedly by German shells in World War I. Its famous cathedral was not fully restored until 1938.

distance ahead. The bitter, numbing cold, which always prevails at these high altitudes, was by this time
an old and familiar experience to me.

We had been sailing along at this dizzy height for
some thirty minutes between Reims and the Argonne
Woods when it occurred to me to look below at the
landscape. And such a spectacle spread itself out before my eyes when I at last did look over the side of my
little office!

The trenches in this sector were quite old and had
remained in practically the same position for three
years of warfare. To my inexperienced view there appeared to be nothing below me but old battered
trenches, trench works, and billions of shellholes that
had dug up the whole surface of the earth for four or
five miles on either side of me. Not a tree, not a fence,
no sign of any familiar occupation of mankind, nothing but a chaos of ruin and desolation. The awfulness
of the thing was truly appalling.

Perhaps this feeling got the best of me for a moment.
I don't know of what Campbell was thinking and I
suppose Major Lufbery was far too accustomed to the
situation to give a thought to it.

But just when I had gained enough equilibrium of
mind to keep my place in formation and at the same
time take an interest in the battlefields below me, I
began to feel a terrible seasickness. A stiff wind was
blowing and no ship on the high seas ever rolled and
pitched more than my Nieuport, while I was attempting to follow Major Lufbery's maneuvers.

I didn't want to confess even to myself that I could get sick in the air. This was what would be expected from a brand new aviator on his first trip over the lines. It would be wonderfully amusing to Lufbery and the rest of the boys in the squadron when I got back to the field—if I ever did—to advise me to take along a bottle of medicine next time I tried to fly. I grew cold with the thought of it. Then I set my teeth and prayed that I might fight it off. I determined to look forward and fly straight ahead and concentrate my whole mind on the task of sticking it out.

I had hardly gotten control of myself when I was horribly startled by an explosion that seemed only a few feet to my rear. I didn't even have time to look around, for at the same instant the concussion caught my plane and I began to roll and toss much worse than I had ever realized was possible. The very terror of my situation drove away all thoughts of sickness. In the midst of it several more shocks tipped my machine and repeated sounds of nearby explosions smote my ears. No matter what happened, I must look around to see what awful fate was overtaking me.

All that I could see were four or five black puffs of smoke some distance behind and below my tail.

I knew what they were right enough. They were "Archy!"[6] They were eighteen-pound shells of shrapnel that were being fired at me by the Germans. And

[6]"Archy": an expression of contempt for enemy antiaircraft fire that had originated in the British sector.

the battery that was firing them was only too well known to me. We had all been told about the most accurate battery that Allied aviators had met in this sector. It was situated just outside of the small town of Suippes. There was Suippes down there just under my left wing. A mile north of Suippes was the exact location of this famous shooting battery. I looked down and picked it out quite clearly. I knew they could see me and were seeing me much more plainly than I was seeing them. And probably they had quite a few more of those shells on hand that they were contemplating popping up at me.

I shall never forget how scared I was and how enraged I felt at the old pilots at home who pretended to like the Archies. The latter were bursting all around me again and were terribly close, and I felt a vengeful desire to get home just once more in order to take it out on those blasé pilots who had been telling us newcomers that antiaircraft guns were a joke and never did any damage. They used to count up the cost of each shell at five or ten dollars apiece and then figure that they had cost the German government about a million dollars for their morning's amusement. Any one of those shells might happen to hit me just as well as happen to burst 100 yards away. It was due entirely to my own good luck, and not all to those scoffers' silly advice, that one of them hadn't hit me already. I was more indignant with the boys who had been stuffing me with their criminal wit than I was with the gunners who were firing at me.

Never before did I and never again will I quite so much appreciate the comfort of having a friend near at hand. I suddenly noticed that Major Lufbery was alongside me. Almost subconsciously I followed his maneuvers and gradually I began to realize that each maneuver he made was a direct word of encouragement to me. His machine seemed to speak to me, to soothe my feelings, to prove to me that there was no danger so long as I followed its wise leadership.

Little by little my alarm passed away. I began to watch the course of the black puffs behind me. I grew accustomed to the momentary disturbance of the air after each explosion, and almost mechanically I met the lift of the machine with the gentle pressure of my joystick, which righted my Nieuport and smoothed its course.

I suddenly discovered that Major Lufbery was leading us homeward. I glanced at the clock on my dashboard. It was nearly ten o'clock. We had been out almost two hours and our fuel supply must be running low. These fast-flying fighting machines cannot carry a large supply of gasoline and oil, as every pound of weight counts against the speed and climbing powers of the aeroplane.

Gradually we descended as we approached the vicinity of our aerodrome. We circled once about the field and, shutting off the motor, slid gently down into the mud, which quickly brought the machines to a full pause. Quickening the speed of the propellers, we taxied one by one toward the door of the hangar before which every pilot and mechanic stood awaiting us with open-armed expectancy. They were eager to hear the details of our first flight into enemy territory and to see how two beginners, like themselves, had withstood the experience.

Just here Major Lufbery broke into the conversation and asked us particularly what we had seen. I didn't like the sound of his customary little chuckle on this occasion. But we both repeated as easily as we could that we hadn't seen any other aeroplanes in the sky.

"Just what I expected. They are all the same!" was the major's only comment.

We indignantly asked him what he meant by addressing two expert war pilots in such tones.

"Well," said Lufbery, "one formation of five Spads crossed under us before we passed the lines, and another flight of five Spads went by about fifteen minutes later and you didn't see them, although neither one of them was more than 500 yards away. It was just as well they were not German!

"Then there were four German Albatros two miles ahead of us when we turned back and there was another enemy two-seater nearer us than that at about 5,000 feet above the lines. You ought to look about a bit when you get in enemy lines."

Campbell and I stood aghast, looking at each other. Then I saw he was thinking the same thoughts as I. The major was ragging us from a sense of duty, to take some of the conceit out of us. But it was only after weeks of experience over the front that we realized how true his statements probably were. No matter how good a flyer the scout may be and no matter how perfect his eyesight is, he must learn to see before he can distinguish objects either on the ground or in air. What is called "vision of the air" can come only from experience, and no pilot ever has it on his first arrival at the front.

Then sauntering over to my machine the major bucked me up very considerably by blandly inquiring "How much of that shrapnel did you get, Rick?" I couldn't help laughing at his effort to put me in a heroic picture frame for the benefit of the boys who were listening. Imagine my horror when he began poking his finger in one shrapnel hole in the tail; another fragment had gone through the outer edge of the wing, and a third had passed directly through both wings not a foot from my body!

The boys told me afterward that I stayed pale for a good thirty minutes and I believe them, for a week passed before the major suggested to me that I again accompany him into the German lines.

II

The Aerodrome

I OFTEN WONDERED whether the mothers and friends of our pilots formed a true conception back home of the surroundings and daily doings of their loved ones in France. Even the term "aerodrome"—where it is known that aeroplanes are landed, kept and cared for, where the pilots live and start from in their trips over the lines and where they are anxiously awaited at the end of their patrol by their comrades—even "aerodrome" must convey a more or less uncertain picture to those who have never actually seen one.

Picture in your minds a smooth field covered with sod and occupying a situation near a town and good highway. It is on comparatively level ground and is square in shape, and each of the four sides is about half a mile in length.

Such a field accommodates very nicely four squadrons of fighting machines, which means eighty or ninety aeroplanes and as many pilots. The road skirts one side of the square. Close to the road in each corner of the square are placed two large sheds, or hangars, to house the aeroplanes. Each hangar will hold comfortably ten or twelve machines of the small type. There they spend the night and each machine is carefully inspected by the mechanics who "belong to it." Each pilot has three mechanics who are responsible for his aeroplane, and it is seldom that any defect can escape their jealous attention.

Around the edges of the field, then, these eight or ten large hangars stand facing inward, with wide open doors through which the aeroplane can pass onto the ground. A short distance away are situated the mess and sleeping quarters for the officers of each squadron. As there are but twenty pilots to each squadron, the officers of two squadrons frequently mess together. The enlisted men, including the mechanics, truck drivers, workmen, and servants, occupy quarters of their own at a little distance behind the hangars. As each squadron requires almost 200 enlisted men to take proper care of its many details, it is seen that the entire personnel of the average aerodrome group numbers quite 1,000 men when the Headquarters, Searchlight Company, Telephone Squad, Lighting Plant, Red Cross, and Y.M.C.A. personnel are added to it. The antiaircraft gunners who have charge of the defense of the aerodrome against enemy raids are not attached to the Air Service and are not properly part of the aerodrome membership.

Such then is the rough arrangement of the pilots' aerodrome. From the sky an aerodrome can be seen many miles away by an experienced observer and although every effort is made to camouflage hangars, huts, and aeroplanes, no flying fields can long be in use by either side before they are discovered by the enemy.

We were but three weeks in the aerodrome at

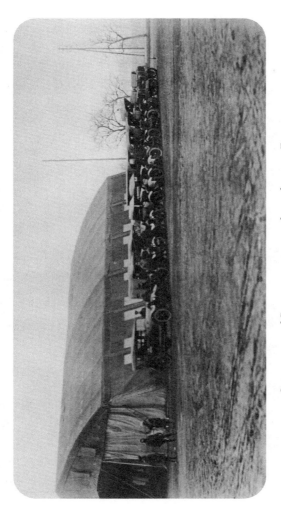

Canvas-covered Bessoneau-type aerodrome hangar, France

Courtesy Auburn University Archives

Villeneuve, at which time the weather was so severe that comparatively little flying was undertaken by the first of our American pilots who formed this unit. March 1918 had snow storms, heavy rains, and high winds. Our aeroplanes were not of the best, and they had not yet been fully equipped.

An amusing episode occurred in this connection, which seems funnier now than it did at that time. The French authorities very kindly made arrangements to help train the new pilots of our squadron in combat fighting over the lines. Accordingly, every day or two an experienced French airman would drop down upon our field and take away with him two of our in-experienced freshmen for a trip into Germany, just as Major Lufbery had taken Campbell and myself. Naturally all of our pilots were anxious to go.

After two weeks' patrolling over enemy territory in this manner, you can imagine the consternation of these French flight leaders when they discovered that the American machines that had accompanied them carried no aeroplane guns! Our machine guns had not yet arrived![1]

It was at this period that we lost one of my dearest friends and a commander who was respected and loved by all the pilots. Captain James Miller had left

[1]The squadron's planes were armed with machine guns by 18 March 1918. Contrary to many accounts based on this passage, EVR's first patrol with Lufbery and Campbell was armed with machine guns. The unarmed patrols mentioned here were flown by Squadron 95, which had come to Villeneuve-les-Vertus earlier than the 94th.

family and home and a prosperous business in New York to serve his country over the battlefields of France. He was a light-hearted, lovable companion, but I had long ago discovered the stern, determined qualities of his character. He had often told me that his greatest desire was to go into the skies and win a combat against an enemy aviator. The long delays in Paris irritated him, and his work in organizing the Aviation School at Issoudun for the training of American pilots did not satisfy him. He burned for an opportunity to get over the lines in a fighting plane.

I found Captain Miller at the Villeneuve aerodrome when I arrived there. He had command of the fighting squadron adjoining mine, the 95th. But he had no machines and no equipment and apparently he was as remote from air combats there as he had been in Paris. Still dominated with the one idea of getting into a fight with the enemy, it was especially difficult for him to be patient.

One day toward the middle of March we received a visit from Major [Davenport] Johnson and Major [Millard F.] Harmon, who were then temporarily attached to one of the French Spad squadrons in the vicinity. I shall never forget the boyish delight with which Captain Miller came to me after their departure and confided to me what he considered the most cherished secret in his life. Major Johnson had promised him that he might call at his aerodrome the following day and take a flight over the lines in one of their machines. He was happy over the prospect.

I never saw him again. The following evening we were notified through military channels that Captain James Miller was missing. Not until several days later did I learn the details of his disappearance. Then I learned that Major Johnson himself had accompanied Miller on his first flight and that they had passed over Reims and proceeded toward the Argonne Forest—the very same patrol on which Lufbery had taken me but a few days before.

Two squadrons of enemy machines were discovered some distance within the enemy lines and Miller, not observing them, flew in and was attacked. The enemy aeroplanes were two-seaters, carrying machine guns in front and behind. Major Johnson did not warn Miller, but returned to his field and landed, stating that his guns had jammed. Captain Miller was never seen again.

A month later a German official report reached us that Captain James Miller of the American Air Service had been wounded in combat and had fallen within German territory where he died a few hours later.

Poor Jim! His was the first and most sorrowful loss that had come to our new group. Then it was I learned that I must not permit myself to cherish friendships with my pilot comrades so intimately that their going would upset the work I had to do.[2]

These days of March 1918 were trying ones for our

[2]Miller, a Wall Street banker, had become friends with EVR on the *Baltic* when it took Pershing and his entourage to Europe in 1917, and had also helped EVR secure appointment as engineering officer at Issoudun.

Allies in the British and French armies. It was known that the enemy was preparing for a conclusive and tremendous push within a few days with which to gain the Channel ports against the British before U.S. troops could be in position to aid them.

The Germans knew better than did our own countrymen at home just how difficult would be our preparations for a really important force of aeroplanes. They had seen the spring months pass; instead of viewing with alarm the huge fleet of 20,000 aeroplanes sweeping the skies clear of German Fokkers, they had complacently witnessed the Fokkers occupying the air back of our lines whenever they desired it, with never an American plane to oppose them.[3]

On 21 March 1918, the great German attack was launched against the British in the north. We heard serious rumors about the numbers of prisoners captured by the enemy and the rapid advances they were making in each push.

Our aerodrome at Villeneuve was at that time but eighteen miles from the lines. In clear weather we could distinctly see our line of observation balloons that stretched along the front between us and the lines. The booming of guns sounded continuously in our ears. On 30 March we were ordered to move our squadrons to another aerodrome farther away from the front. We went to Epiez that day, where we

[3]This paragraph is a mordant comment on unfulfilled American plans to supply 20,475 planes to the Allied war effort within a year after the United States entered the war.

found ourselves about thirty miles from the front lines.

Here at Epiez, Squadron 94 was joined by Captain James Norman Hall, the author of *Kitchener's Mob* and *High Adventure*;[4] also Captain David McK. Peterson, of Honesdale, Pennsylvania. Both of them were experienced pilots who had become celebrated for their air work in the Lafayette Escadrille and who did much to hearten and instruct us during this forlorn period. We had all heard of these boys and idolized them before we had seen them. I cannot adequately describe the inspiration we all received from the coming of these two veteran air fighters to our camp. A day or two after we had settled down in our new aerodrome we heard the buzzing of an approaching machine. All hands rushed out to see what it meant. A Nieuport bearing American colors assured us it was a friend and probably another new member of our squadron, since he was preparing to land on our field.

He shut off the motor and glided down until the wheels skimmed the ground. The next instant her nose struck the mud and in a twinkling the machine had somersaulted over onto her back and slid along toward us tail foremost. We walked out to the wreck to secure the remains of the raw pilot who hadn't learned yet how to land a machine, and some of us made rather

[4]*Kitchener's Mob* (1916) was based on Hall's experiences as a machine gunner with the British army in 1915; *High Adventure* (1918) dealt with his experiences in the Lafayette Escadrille. Hall later became famous as coauthor with Charles B. Nordhoff of the best-selling trilogy *Mutiny on the Bounty, Pitcairn's Island,* and *Men Against the Sea.*

caustic comments about the authorities sending us such unsophisticated aviators. Imagine our stupefaction when we discovered the grinning face of Captain Hall himself looking at us upside down!

Fortunately he wasn't hurt in the slightest, and I think he would be glad if he could know how much good it did all of us young pilots to discover that even the best airmen can sometimes come a cropper.

Hall climbed out of his wreckage, and coming over to me told me that there was another machine still at our old aerodrome that must be flown over. I was directed to get a motor car and drive back to Villeneuve and, after making certain that everything was in order with the Nieuport, fly home with it on the morrow.

I accordingly got myself ready and set out. It was late at night when we started. Shortly before midnight we entered a small village just south of Châlons on the Marne River. Suddenly we noticed people running excitedly about the streets and as they came under the glare of my headlights I saw they were absolutely stricken with terror. I stopped the car as an old man came running up to me and asked him what was the trouble.

"The Boches are overhead!" was his reply, pointing upward into the night. "Please, *M'sieur,* put out the lights of your car!"

I snapped out the headlights and stood there for a moment, watching those poor people scurrying about for shelter. Old women whose backs were bent with age and toil were running helter-skelter through the streets for the open country, small children clinging to their skirts. They did not know where they were going, and many of them ran into each other as they crossed to and fro. Their one idea was to get away from their beds where they imagined the bombs from the enemy airplanes would be certain to find them. In truth that would have been the safest place for them to remain.

We proceeded through the village and a moment later came to a rise in the ground from which we could see the antiaircraft shells bursting above the city of Châlons a few miles ahead of us. Many sweeping searchlights were scanning the heavens with yellow fingers itching to grasp the path where the enemy planes were pursuing their way. For almost an hour we stood on this hill and regarded the spectacle with the same critical interest we had often experienced in watching an opera.[5] Then suddenly the lights were extinguished and the booming of exploding shells ceased. We regretfully climbed back into our car and continued on our way. The show was over!

The next morning we proceeded on to the old aerodrome where I found the last of our Nieuports, and had it run out and tested. After half an hour's inspection I found everything right, climbed aboard the little bus and waved my two mechanics good-bye. In thirty minutes I was over the Epiez field.

Squadron 95, which hadn't yet learned how to shoot in the air, was sent back to the Cazeau school, while 94, destined to become the greatest American

[5]EVR, who loved music, had attended performances of *Thaïs* and *Faust* in Paris on 2 and 3 March 1918.

squadron in France in the number of its victories
over the enemy, was ordered to vacate the Epiez aerodrome and move on eastward and north to Toul.[6] On
10 April 1918, we took our departure, flying our Nieuports over to an old aerodrome east of Toul that had
been vacated by the French for our use.[7] Supplies,
beds, mess-furniture, oil and gasoline, and all the
multitudinous paraphernalia of an aviation camp followed us in lorries and trucks. For a day or two we
had our hands full with settling ourselves in our new
quarters and acquainting ourselves with our sector
of the map. We were two miles east of Toul, one of
the most important railroad connections on our side
of the front and a town that the enemy tried almost
daily to demolish with aeroplane bombs. We were
barely eighteen miles from the lines and in a country
covered with rolling hills and extensive forests.

Nancy lay fifteen miles to the east of us, Lunéville
twelve miles farther east and the highway from Toul
to Nancy to Lunéville lay parallel to the enemy lines
and within easy shelling distance of the German
guns. But along this highway one would not have realized that a war was on. East of this point no efforts
had been made at an offensive by either side. Business went on as usual in Lunéville. Children played

[6]This move was related to the withdrawal of the French 1st Division from the Toul sector in early April and its replacement by
the 26th (Yankee) Division, one of the earliest American contin-
gents to see combat in World War I.
[7]The aerodrome was located at Gengoult.

in the streets and traffic pursued its leisurely way. An occasional German sentry faced a French sentry along the lines from Lunéville to Switzerland, at intervals of 100 yards or so, but it was said that these sentries messed together and slept together for the sake of companionship. This unnatural situation was considerably altered later, when the Americans came in. The country of the Vosges Mountains was thought to be too rough to permit invasion by either side.

The squadron at that time was commanded by Major John Huffer. He was one of America's best pilots and finest fellows, but curiously enough, he had been born in France and had never been in America nor in any English-speaking country. Major Huffer had served in the Ambulance Division since the early days of the war, later joining the Foreign Legion with William Thaw, Victor Chapman, and other American boys. When the American escadrille was formed, he entered aviation and thus was a veteran war pilot long before America came into the war.[8]

When he discovered that our beloved squadron was to receive the distinction of being the first actually to begin fighting for America, the question of a significant and proper squadron insignia became of prime

[8]Huffer did not belong to the Lafayette Escadrille but to the Lafayette Flying Corps, a broader term applied to Americans who flew for *any* French unit before the United States entered the war. Cited five times for valor, Huffer served in four French squadrons and also flew on the Italian front.

importance to us. We were busy those first days in Toul painting our machines with the American Red, White, and Blue, with our individual markings and with the last finishing touches that would prepare them for their first expedition over the lines. Then came the ideas for our insignia!

Major Huffer suggested Uncle Sam's Stovepipe Hat with the Stars-and-Stripes for a hatband. And our post surgeon, Lieutenant [Gary] Walters of Pittsburgh, Pennsylvania, raised a cheer by his inspiration of the "Hat-in-the-Ring." It was immediately adopted, and the next day designs and drawings were made by Lieutenant John Wentworth of Chicago, soon culminating in the adoption of the bold challenge painted on the sides of our fighting planes, which several scores of enemy airmen have since been unfortunate enough to dispute.[9]

Toul then saw the launching of America's first fighting squadron. And it was from this aerodrome that I won my first five victories in the following thirty days.

[9]Walters was flight surgeon of the 94th; Wentworth, an architect whose drawing skills resulted in his being chosen to design the insignia. The symbol, which became one of the world's most famous military emblems and continues to be used by the 94th Fighter Squadron, was derived from an old American custom of throwing a hat into the ring as an invitation to battle.

III

Our First Sorties

O N THE EVENING of 13 April 1918 we were indeed a happy lot of pilots, for we were reading on our new Operations Board the first war-flight order ever given by an all-American squadron commander to all-American pilots. It stated in simple terms that Captain Peterson, Lieutenant Reed [M.] Chambers[1] and Lieutenant E. V. Rickenbacker would start on a patrol of the lines tomorrow morning at six o'clock. Our altitude was to be 16,000 feet; our patrol was to extend from Pont-â-Mousson to St. Mihiel and we were to return at eight o'clock—a two hours' patrol. Captain Peterson was designated as leader of the flight.

Picture the map of these French towns, as every pilot in our Squadron 94 had it indelibly pressed into his memory. While flying in the vicinity of enemy territory it is quite essential that one should know every landmark on the horizon. Every river, every railroad, highway, and village must be as familiar to the airman as are the positions of first, second, and third bases to the home-run hitter.

[1]Chambers, who won seven victories and received numerous decorations for valor, became one of EVR's lifelong friends and business associates. In 1919, he succeeded EVR as commander of the 94th PS.

Toul is eighteen miles almost directly south of Pont-à-Mousson, St. Mihiel is directly west of Pont-à-Mousson about the same distance. The battle lines ran straight between Pont-à-Mousson and St. Mihiel; then they turned north to run another eighteen miles to the edge of Verdun. Metz is situated some twenty miles straight north of Pont-à-Mousson. And around Metz, several squadrons of enemy bombing aeroplanes and fighting machines had their lairs on a hill-top, from which they surveyed the lines that we were to patrol on 13 April. In short, the sector from Pont-à-Mousson to St. Mihiel was fairly alive with air activity when weather conditions permitted the use of aeroplanes at all.

This was the beat on which Captain Peterson, Chambers, and I would find ourselves tomorrow at six. Lieutenant Douglas Campbell and Lieutenant Alan Winslow were directed in the same order to stand by on the alert at the hangar from six o'clock until ten the same morning. This "alert" was provided for any sudden emergency; such as an enemy bombing raid in our direction or a sudden call for help against an enemy aeroplane within our lines.

Immediately after dinner that night Reed Chambers and I retired with Captain Peterson to his room, where we talked over the coming event. The captain gave us some curt directions about the precautions we should take in case of an attack, instructed me particularly that I was to lead the flight if anything happened to him or his motor, and under these circumstances I was to

The men and aircraft of the 1st Pursuit Squadron, France, 1918

Courtesy United States Air Force, 1st Fighter Wing History Office

continue our patrol until the time was up. Then he summoned an orderly and gave orders to call all five of us at 5:00 A.M. Advising Reed and me to sleep tight and try not to dream about Fokker aeroplanes, off he went to bed.

We knew very well what we would dream about. Try as I might, I could not get to sleep that night for hours. I thought over everything I had ever read or heard about aeroplane fighting. I imagined the enemies coming at me from every direction. I pictured to myself the various ways I would circumvent them and finally bring them tumbling down to their final crash. At last I dropped off to sleep and continued dreaming the same maneuvers. Just as I was shooting down the last of a good-sized number, the orderly punched my elbow and woke me up. It was five o'clock.

A wonderful morning greeted us, and the five of us had a merry breakfast. We advised Campbell and Winslow to keep a sharp lookout above the aerodrome that morning, for we intended to stir up the enemy, and undoubtedly there would be droves of them coming over our field for revenge.

But upon reaching the field after breakfast we found that the atmosphere was bad and the mist so heavy that the ground was completely hidden a short distance away. Captain Peterson sent Chambers and myself up to reconnoiter at 1,500 feet. Away we went. After circling the field two or three times, we noticed Captain Peterson take off and climb up to join us. We continued climbing and just about the time we had attained the frigid altitude, 16,000 feet, I noticed the captain's machine gliding back to the field.

Unsophisticated as I was, I did not know the danger into which I was leading my companion, and as Chambers knew less about the country than I did, he readily followed my lead and away we flew.

We picked up the valley of the Moselle River and proceeded blandly on our way and would probably have kept on to the Rhine but for a sudden bark under the tail of Chambers's machine announcing that we were discovered over German guns. I had been shot up by Archy before and now gloried in the utter contempt I felt for him, but this was Reed's first experience with German antiaircraft artillery and, as he admitted later, he thought it was all over for him. He sheered in so close to me that we nearly collided. Gradually we maneuvered out of the zone of fire and eventually became so disdainful of the shellbursts that we proceeded grandly on our way without paying any attention to them.

I located Pont-à-Mousson and from there set our course for St. Mihiel. Four times we made the round trip between these two towns amid intermittent Archy fire, but without seeing any aeroplanes in the sky. Then I decided we must turn toward home if we were to close our first patrol at the designated time. To my horror I discovered the whole landscape to the south of us was covered with a dense covering of fog. The whole area was covered, and under the blanket, somewhere in France, was the field upon which we were supposed to land. Land we must in a short half hour, for our fuel would be consumed and we would drop that instant. I began to realize then why Captain Peterson had gone back to the field, and I felt cold chills run down my spine as I contemplated the various kinds of mishaps that were in store for Reed and me.

There was nothing for it but a dive through the thick fog clouds. I stuck down my nose, entered them and lost Chambers immediately and only hoped that he had not come in directly behind me. I flew by compass, all the while watching the needle drop down the altimeter. Cautiously, I flattened out at 1,000 feet, for there are high hills in this sector, and some tall trees might show up ahead of me at any instant. Again I put down her nose and crept nearer the earth. At last I saw something below me and immediately zoomed up into the mist again. The nervousness of that foggy ride homeward I shall never forget.

By the sheerest good luck I caught a brief glimpse of a Y and a railroad tunnel that somehow seemed familiar to me. I circled back and got another view of it. Imagine my joy when I discovered it was a landmark near Commercy that I had flown over just once before when coming from Epiez to Toul. I put about, and flying only 100 feet above ground, continued straight into Toul, from which location I easily found the flying field, and landed quite perfectly.

Captain Peterson came up to me and informed me I was a bloody fool for flying off in a fog, which I knew was a fact and cheerfully admitted. Then I asked about Reed Chambers and felt a return of all my previous fear when I learned they had heard nothing from him.

With a heavy heart I got out of my flying clothes and walked over to headquarters to make out my report. I was positive the telephone would ring within a few minutes to inform us that Chambers had crashed and killed himself in the fog. I had barely begun my writing when the telephone did ring. I stood quivering in my shoes while the operations officer answered the call. Then he shouted:

"Quick! Two Boche aeroplanes are reported over Foug. Send in an alert!"

But at the same instant we heard two of our machines taking off the field. It was Campbell and Winslow, who had been standing by all morning for a chance nobody had expected them to get. I started to run toward the hangars, but before I reached the field a private rushed to me saying, "A German aeroplane has just fallen in flames on our field!"

It was true. I could see the flames from where I stood. Before I could reach the spot, however, another yell aroused my attention and I turned and saw a second machine fall nose down into a field not 500 yards away. The first had been destroyed by Alan Winslow who had shot it down in flames within three minutes after leaving the field. The second was forced down by Douglas Campbell, and it crashed in the mist before the pilot could discover his proximity to the ground. These were the first two enemy aeroplanes brought

down by any American squadron and both had miraculously crashed on the very doorstep of our aerodrome on the first day we had begun operations!

Neither of the German pilots was seriously injured.
Upon our questioning them as to how they happened
to be about in such weather, they informed us that
they had been summoned to go up to attack two patrolling machines that were being "Archied" between
Pont-à-Mousson and St. Mihiel. They had followed
Chambers and me until they lost us in the fog. Then
they tried to find their own way home to their aerodrome near Metz. They discovered our field and came
down low thinking it might be their own, when
Winslow and Campbell flew up and attacked them at
about 500 feet above ground.

This was indeed a wonderful opening exhibition
for our squadron, and had the stage been set and the
scene arranged for it, could not have worked more
perfectly. Then it was added to our joy to receive the
congratulations and praise of the French inhabitants
of Toul who had endured so many bombing raids
from these machines without seeing any Allied planes
on the defense of their beloved little city. When they
learned that two enemy machines had been shot down
on the very first day of the arrival of the Americans
their delight knew no bounds. They wrung our hands,
kissed us, toasted us in their best Moselle wine and
yelled: *"Vive la France!" "Vivent les Americains!"* until
they were hoarse. We each took a souvenir from the
German machines, which were to be the first of our

long series of *descendus*,[2] and the remains of the captured prizes we rolled into Toul, where they remained
upon exhibition in the city square until the last vestiges
of them disappeared. To complete our joy, we learned
that Reed Chambers had landed a short distance away
from our 'drome. The date of this first American victory was 14 April 1918.

For several days following, bad weather kept us idle
on the ground. But on 18 April an *alerte* was sounded
informing us that an enemy plane was seen over Pont-
à-Mousson. Reed Chambers and I applied for the job
of landing this fellow, and after obtaining permission
we jumped into our machines, which were warmed up
and ready, and off we started. I was determined to
bring down the next victim for our squadron and had
it planned in my mind just how it was to be done.

It was a thick day and the clouds hung about 3,000
feet above ground. We plunged boldly into them and
flew straight on. Finally we got above the clouds and
began circling about in wide sweeps, looking everywhere for the bold German. After thirty minutes or
more of desperate searching, I decided to drop back
below the clouds to see where we really were. Certainly
there were no Germans in this sector, after all.

In ten minutes I was below the clouds skimming
along the landscape with an eye out for landmarks.
Suddenly I discovered a large city ahead that looked
strangely like Nancy, except that it was in exactly the
wrong direction. I drew nearer and couldn't believe

[2] *"Descendus"*: enemy planes shot down in combat.

my eyes when a closer scrutiny proved that it was Nancy. I had been trusting to my boasted sense of direction all during this flight and had not even consulted my compass. Consequently I had been turned completely around and had led Chambers in exactly the opposite direction from the spot where the enemy was waiting for us. We had not been within ten miles of the lines the whole morning.

In great disgust I led the way homeward. Landing my machine I went over to the office and put in a very brief report to the effect that there were no enemy machines to be seen in our patrol. Quite true as far as I went, but I could not bring myself to state just why there were no Germans that morning. But I learned a very valuable lesson that day and have never had cause to regret the short discomfiture it gave me.

I was standing by on the aerodrome on 23 April when at about noon we received a warning by telephone that an enemy aeroplane had just been sighted between St. Mihiel and Pont-à-Mousson, flying from west to east. Major Huffer sent me word to get off immediately and find him. I set off alone.

I took off the field and pulling up her nose, I lifted my little Nieuport straight upward as steeply as she would climb and set a direct course for Pont-à-Mousson. In five minutes I picked up the river and the little city of Pont-à-Mousson crowded along its bank.

The French now held Pont-à-Mousson. Enemy artillery had been doing considerable damage to the bridge and buildings, and this now disclosed itself to

my eyes. Many roofs were torn off and the whole town
was badly knocked about. I began to search the skies
for a moving speck.

A sudden palpitation of my heart indicated that I
did see a speck, on the very first glance I shot toward
Germany. There, at about my own altitude, was the
wasp-like edge of an aeroplane coming directly toward me. I began to shiver lest he had seen me first
while I was joyriding over Pont-à-Mousson and had
thus had time to form a plot of his own before I had
formulated any of mine. Both of us continued dead
ahead at each other for twenty seconds or so until we
arrived almost within shouting distance, when I discovered to my great relief that he wore the blue center
cocarde[3] of a Frenchman and his machine was a Spad.
We had fortunately neither of us fired a shot.

Suddenly I saw the French pilot zoom up over me
and attempt to get on my tail. Whether joking or not,
I couldn't permit such a maneuver, so I quickly darted
under him and got the best position myself. The Nieuport can outmaneuver a Spad and has a little faster
climb; so the stranger soon found he had his match.
But to my amazement the fellow kept circling about me
continually trying to bring his guns to bear upon me.
I began wondering then whether he was some idiot

---

[3]"Cocarde": a roundel with three concentric circles on the
wings of an Allied plane, identifying its nationality. The French
roundel had a blue center surrounded by white middle and red
outer rings. The corresponding sequence on a British plane was
red, white, and blue; on an American aircraft, white, blue, and red.

who did not know an ally when he saw one, or was he a real German flying over our lines in a captured French machine? The former was evidently the correct solution, for as soon as I came by him again I turned flat over in front of him and let him have a long look at my American white center cocardes on my wings. This performance apparently satisfied my persistent friend, for he soon swerved off and went on home, leaving me to proceed on my mission. This little episode taught me another lesson. Since that day I have never taken any chances with any aeroplane in my vicinity, whether it was friend or foe. Some friends are better shots than are casual enemies.

My real quarry had made his escape during my little tourney with the Frenchman and I found no game in the sky, though I flew a full two hours along the lines. When I returned home, however, I found myself surrounded by the whole force as soon as my Nieuport stopped rolling along the ground. They fairly overwhelmed me with congratulations for bringing down a German, who had been seen to fall by one of our artillery batteries. As he fell in the very sector that I was then patrolling, they naturally credited me with the victory. It was a pity to undeceive them, but it had to be done.

The curious climax to this affair was that we never did discover who shot down that machine. He was never claimed by anyone else. I was convinced I certainly could not have accomplished my first victory without firing a shot or even seeing my enemy.

Thus, I had all the fruits of a first victory without

having won it. But what was far more important to me, I had learned something more in the art of war flying. I had undoubtedly saved my life by keeping out of the gunsight of a friendly machine!

The very next day I learned another lesson.

Again it was about noon and I was on duty when an alarm came in that an enemy plane was flying over St. Mihiel. It was a day of low-hanging clouds. I was absolutely determined that day to get my German despite every obstacle, so I flew straight into the enemy's lines at about 3,000 feet altitude. At that low height my machine was a splendid target for Archy, for after the first shot at me they found exactly the level of the clouds, and they could see that I was just under them. Consequently, I knew I was in for a warm time with the shellbursts, and I did some extraordinary dodging across two or three of their batteries.

I passed just north of St. Mihiel, and within a minute after the Archy began firing at me I sighted an enemy plane just ahead. I was coming in on him from the rear, for I had decided that it would be a brilliant idea to cross the lines halfway to Verdun and catch the enemy from a quarter that might be unsuspected. It had worked perfectly, though I couldn't understand why he had been so blind as to let the black bursts of shellfire around me pass unnoticed. But still he sat there with apparently no intention of trying to get away. I began to get nervous with the idea that this was almost too much of a good thing. Was he really the enemy?

As this was in reality the first German machine I had

ever seen in the air and I had judged his status from the shape of his planes and fuselage, I thought perhaps I had better actually take a look at his markings before firing and see that he really had a black cross[4] painted on his machine. So I dropped my finger from the trigger of my gun and dived a little closer.

Yes! he was a German. But instead of having a black cross he wore a black cocarde! It was a black cocarde with a white center. This must be something new, as no such markings had ever been reported at our headquarters. However he was no friend of mine and I would now proceed to down him. Why did he linger so complacently about my guns?

Suddenly I remembered the often-repeated instructions of Major Lufbery about attacking enemy observation machines. "Always remember it may be a trap!" I hurriedly looked over my shoulder—and just in time! There, coming out of a cloud over my head, was a beautiful black Albatros fighting machine that had been hiding about, waiting for me to walk into his trap. I gave one pull to my joystick and zoomed straight upward on my tail without giving a second thought to my easy victim below me.

To my delight I found that I could not only outclimb my adversary, but I could outmaneuver him while doing so. I got above him after a few seconds and was again pressing my triggers to fire my first shots in

[4]A black cross, either of the Maltese variety or (after 15 April 1918) with straight borders, was the German counterpart of the roundels on Allied planes.

the great war when it occurred to me that I had better look again and see that nobody else was sitting farther upstairs watching this little party with a view of joining in while my attention was diverted.

Instantly I forgot all about bringing down enemy aeroplanes and felt overwhelmed with one immense desire to get home as quickly as possible. Two aeroplanes from Germany were coming head-on at me not 500 yards away. How many more there were behind them I didn't wait to determine.

On that homeward trip, I climbed, dived, tailspun, circled, and stalled. They beat me at every maneuver and continued to overhaul me. Just when I had begun to despair of ever seeing my learned instructors again I ran into a cloud. Dimly I realized I was in a position of advantage for the moment, so I improved it to the utmost. Halfway in I reversed directions and began climbing heavenward. After thirty minutes industriously occupied in throwing my pursuers off my trail, I ventured out of concealment and gratefully made my way home.

IV

Downing My First Enemy

Aᴘʀɪʟ in France is much like April anywhere else.
Rains and cloudy weather appear suddenly out
of a clear sky, and flying becomes out of the question
or very precarious at best. On 29 April 1918 we rose at
six o'clock and stuck our heads out of doors as usual
for a hasty survey of a dismal sky. For the past three or
four days it had rained steadily. No patrols had gone
out from our aerodrome. If they had gone, they would
not have found any enemy aircraft about, for none had
been sighted from the lines along our sector.

About noon the sun suddenly broke through and
our hopes began to rise. I was slated for a patrol that
afternoon, and from three o'clock on I waited near the
hangars watching the steadily clearing sky. Captain
Hall and I were to stand on alert until six o'clock that
night at the aerodrome. Precisely at five o'clock Captain Hall received a telephone call from the French
headquarters at Beaumont stating that an enemy two-
seater machine had just crossed our lines and was flying south over their heads.

Captain Hall and I had been walking about the field
in our flying clothes; our machines were standing side
by side with their noses pointing into the wind. Within
the minute we had jumped into our seats and then our

mechanics were twirling the propellers. Just then the telephone sergeant came running out to us and told Captain Hall to hold his flight until the major was ready. He was to accompany us and would be on the field in two minutes.

While the sergeant was delivering the message I was scanning the northern heavens, and there I suddenly picked up a tiny speck against the clouds above the Forêt de la Reine, which I was convinced must be the enemy plane we were after. The major was not yet in sight. Our motors were smoothly turning over and everything was ready.

Pointing out the distant speck to Jimmy Hall, I begged him to give the word to go before we lost sight of our easy victim. If we waited for the major we might be too late.

To my great joy, Captain Hall acquiesced and immediately ordered the boys to pull away the blocks from our wheels. His motor roared as he opened up his throttle, and in a twinkling both our machines were running rapidly over the surface of the field. Almost side by side we arose and climbing swiftly, soared away in a straight line after our distant enemy.

In five minutes we were above our observation balloon line that stretches along some two miles or so behind the front. I was on Jimmy's right wing and off to my right in the direction of Pont-à-Mousson I could still distinguish our unsuspecting quarry. Try as I might, I could not induce the captain to turn in that direction, though I dipped my wings, darted away from him, and tried in every way to attract his attention to the target that was so conspicuous to me. He stupidly continued on straight north.

I determined to sever relations with him and take them on alone, since he evidently was generous enough to give me a clear field. Accordingly, I swerved swiftly away from Captain Hall, and within five minutes overhauled the enemy and adroitly maneuvered myself into an ideal position just under his sheltering tail. It was a large three-seater machine and a brace of guns poked their noses out to the rear over my head. With fingers closing on my triggers I prepared for a dash upward and quickly pulled back my stick. Up I zoomed until my sights began to travel along the length of the fuselage overhead. Suddenly they rested on a curiously familiar-looking device. It was the French circular cocarde painted brightly under each wing! Until this time I had not even thought of looking for its nationality, so certain had I been that this must be the German machine that had been sighted by the French headquarters.

Completely disgusted with myself, I then *viraged* abruptly away from my latest blunder, finding some little satisfaction in witnessing the startled surprise of the three Frenchmen aboard the craft, who had not become aware of my proximity until they saw me flash past them. At any rate I had stalked them successfully and might have easily downed them if they had been Germans. But as it was, it would be a trifle difficult to face Jimmy Hall again and explain to him why I had left him alone to get myself five miles away under the tail of a perfectly harmless Ally three-seater. I looked about to discover Jimmy's whereabouts.

There he was cavorting about amidst a thick barrage of black shellbursts across the German lines. He was halfway to St. Mihiel and a mile or two inside enemy territory. Evidently he was waiting for me to discover my mistake and then overtake him, for he was having a delightful time with the Archy gunners, doing loops, barrels, sideslips, and spins immediately over their heads to show them his contempt for them, while he waited for his comrade. Finally he came out of the Archy area with a long graceful dive, and swinging up alongside my machine he wiggled his wings as though he were laughing at me, and then suddenly he set a course back toward Pont-à-Mousson.

Whether or not he knew all along that a German craft was in that region I could not tell. But when he began to change his direction and curve up into the sun I followed close behind him knowing that there was a good reason for this maneuver. I looked earnestly about me in every direction.

Yes! There was a scout coming toward us from north of Pont-à-Mousson. It was approximately at our altitude. I knew it was a German the moment I saw it, for it had the familiar lines of their new Pfalz.[1] More-

[1]The plane was a Pfalz D-III, a streamlined single-seater designed to replace the obsolescent Albatros D-III. It was not "new" in April 1918, having been introduced the previous summer. Guides on which EVR may have based his identification, however,

over, my confidence in James Norman Hall was such that I knew he couldn't make a mistake. And he was still climbing into the sun, carefully keeping his position between its glare and the oncoming fighting plane. I clung as closely to Hall as I could. The German was steadily approaching us, unconscious of his danger, for we were full in the sun.

With the first downward dive of Jimmy's machine I was by his side. We had at least a 1,000-foot advantage over the enemy and we were two-to-one numerically. He might outdive our machines, for the Pfalz is a famous diver, while our faster-climbing Nieuports had a droll little habit of shedding their fabric when plunged too furiously through the air. The German hadn't a chance to outfly us. His only salvation would be in a dive toward his own lines.

These thoughts passed through my mind in a flash and I instantly determined my tactics. While Hall went in for his attack I would keep my altitude and get a position the other side of the Pfalz to cut off his retreat.

No sooner had I altered my line of flight than the German pilot saw me leave the sun's rays. Hall was already halfway to him when he stuck up his nose and began furiously climbing to the upper ceiling. I let him pass me and found myself on the other side just as Hall began firing. I doubt if the enemy pilot had seen Hall's Nieuport at all.

---

still classed it as new because no specimens had been captured intact and little was known about the plane.

Surprised by discovering this new antagonist, Hall, ahead of him, the Pfalz immediately abandoned all idea of a battle, and banking around to the right, started for home, just as I had expected him to do. In a trice I was on his tail. Down, down we sped with throttles both full open. Hall was coming on somewhere in my rear. The German had no heart for evolutions or maneuvers. He was running like a scared rabbit, as I had run from Campbell. I was gaining on him every instant and had my sights trained dead on his seat before I fired my first shot.

At 150 yards I pressed my triggers. The tracer bullets cut a streak of living fire into the rear of the Pfalz tail. Raising the nose of my aeroplane slightly, the fiery streak lifted itself like the stream of water pouring from a garden hose. Gradually it settled into the pilot's seat. The swerving of the Pfalz course indicated that its rudder no longer was held by a directing hand. At 2,000 feet above the enemy's lines I pulled up my headlong dive and watched the enemy machine continuing on its course. Curving slightly to the left, the Pfalz circled a little to the south and the next minute crashed onto the ground just at the edge of the woods a mile inside their own lines. I had brought down my first enemy aeroplane and had not been subjected to a single shot!

Hall was immediately beside me. He was evidently as pleased as I was over our success, for he danced his machine about in incredible maneuvers. And then I realized that old friend Archy was back on the job. We were not two miles away from the German antiaircraft batteries, and they put a furious bombardment of shrapnel all about us. I was quite ready to call it a day and go home, but Captain Hall deliberately returned to the barrage and entered it with me at his heels. Machine guns and rifle fire from the trenches greeted us and I do not mind admitting that I got out quickly the way I came in without any unnecessary delay, but Hall continued to do stunts over their heads for ten minutes, surpassing all the acrobatics that the enraged Germans had ever seen over their own peaceful aerodromes.

Jimmy exhausted his spirits about the time the Germans had exhausted all their available ammunition and we started blithely for home. Swooping down to our field side by side, we made a quick landing and taxied our victorious machines up to the hangars. Then, jumping out, we ran to each other, extending glad hands for our first exchange of congratulations. We then noticed that the squadron pilots and mechanics were streaming across the aerodrome toward us from all directions. They had heard the news while we were still dodging shrapnel and were hastening out to welcome our return. The French had telephoned in a confirmation of my first victory before I had time to reach home. Not a single bullet hole had punctured any part of my machine.

The following day I was notified that General Gerard, the commanding officer of the Eighth French Army, had offered to decorate Captain Hall and me in the name of the French government for our victory the day before. We were then operating in conjunction with this branch of the French Army. The *Croix de Guerre* with palm was to be accorded each of us, provided such an order met the approval of our own government. Both Jimmy and I had been included, as such was the French rule where two pilots participated in a victory.

The truth was that in the tense excitement of this first victory, I was quite blind to the fact that I was shooting deadly bullets at another aviator; if I had been by myself, there is no doubt in my own mind that I should have made a blunder again in some particular that would have reversed the situation. Captain Hall's presence, if not his actual bullets, had won the victory and had given me that wonderful feeling of self-confidence that made it possible for me subsequently to return to battle without him and handle similar situations successfully.[2]

[2]This account of EVR's first victory differs significantly from the one in the original text. Discrepancies between the two accounts are too numerous to note, but EVR stated that being given a share of the kill "was a great deal like taking something that did not belong to me rightfully, as I shall always be convinced that it was Captain Hall's victory and not mine." The vivid prose in the published text, including the famous "garden hose" passage, does not appear in the original text. Driggs probably embellished the details of the combat to tell a better story.

V

Jimmy Meissner Strips His Wings

Fᴿᴏᴍ ᴛʜᴇ ᴇɴᴛʀɪᴇs in my diary of this April period, one would get rather an unfavorable opinion of that quarter of France in which our squadron was located. "Rain and mud!" "Dud weather!" "No flying today!" are a few of the samples. None of the pilots or enlisted men of our American flying squadrons will be easily enraptured in the days to come with descriptions of the romance of *La Belle France*.

The day after my first enemy machine was brought down we were unable, on account of the fog, to carry out our air patrols. That afternoon a group of American newspapermen came out to the aerodrome to talk to me about my sensations in shooting down another man's machine. They took photographs of me and jotted down notes, and finally requested me to make a short flight over the field and perform a few stunts. The weather was not too rough for such an exhibition, so I gladly complied, and for half an hour I rolled and looped and dived about the clouds 1,000 feet or so above the aerodrome. But the visibility was so bad that I could not see the ground a mile away from the field.

On 1 May Major Lufbery and I made a small attempt to get a kill. However, it ended in a somewhat ludicrous fiasco. Luf was attached to 94 at that time, not as a commanding officer, but as a pilot for instruction. He was America's Ace of Aces and our most distinguished pilot. His long and successful experience in air-fighting was naturally of the greatest benefit to all of us younger pilots and every one of us considered it an honor to be sent out on an expedition with him.

We were sitting near the hangars talking and smoking at about five o'clock that afternoon when the telephone rang and Major Lufbery was informed that a German aeroplane had been sighted over Montsec, just above St. Mihiel. Lufbery hung up the phone, grinned his confident smile and began putting on his flying suit. I suspected something was up, and walking quickly over to where Lufbery was dressing, I asked him if I might go with him.

"Where do you want to go?" asked Lufbery.

"Wherever you go!" I replied.

My answer evidently pleased the major, for he grunted his customary chuckle and then said, "Come ahead."

I was delighted at the opportunity of accompanying Lufbery anywhere, and I was inside my flying clothes as soon as he was. As we walked out to our Nieuports, he told me we might get a German. All I had to do was to follow him and keep my eyes open.

We flew over Montsec for half an hour without getting a sign of the enemy. Thick as the day was, we would have been able to see the French antiaircraft shells bursting if any enemy aeroplanes had been in that sector. So, after cruising about once more over the German lines, Lufbery started for home in the direction of Pont-à-Mousson. We passed directly over the town at an altitude of 6,000 feet.

Suddenly Lufbery started diving directly down. I immediately nosed over and followed in hot pursuit, thinking he had spotted an enemy below and was about to open an attack. But a minute later I saw that the major was very evidently in trouble. His propeller had stopped turning and he was anxiously looking about and circling away for a favorable landing place.

Following him at a little distance behind, I saw him settle down into a very respectable field just south of Pont-à-Mousson. His machine dropped gently down to the mud, rolled along a few feet, then to my astonishment it stuck its nose in the mud, stood with tail pointing heavenward, hesitated there for a second or two and as I passed about 100 feet overhead, his Nieuport turned gently upside down and lay there on its back. I dare say Lufbery was swearing softly to himself as he saw me glide past.

Circling back I was highly amused to see the major crawling out on his hands and knees through the mud. He waved a dripping hand to me to indicate he was all right. I put on speed and hurried on home to send him help. His machine had somersaulted less than three miles from the enemy's lines.

Major Huffer himself took down from my description the exact location of the *panne*, and jumping into a motor car, he ran up to the spot I had indicated. There

he found Lufbery, none the worse for his forced landing, except for a slight scratch alongside his nose. One
of his cylinders had blown out and he had found himself at just a sufficient height to glide down and land at
a spot safely behind the observation of the enemy.

It was on the very next day that Lieutenant Jimmy
Meissner had another very trying experience with the
Nieuport machine. At about noon he and Lieutenant
[Philip W.] Davis were sent out to protect a French
observation machine that had been ordered to take
photographs of the enemy's positions behind Pont-à-
Mousson. The photographing machine went down
to 7,000 or 8,000 feet and was proceeding calmly on
its work, leaving the matter of its defense to the two
American pilots sitting upstairs some 4,000 or 5,000
feet overhead.

Suddenly Meissner discovered two Albatros fighting machines almost upon him, coming out of the sun.
They were already on the attack and were firing as they
dived swiftly upon the two Nieuports.

Jimmy made a quick maneuver and zoomed up
above the nearest Albatros. Instantly he utilized his advantage now that he had the upper floor,[1] and in a trice
he headed downward upon the tail of the enemy, firing long bursts from his machine gun as he plunged
after the fleeing German. But the Albatros pilot was an
old hand at this game, and before Meissner could overtake him he had thrown his machine into a tailspin,

[1] It was advantageous to attack a plane from above and behind,
especially if the enemy pilot had the sun in his eyes.

Lieutenant Hamilton Coolidge   *Lieutenant James A. Meissner*

Courtesy United States Air Force, 1st Fighter Wing History Office

which not only presented a target difficult to hit, but almost persuaded Jimmy that the machine was falling out of control.

Jimmy had heard many stories of this sort of "playing possum," however. He determined to keep after the spinning Albatros and see the end of the combat. Accordingly he opened his throttle and dived headlong down. One thousand, 2,000, 3,000 feet he plunged, mindless of everything but the occasional target that whirled periodically before his sights. At last he got in a burst that produced immediate results. The Albatros sent out a quick puff of smoke that was immediately followed by a mass of flames. One of Meissner's tracer bullets had set fire to the fuel tank of the enemy's machine. The plucky victor pulled up his Nieuport and took a self-satisfied look around him.

There, scarcely 1,000 feet below him, were the enemy lines. From various directions machine guns and short Archies were directing their fire on him. He grinned at them contemptuously and looked away for the expected view of Lieutenant Davis's Nieuport and the other Albatros. Neither was to be seen. Perhaps they were on his other wing. One glance around to the left and Jimmy's heart was in his throat.

He saw that the entire length of his left upper wing was stripped of fabric! And as he turned a horrified gaze to the other wing, he saw that its fabric, too, was even at the moment beginning to tear away from its leading edge and was flapping in the wind! So furious had been his downward plunge that the force of the wind's pressure had torn away the fragile covering on both his upper wings. Without this supporting surface his aeroplane would drop like a stone. Although it couldn't make much difference whether it dropped into German lines or within his own so far as his life was concerned, Meissner admitted later he always wanted a military funeral; so he eased off his speed and tenderly turned his wobbling machine about and headed back toward France.

Using only the slightest possible engine power and nursing his crippled little 'bus with great delicacy, Meissner succeeded in gaining No-Man's-Land, then passed over the American trenches. He did not dare to alter either his direction or speed. Less than half a mile further his machine glided into the earth and crashed beyond repair. Meissner crawled forth from the wreckage and felt himself all over carefully, to try to make himself understand that he was in reality in the land of the living—and free.

Such was the climax of Meissner's first victory, and the squadron's fourth. Meissner lived to repeat his success many times and to add much luster to the reputation of his squadron. But a narrower escape from death has rarely favored any pilot at the front.[2]

Again did the news of the squadron's victory pre-

---

[2] This account is misleading in stating that Meissner's plane "crashed beyond repair" and that Meissner "crawled forth from the wreckage." Because the ailerons of the plane were in the lower wings, which were unaffected by the dive, Meissner landed without crashing, and only his upper wings were stripped of fabric.

cede the arrival of the victor. When Meissner arrived
at the aerodrome by automobile an hour or two later,
the American photographers and newspapermen had
already arrived, and he was begged to stand for his
photograph. Like an embarrassed schoolboy, Jimmy
pushed them away exclaiming, "Nobody saw the machine fall in flames but me. It may not be confirmed."

Great was his surprise when he learned that a
French observation post had witnessed the whole
combat and had already telephoned us, not only with
the result of the fight but the position where Meissner
had been forced to land. We all took a hand then and
forced the embarrassed pilot to stand and face the
camera. It was a custom with which most of the 94's
pilots became acquainted within the next six months.

But our happiness and satisfaction were short-lived.
Later in the afternoon Captain Peterson returned from
his patrol over enemy's lines and brought back with
him but two of the three companions who had gone
out with him. We all walked out to get the news. Peterson had shot down another enemy aeroplane in
flames, totaling five for the squadron with this double
in one day. But during his combat, in which five Pfalz
monoplanes had been attacked by our four pilots, Peterson saw one of his Nieuports pass swiftly by him,

---

The original text merely says that Meissner "gained such terrific
speed that (. . .) the entire leading edge and linen was ripped off
his upper wings, and only by coolness and determination was he
able to land safely within a kilometer behind our front line trench."
Here again, Driggs embellished the facts to tell a better story.

ablaze from stem to stern. He collected his patrol quickly about him and rapidly scanned their markings. Charley Chapman's was missing! All were present but Chapman's well-known machine.

Then Peterson remembered seeing Chapman leave the fight to attack a two-seater German machine below him. Other pilots later filled in the details that were lacking. Chapman had no sooner dived to the attack than one of the hostile fighting machines was on his trail. Chapman turned to meet his pursuer and in doing so he brought himself full into the range of fire of the two-seater. Set on fire by the first burst, the mounting flames soon were quickly swept over the whole structure of Chapman's machine by the rush of the wind.

It was our first loss in combat, and sadly did we feel that loss. Charley Chapman was one of the best-loved of our little band and the sudden pang came to each one of us that we would never see his jolly good-natured smile again. The horror of his fate was not lost on us, one may be sure. No form of death is so dreaded by the pilot as falling to the earth in flames. Later on our most noted member leaped overboard to his death to avoid the slower torture of being burnt alive.[3]

---

[3]This sentence foreshadows the fiery death of Raoul Lufbery, which will be related in Chapter X.

VI

Jimmy Hall's Last Fight

O N MONDAY, 6 May 1918, the monotony of another "dud" day was happily broken by the arrival at our aerodrome of our old comrades of Squadron 95, who had been with us at Epiez. They had just completed their gunnery training at Cazeau and were now ready for the great war. From that day to the end of the conflict Squadrons 94 and 95 continued to occupy the same aerodrome. No other two American squadrons in France ever equaled their victories and number of hours flying over the lines.

At about eight o'clock on the morning of 7 May 1918, the French alerted us by telephone. Four enemy aeroplanes were flying over Pont-à-Mousson and were headed for the south. Flight No. 1—my own—was on duty at the time—very luckily for us, as Jimmy Hall, Eddie [M. Edwin] Green, and I thought. We jumped for our machines and anxiously watched the mechanics swinging the propellers.

"Switch off!" yelled the mechanic.

"Coupez!" I replied as I cut the switch with one finger while wriggling the rest of them into my fur gloves.[1] Three or four downward strokes of the stick and the

---

[1]The pilot had to tell the mechanic when the ignition switch was off and on so that the mechanic could use caution in swinging

mechanic paused a moment to look up over the fuselage to my face.

"Contact?" he yelled determinedly.

"Contact it is!" I called back, snapping on the switch. The well-groomed motor caught with a roar at the first heave, and at almost the same time I saw that Hall and Green were in equal readiness for the business of the day. A moment later, the three machines lifted their spinning wheels from the ground and heading straight toward the little city of Pont-à-Mousson on the Moselle, we began climbing as we flew.

When I looked down and found the roofs of Pont-à-Mousson below me, my altimeter indicated an elevation of 12,000 feet. Nothing appeared to be in sight inside the German lines, so I turned my scrutiny to the west toward St. Mihiel. The winding river there traced an indistinct line around the hills near St. Mihiel, and finally disappeared in the direction of distant Verdun. I drew my focus a little closer and instantly detected a moving shadow some two or three miles inside our lines in the vicinity of Beaumont, about halfway to St. Mihiel. It was a German—this I saw at the second glance. It looked like a two-seater and was evidently regulating the enemy's artillery fire against some American position back of Beaumont. I dipped my wings to signal the news of my discovery to my companions and as I did so I saw Jimmy Hall's Nieuport

---

the propeller. Because mechanics might be French, American pilots habitually used French terminology.

play the same maneuver. The three of us began our direct *piqué* together.

As we neared the vicinity of our unsuspicious prey I noticed a German Archy shell break, not near me but in close proximity to their own machine. The German shells emit a black smoke upon bursting that distinguishes them from the Allies' shells, which show a white smoke. Instantly the two-seater Albatros turned and dived for Germany.

A moment later three more German shells burst ahead of the retreating two-seater. And these three bursts were at about our present altitude. It seemed to be a previously arranged method of conversation that the gunners below were carrying on with the aeroplane high above them. They were telling the Albatros that our three fast fighting-machines were approaching from the east, and they indicated by the smoke-bursts the precise altitude at which we were flying.

Many times since have I noticed this marvelous signaling arrangement between the antiaircraft gunners and the German aeroplanes. On one occasion I saw a shellburst informing the opposing pilots of my presence above a cloud when I was hiding and planning a surprise party for their oncoming colleagues. This admirable liaison between German artillery and their aviators might be imitated with great advantage by our own army. For not only does the threatened machine get this valuable warning, but aeroplane reinforcements far distant can see these smokebursts and fly to the rescue with full information as to the number, altitude, and perhaps the type of hostile machines ahead of them. Almost invariably an overpowering enemy formation appeared shortly after these signals were sent up.

Still another signal was adopted by the German batteries to indicate the formation of our machines to their pilots. Through their powerful telescopes they ascertained the relative position of each machine in our formation. If one of our machines climbed high above the rest of the formation in order to perch well upstairs and guard against a surprise from the ceiling, this maneuver was communicated to their pilots by sending up one shell that burst well above the others. Immediately the German pilots were on their guard against an antagonist who was hiding in the glare of the sun and could not be seen by them. The single high burst notified them that he was there.

As Captain Hall, Lieutenant Green, and I drew nearer to the slower two-seater machine, another smokeburst signal came from the batteries below I turned my head and looked about me to see if enemy machines were coming in answer to these signals. Back toward Pont-à-Mousson I thought I saw something in the sky. Keeping my gaze fixed in that direction, my suspicions were soon verified. Four Pfalz scouts were in hot pursuit after us and were diagonalling our course so as to cut off our retreat.

Sheering in ahead of Captain Hall, I wigwagged my wings and headed away to the right. This is the signal given to the leader of a flight, to draw his attention to a danger that he has overlooked. The next moment Captain Hall had again taken the lead and all three of our machines had turned and were headed eastward. The oncoming enemy formation was flying much below us, which gave us a decided advantage. We could dive down to the attack when we chose and could keep out of their reach so long as we kept above them. Our machines were at that time some three or four miles inside the German lines.

For some unexplained reason Captain Hall began turning more and more into Germany. I wondered what could be the trouble. Either he saw something in that direction, or else he still was ignorant of the near presence of the four Pfalz machines. I debated the matter for an instant, then darted in ahead of Jimmy and gave him another signal. Fully convinced now that he must see the enemy formation that was hardly more than a mile from us, I came out of my *virage* and headed down for the attack. With a man like Captain Hall behind me, I did not fear for the outcome. His machine followed close behind mine.

From our superior height we soon accumulated a speed that brought us into a very favorable position. I selected the rear Pfalz scout and got my sights dead on him and prepared to shoot. My aim never wavered as the distance between us narrowed. At 200 yards I pressed my trigger and watched my tracer bullets speeding ahead into the Pfalz's wings. My gun continued to fire steadily until I had approached to within fifty yards of the Pfalz. Then the enemy machine turned over and fell into a *vrille*. I did not dare to follow him farther. I zoomed up until I stood fairly upright on my tail, and looked around me.

My first thought was that during the intentness of my pursuit against my victim one of his companions might be getting a similar position over my tail. To my great relief no enemy was behind me. But off to the right, not 100 yards away, I saw a Nieuport diving steeply down, and on his tail was a diving Pfalz pouring streams of living fire into the fuselage and cockpit of the American machine. Even as I watched this frightful death chase, the tables were suddenly turned. Hall or Green, whichever it was, seeming to tire of the monotony, zoomed quickly upward and looped his machine completely over, coming out of the loop just as the Pfalz went under him. In a twinkling the situation was reversed and the Nieuport was pouring bullets at the rate of 650 per minute into the German machine, ahead.

The Pfalz fell, and I *piquéd* down and flew alongside the victorious Hall. My surprise can be imagined when I discovered not Hall, but Green looking across at me from his seat! And no other machine was in the sky. What could have happened to Hall?

We flew homeward together, Green and I, encountering a furious storm of Archy as we crossed the trenches. Arrived at the landing ground, I immediately ran over to Green to inquire for news. My heart was heavy as lead within me, for I was certain as to what the answer would be.

"Went down in a tailspin with his upper wing gone!" Green informed me without my speaking. "I saw him dive onto a German just as I began my attack. The next I saw of him, he was going in a *vrille* and the German was still firing at him as he was falling. He must have struck just back of those woods behind Montsec."

I cannot describe the joy that came to the squadron about a month later when we received a letter from Hall himself. He wrote from a hospital in Germany, where he was laid up with a broken ankle. He had not been shot down in the combat, as we had supposed, but had dived too swiftly for the weak wing structure of a Nieuport. His upper wing had collapsed in full flight; and not until he had almost reached the ground had he been able to straighten out his aeroplane. In the crash he had escaped with merely a cracked ankle. In another fortnight he hoped he would be as good as ever.

On 19 November 1918, when the day came for the French army to march in and occupy the fortress and city of Metz, several of the officers from our squadron flew over from our aerodrome at Rembercourt to witness the ceremony. We appeared to be the first Americans that the Metz populace had seen. One of the first citizens who spoke to us while we were overlooking the triumphal procession through the Plaza asked us if we knew an American aviator named Captain Hall. We immediately gathered around him and drew him to one side.

"Well," he said, half in French and half in German, "your Captain Hall was confined in the hospital here for many weeks and then was in a prison. Only yesterday the Germans evacuated Metz, and all their prisoners were set at liberty. Captain Hall left here yesterday in the direction of Nancy. He walked away quite nicely with the aid of a cane, and perhaps he will be able to get a ride part of the way."

Upon our return to the aerodrome from Metz next day, we learned that Jimmy Hall had indeed come through the lines. He had gone to Paris for a rest. A number of his old friends immediately got into their machines and flew to Paris, where they greeted their long-lost comrade with appropriate ceremonies at the justly celebrated Inn of Monsieur de Crillon—that American aviator's rendezvous and oasis in Paris.

And from Hall himself we learned the true facts of his accident that day over Montsec. He had overtaxed his Nieuport by too fast a dive. A wing gave way and threatened to drop him into the woods below. But by nursing his machine along with engine half on, he was succeeding, just as Meissner had done the day before, in making appreciable headway toward home, when he felt a violent blow on his engine. His motor stopped dead. Again he dropped utterly out of control and eventually crashed in an open field, suffering a badly broken ankle.

One of the pilots with whom we had just been fighting landed nearby and came over and made him prisoner. A brief inspection of his motor showed that the violent blow he had felt in midair was the result of a direct hit by a dud shell! By some miracle it had failed to explode!

The Pfalz pilot took Hall to his own squadron quarters where he dined that night with the German aviators. They admitted to him that they had lost two machines in the fight with our formation that day.

Two machines! Green shot one down, but who got the other? I had seen my man fall in a *vrille,* but having no time to follow him down, I had concluded that he was shamming and was in reality quite unhurt. I had not even thought that I had won a victory in that combat. Imagine my surprise when Captain Hall later described how he himself had seen my antagonist burst into flames and crash, burnt to a crisp! And the surviving pilots of his squadron admitted to Hall that they had lost two machines in that day's fight! Thus do victories sometimes come to the air fighter without his realizing it. This enemy machine was never claimed and never credited to me.[2]

Hall's disappearance that day was known to the whole civilized world within twenty-four hours. Widely known to the public as a most gifted author, he was beloved by all American aviators in France as their most daring air fighter. Every pilot who had the privilege of his acquaintance burned with a desire to avenge him.

[2]Rickenbacker *did* receive official credit for this victory in 1960 when an affadavit signed by Hall was recovered after being lost for many years.

Within fifteen minutes after I had landed from Hall's last patrol I encountered old Luf walking toward the aerodrome with a set look of determination on his usually merry features that denoted no mercy to the enemies he had in mind. He was, I knew, one of Jimmy's very intimate friends. For many months they had flown together in the famous old Lafayette Escadrille.

His mechanics, seeing his approach, anticipated his wishes and began pushing out his plane and collecting his flying equipment for him. Without uttering a word, Lufbery pulled on his flying suit, climbed into his machine, and set out toward Germany.

He flew for an hour and a half without encountering an enemy plane. Then with but a half-hour's petrol remaining, he flew deeper into Germany to attack single-handedly three fighting machines that he detected north of St. Mihiel. One of these he shot down, and the others took to their heels. The following day his gallant victory was confirmed by an advanced post that had witnessed the combat.

Pathetic and depressing as was the disappearance of James Norman Hall to all of us, I am convinced that the memory of him actually did much to account for the coming extraordinary successes of his squadron. Every pilot in his organization that day swore to avenge the greatest individual loss that the American Air Service had yet suffered.

VII

New Responsibilities

IT WAS on 8 May 1918, the day following the melancholy disappearance of Captain Jimmy Hall, that I was notified that I was to take his place and henceforth was to command Flight No. 1 in our squadron. While very much gratified by this promotion, I could not help realizing that before the day was over some other man in my flight might be taking over the command in my place just as I was taking it from Captain Hall.

Many small ideas that might enable me to prolong my life in aviation had made indelible impressions upon my mind during the past weeks. Several of them had come to my attention through the ludicrous blunders I had been making. The more foolish I had felt over each mistake, the deeper became the lesson to me. I resolved as soon as I became flight commander, that I should begin by schooling the pilots under my care in some of the lifesaving tricks that I had learned. The dangerous frailty of the Nieuport's wings was one item to bear in mind.

Another of these little precautions that might spell the difference between life and death was the habit I forced upon myself always to make one or two complete circles of the aeroplane before landing at the end of a patrol. The necessity for such trifling precaution is reasonable. Diving swiftly and suddenly from 15,000 feet altitude where the air is thin and very cold, to the ground level where the change in the pressure upon the temples is often severe, may very easily make the airman dizzy. He may misjudge his distance above the earth and crash violently when trying only to skim the ground. A circuit or two just above the surface of the landing field will give him time to adjust his vision and accustom himself to the change in the air pressure. It takes but a minute and may save a life. Incidentally one can look about and see that no other planes are preparing to land in the same spot at the same time.[1]

Two days after assuming my new command I was returning with my flight late in the afternoon from a patrol. As we circled about our field I noticed a plane flattening out for a landing below me. I watched him for a moment and saw that he was coming in perfectly. The next instant I noticed another plane coming in to land from exactly the opposite direction. The wheels of both machines touched earth at the opposite ends of the field at approximately the same moment. I was powerless to do more than watch the climax of this stupid proceeding, though I believe I did try to shout to each of them to look out for the other fellow. Of course

[1]When landing, the pilot's downward visibility was blocked by the engine, requiring him to sideslip in his final approach in order to see where he would land. The same problem required that the pilot taxi in a "fishtail" manner while on the ground in order to see forward. To understand the accident that follows, it is also necessary to know that a Nieuport had no brakes; once it touched the ground, its tailskid brought it to a stop.

I could not make myself heard by anybody, but I couldn't help shouting, for I knew instinctively that they were in for a jolly good crash.

The two machines raced gracefully toward each other head on, very much like a staged railroad collision at a county fair. Exactly in the middle of the field they met, the two wings embraced each other in an "aleman left" figure[2] of the dancers and around and around they went, spinning like a top. In the midst of the revolving dance, the synchronizing mechanism on Captain [Kenneth] Marr's[3] machine guns became involved and flaming tracer bullets and incendiary bullets shot out of the merry-go-round at the rate of 650 shots per minute. From my box seat above it looked very much like a Fourth-of-July celebration, with a gigantic pin wheel shooting out living sparks in every direction.

Fortunately not a soul was hurt during the entire celebration, as seems to be the usual lucky outcome of mimic war maneuvers. Both pilots crawled out of the wreckage, shook hands and walked over to the hangars to tell the men in shelter that the show was over.[4] Then we made our landing.

The next day Reed Chambers accompanied me on a patrol across the German lines and we made another

[2]"Allemande left": a dance step with intertwined arms.
[3]Marr, a Californian, enlisted early in World War I as an ambulance driver and later became a pilot in the Lafayette Escadrille. Soon after the incident mentioned here he was promoted to major and put in command of the 94th, succeeding Huffer.
[4]The original text indicates that both wings were torn off both of the planes involved in the accident.

rather interesting discovery. Four splendid Albatros machines were approaching us from over Thiaucourt which was about four miles inside the enemy's territory. They were in good formation and were at about our altitude. I wigwagged over to Reed and he wigwagged back to me. We both understood each other. We were two against the enemy four, but the two on our side had full confidence in each other and both were fairly well bucked up over the recent successes of our squadron. Perhaps the opposing four might be lacking in this mutual confidence. At any rate, it was worth the chance of trying a bluff to see if we could not get them separated.

It is half the game to know thoroughly one's partner and his capabilities in air fighting, as it is in any other accomplishment. Reed Chambers was a daredevil to all appearances, and was always an eager flyer, but I had noticed that he combined a rare caution with his recklessness, making him an excellent and reliable comrade in a fight. Subsequently, Reed accumulated seven official victories to his credit, and at the end of the war he stood next to me in the number of hours flying over enemy's lines.

As we simultaneously turned toward the Albatros group, we put on our motors and headed directly into them. We didn't swerve an inch from our parallel course as we shot straight at the center of the approaching quartet. Whether they thought we were two furious expert fighters from the United States or two crazy amateurs who might ram them in midair I do not know, but before we had arrived within fair shooting range, the leader banked over, turned tail, and the rest of the formation sheepishly following him; all four diving steeply down into Germany, leaving us a vacant sky over Thiaucourt. We had bluffed out a superior formation through sheer impudence.

Twelve May was "dud" as far as aviation was concerned, but it was brightened by one of the pleasantest incidents that marked my stay in France. Colonel Mitchell telephoned over to the aerodrome to invite several of us to make a call with him at Château Sirur, a magnificent estate of an old French family, situated some fifty miles south of our aerodrome. Major Huffer, with several other officers from our squadron, left the mess with me immediately after lunch and we reached the château within a few minutes of the arrival of Colonel Mitchell and Major Hall. The countess gave us a most cordial greeting, then took us over a part of the estate, which consisted of a park some ten miles square. The grounds were heavily wooded and beautifully kept. Through the woodland curved a winding stream that was spanned at intervals with quaint and ancient stone bridges. Fish ponds and shooting preserves provided the château with wild game the year around. Several wild boar crossed our road a few paces in front of us during our walk. Shooting wild boar, we were told, was one of the favorite pastimes of the occupants of the château.

During tea, the countess very graciously invited us to make this magnificent old castle our home if at any time American aviators became worn out with work at the front. I must confess to the good countess some day that a scandalous number of our overtired aviators, and perhaps still greater a number of not-at-all tired American aviators, did subsequently avail themselves of her very generous invitation.

After cordial goodbyes to our hospitable hostess we motored back to Chaumont where we dined with Colonel Mitchell; then with another long drive we finally reached home tired but happy at 3:30 in the morning. There, staring me in the face was an order directing me to lead my patrol over the lines in the morning at five o'clock sharp! An hour-and-a-half sleep for an utterly worn-out aviator!

Heaven must have heard my prayers for rain that night, for the next morning when I woke up at eleven o'clock and rushed to the window, I found the rain falling in sheets. The orderly had omitted to call me at the appointed hour because he saw that the weather was too thick for flying.

Decorations for valor and heroism were coming to several of the boys in our squadron on 15 May; we all woke up that morning to find a beautiful day dawning. While all of us assumed a truly American disdain for performances of this kind, we nevertheless clearly indicated by our nervousness the pride that we really felt in receiving this award.

General Gerard, commander of the Eighth French Army, was to arrive at our field shortly after lunch. All the forenoon I tried to avoid my gallant messmates, who were continually seeking me out to advise me to shave again and to use plenty of powder on the cheeks where the general would kiss me. Both Lieutenant Jimmy Meissner and I were quite new to this decoration business and we were nicely stuffed by the other fellows who claimed to know all about it. Major David Peterson was also receiving the *Croix de Guerre,* but he had been through many ceremonies of this kind and was little worried by the prospect. Captain James Norman Hall, whom we considered killed in combat, and Lieutenant Charles Chapman, who had been shot down a fortnight before, were both summoned to appear for their well-earned distinctions, but neither, alas, could answer to his name.

Shortly after one o'clock, three companies of a crack *poilu*[5] regiment marched onto our field behind a gorgeous French military band of music. Then came several more companies of infantry from the famous American 26th Division, the New England boys. They had a good snappy American band at their head. Both French and American soldiers drew up their ranks in the form of a hollow square in the center of our aerodrome.

In the meantime we had run out all the Nieuports from the hangars and they stood cheek-by-jowl across the field, shining brightly with their red, white, and blue markings. All the men formed ranks behind the aeroplanes, awaiting the ceremony.

[5]"Poilu": a French infantryman, particularly one in the front lines.

Jimmy Meissner and I stood shaking in our well-polished boots, while our cheery comrades came by for a last word of comforting advice. Then, with Major Peterson beside us, we waited for the fatal word of advance into the awful presence. Suddenly, amidst a blare of both bands, the general's party appeared from behind one of the hangars where they had been in hiding all this time. I tried one minute to think of how proud my old mother would be of me, and the next would attempt to stretch my face up to such a height that no ordinary general would ever be able to reach it with his lips. This was the last piece of excellent advice that a delegation of my oldest friends had crossed the aerodrome to give me.

Suddenly a faraway band began playing something that sounded somewhat familiar. It turned out to be the National Anthem, "Oh, Say! Can you see . . . ?" Everybody jerked to attention and stood at the salute until it ended. Then from far away in front of me Colonel Mitchell, the head of our air service, began a brief speech congratulating us upon the honors that the French Army was conferring upon us. And then General Gerard, a kindly looking man with a business-like military efficiency in his features and movements, approached our little line of three. He was carrying in his hands the *Croix de Guerre* and a printed list of citations from the French Army. Pausing immediately in front of us, he began reading them aloud in French.

The *Croix de Guerre* is a beautiful medal in bronze, artistically designed and executed. It hangs suspended from a ribbon of striped red and green upon which are fastened the palms or stars for each particular citation given by the army or division. If any individual soldier is mentioned for an act of heroism in especial terms by an army order he is presented with an additional palm for each of such citations. Some of the French airmen have received so many citations that the medal itself would hang down below the waist if the ribbon were properly lengthened to accommodate every palm awarded. I have seen René Fonck, the French Ace of Aces, who has been cited twenty-nine times for his victories, wearing his *Croix de Guerre* in two sections so as to accommodate all the palms that must be worn upon ceremonial occasions. If the citations come from a division instead of an army, the decoration to be worn above the *Croix de Guerre* is a star instead of a palm. Colonel William Thaw wears two stars and three palms among his many other decorations.[6]

With a quick fastening of the much-prized honor upon the breast of our tunics and a hearty handclasp of congratulations, General Gerard left us with a very dignified salute, which we all returned simultaneously. The discriminating commander had not made an attempt to kiss us at all!

Within five minutes the field was cleared. We ran up our motors for a prearranged exhibition in stunt flying,

[6]Whereas the Germans were highly restrictive in awarding the *Ordre Pour le Mérite*—the famous "Blue Max"—the French were very liberal in awarding the *Croix de Guerre*, which in any case was less coveted than their highest decoration, the Legion of Honor.

formation flying, farce combats, and acrobatics. We flung our lithe little Nieuports about the warm sky in every variety of contortion for half an hour, at the end of which we landed and again received a handshake and a smile of thanks from this most courteous of French officials. The troops disappeared behind the dying strains of the *"Sambre et Meuse"* march[7], the mud-splashed automobiles bore away the last of our distinguished visitors, the mechanics reappeared in their grease-covered overalls and began trundling in the machines.

[7]*Sambre et Meuse:* a popular French march often played on ceremonial occasions; see Barbara Tuchman, *The Guns of August,* 252-253.

VIII

A Victory and a Narrow Escape

REED CHAMBERS and I often used to discuss new tricks and wiles by which we might hope to circumvent the crafty enemy. Taken all in all, this whole game of war aviation is so new that any day some newcomer may happen upon a clever trick that none of us has before thought of. I suppose they are sitting up nights the same as we are, trying to devise some startling innovation in the still-crude science of air fighting. At any rate, Reed and I sat up late very often and rose very early the next morning to carry into execution some little plan that had enraptured us the night before.

On the morning of 17 May 1918, my orderly routed me out at four o'clock sharp, in accordance with orders I had given him the night before.

Over our coffee fifteen minutes later, Reed and I hurriedly discussed our clever little scheme for the morning run. We intended to get away from the ground before daylight, climb clear up out of sight and out of hearing long before the Germans were out of bed. By hanging around their front yard we might pick up a stray machine venturing alone across our lines for photographs. It was a wonderful plan. We wondered why nobody had ever thought of it before.

Up over Toul, Commercy, and Nancy we circled as we climbed, climbed, climbed. At nearly 18,000 feet we found we had enough climbing. It seemed about 18,000 degrees below zero at this great height. Still I hugged myself with much satisfaction over the thought that we surely had the upper hand of any two-seater that might come over; and as the visibility was good we had a tremendous range of view.

We waited and waited. Up and down along the pre-arranged sector, where we expected any reasonable enemy might want to come to get photographs on such a fine morning as this, up and down, back and forth we went. At last I began to get rather fed up with the sport. Our plan had worked perfectly and without a single flaw. Yet the stupid Germans were trying to gum up the whole show by staying home this morning. I finally grew indignant at the thought of our early rising hour, our fortunate weather conditions, our high ceiling cleverly obtained without the knowledge of Archy—all these efforts and accomplishments honestly achieved, only to be nullified by the refusal of the fish to bite.

Major Lufbery used to remind us that it was impossible to get enemy planes by sitting at home in the billets with one's feet before the fire. I considered this sage advice as I turned back on my beat for the twentieth time and estimated I still had an hour's petrol left in my tank. I was nearly perishing with the cold and with hunger. Bitterly I contrasted the cozy mess fire in the breakfast room with the frigid heights at which I

Major Reed Chambers

Courtesy United States Air Force, 1st Fighter Wing History Office

had spent the last hour. I felt I had been badly treated.

Where was Chambers anyway? During my preoc-
cupation I had forgotten to keep an eye upon him. I
examined every portion of the sky, but he was not in
sight. Nothing was in sight. No other fool in the world
was abroad at such an unearthly hour. But still, I had
to admit to myself, Luf was right! It was just like going
fishing.

Perhaps I was selecting a poor fishing place whose
only merit was that it was close and handy. I pulled up
my machine and started off for Metz. I knew the fishing must be good there. It was twenty-five miles back
of the lines and claimed, besides the famous fortress,
one of the best of the German aerodromes.

I was now at 20,000 feet above earth, and as I turned
east I saw the first ray of the sun that shone over France
that day. It lay a huge red ball behind the distant mountains of the Rhine. I headed in that direction in order
to cross the enemy's lines east of Pont-à-Mousson,
where I knew lay concealed several sharp-eyed German batteries. At the extremely high altitude at which
I crossed the lines that early morning the sound of my
motor must have been heard by the gunners below, but
I am sure none of them could have seen me, even with
the most powerful telescopes. At any rate, not a shell
was fired at me during my entire journey to Metz.

The celebrated fortifications soon lay spread below
my wings. Metz herself lies deep down within a valley—the lovely valley of the Moselle River. Practically
sheer bluffs 1,000 feet high rise on either bank of the

river, and a sudden turn of the stream a mile below the city's walls provides almost an entire circumference of fortifications about the sheltered little city below.

Beautiful as Metz appeared to me, I for once regretted that I was not mounted on a bombing machine from which I might drop a few souvenirs of my visit into the crowded camps below. Doubtless, Metz contained hundreds of thousands of troops and many officers of high rank, as this secure little city was the gateway between Germany and her front line on the Meuse. My machine gun could inflict no damage from such a height. Regretfully I made a last farewell circuit over the Queen City of Lorraine and started homeward over the Frascati aerodrome, whose hangars topped the hills, and peeped down into the valley of the Moselle. No aeroplanes from there had yet thought fit to leave the ground.

But one more chance remained to score this morning. I knew of an aerodrome just this side of Thiaucourt where some activity might be expected.

My time was nearly gone, for my fuel must be rather far down. The thought of encountering engine trouble this twenty miles behind the lines made me accelerate my pace a bit. Germany would be a sad place for an enemy named Rickenbacker to land in for the duration of the war. I stuck my nose down a bit more as I thought of this, and further increased my speed. Ah! here comes the vicinity of Thiaucourt. Cutting down my motor, I glided on almost noiselessly and reached the town at about 18,000 feet altitude.

Two or three complete circles were made over Thiaucourt with silent engine. My eyes were all the while set upon the enemy aerodrome that I knew occupied the smooth field just outside the little city. Some activity was apparent there, and even as I sailed above them I noticed three graceful Albatros machines leave the ground one after the other. It was evident from their straightaway course that they were going over the lines, accumulating their elevation as they flew southward. I made myself as inconspicuous as possible until the last of the three had his back well toward me. Then I returned to my course and gradually narrowed the distance between us.

By the time we reached Montsec, that celebrated mountain north of St. Mihiel, I estimated some 3,000 feet separated me from my unsuspicious quarry. I was so eager to let them get over our lines before attacking that I quite forgot that I was now a conspicuous figure to the German Archies. Two quick bursts just ahead of me informed me of my error. Without waiting to see whether or not I was hit, I put on the sauce and dived down headlong at the rearmost of the three.

Again I saw the warning signal sent up ahead of the three Albatros pilots. A single black burst from the battery below caused the German airmen to turn about and look behind them. They had not expected any attack from this quarter.

When the leader made the first swerve aside I was less than 200 yards from the rear Albatros. I was descending at a furious pace, regardless of everything but my target ahead. My Nieuport was flying fully 200 miles an hour. Without checking her speed, I kept her nose pointing at the tail of the rear Albatros, which was now darting steeply downward to escape me. As the distance closed to fifty yards I saw my flaming bullets piercing the back of the pilot's seat. I had been firing for perhaps ten seconds from first to last. The scared airman had made the mistake of trying to outdive me instead of outmaneuvering me. He paid for his blunder with his life.

These thoughts flashed through my mind in the fraction of a moment. All the while, during which my fingers pressed the trigger, I was conscious of the extreme danger of my position. Either or both of the other enemy machines were undoubtedly now on my tail, exactly as I had been on their unfortunate companion. And being alone, I must rely solely on my own maneuvers to escape them.

I believe I should have followed my first target all the way to the ground regardless of the consequences, so desperately had I determined to get him. So I perhaps prolonged my terrific speed a trifle too long. As the enemy aeroplane fell off and began to flutter I pulled my stick back close into my seat and began a sharp climb. The notorious weakness of the Nieuport quickly announced itself. A ripping crash that sounded like the crack of doom to my ears told me that the sudden strain had collapsed my right wing. The entire spread of canvas over the top wing was torn off by the wind and disappeared behind me. Deprived of any supporting surface on this side, the Nieuport turned over on her right side. The tail was forced up despite all my efforts with joystick and rudder. Slowly at first, then faster and faster, the tail began revolving around and around. Swifter and swifter became our downward speed. I was caught in a *vrille*, or tailspin, and with a machine as crippled as mine there seemed not the possibility of a chance to come out of it.

I wondered vaguely whether the two Albatros machines would continue to fire at me all the way down. Twice I watched them dive, firing more bullets into my helpless little craft, notwithstanding the apparent certainty of her doom. I felt no anger toward them. I felt somewhat critical toward their bad judgment in thus wasting ammunition. No, that was not exactly it either. My senses were getting confused. What I felt critical about was their stupidity in believing that I was playing 'possum. They were fools not to know when an aeroplane was actually falling to a crash. The whole spread of my fabric was gone. No pilot ever could fly without fabric on his machine.[1]

Where would I strike, I wondered. There were the woods of Montsec below me. Heavens! how much nearer the ground was getting! I wondered if the whole framework of the machine would disintegrate and fling me out to the mercy of the four winds. If I struck in treetops it was barely possible that I might escape with

[1]It must be remembered that the lower right wing, which contained the aileron, did not lose its fabric. Otherwise, EVR would have plummeted to the ground without hope of recovery.

a score of broken bones. Both Jimmy Meissner and Jimmy Hall had escaped death when betrayed through this same fault of the Nieuport. Never would I fly one again if I ever got out of this fix alive! But no use worrying about that now. Either I should not be alive or else I should be a mangled prisoner in Germany. Which would my mother rather have, I wondered?

This sudden spasm of longing to see my mother again roused my fighting spirit. With that thought of her, and the picture before my mind of her opening a cablegram from the front telling her I was dead, I vividly recalled a whole series of childhood scenes. I have never before realized that one actually does see all the events of one's life pass before one's eyes at the certain approach of death. Doubtless they are but a few recollections in reality, but one's natural terror at the imminence of death multiplies them into many.

I began to wonder why the speed of my *vrille* did not increase. With every swing around the circle I felt a regular jar as the shock of the air cushion came against the left wing after passing through the right. I felt a growing irritation at these monotonous bumps. But although I had been experimenting constantly with rudder, joystick, and even with the weight of my body, I found I was totally unable to modify in the slightest the stubborn spiral gait of the aeroplane. Fully 10,000 feet I had fallen in this manner since my wing had collapsed. I looked overboard. It was scarcely 3,000 feet more—and then the crash! I could see men standing on the road in front of a line of trucks. All

were gazing white-faced at me. They were already exulting over the souvenirs they would get from my machine—from my body itself.

With a vicious disregard for consequences, I pulled
open the throttle. The sudden extra speed from the
newly started engine was too much for the perpen-
dicular tail, and before I realized it the tail was quite
horizontal.[2] Like a flash, I seized the joystick and reversed my rudder. The pull of the propeller kept her
straight. If only I could keep her so for five minutes I
might make the lines. They seemed to beckon to me
only two miles or so ahead. I looked above and below.

No aeroplanes in the sky. My late enemies evidently
were sure I was done for. Below me I saw the landscape
slipping swiftly behind me. I was making headway
much faster than I was falling. Sudden elation began
to sweep over me. I boldly tried lifting her head. No
use! She would fly straight but that was all. Ah! here
comes friend Archy!

It is curious that one gets so accustomed to Archy
that its terror actually disappears. So grateful was I to
the crippled little 'bus for not letting me down that I
continued to talk to her and promise her a good rub-
down when we reached the stable. I hardly realized
that Archy was trying to be nasty.

[2]In other words, he opened the selector switch to its maximum
range and, by turning on all nine cylinders, caused a sudden burst
of power that pulled the plane level. Technically speaking, the
plane had no throttle. EVR's instinctive feeling for machinery had
led him to take the only course of action that could have saved his
life.

Over the lines I slid, a good 1,000 feet up. Once freed from the danger of landing in Germany, I tried several small tricks and succeeded in persuading the damaged craft to one more effort. I saw the roofs of my hangar before me. With the motor still running wide open, I grazed the tops of the old 94 hangar and pancaked flatly upon my field.

The French pilots from an adjoining hangar came running out to see what novice was trying to make a landing with his motor on.[3] Later they told me I resembled a bird alighting with a broken wing.

Early next day the French notified us that they had indeed seen the Albatros machine crash and had noticed my crippled Nieuport staggering homeward from the fight, surrounded by Archy. They thus confirmed my victory without any request on my part. And the extraordinary part of the whole affair was that the dead German pilot—my latest victim—had so fallen upon his controls that the machine flew toward France and landed with his dead body a few hundred yards inside the French line.

[3]When landing in a plane with a rotary engine, a pilot alternately turned the motor on and off with a "blip switch," creating a distinctive succession of sounds that could be easily identified at a distance. In his agitated state of mind, EVR had failed to follow this rudimentary procedure and was landing with his engine wide open.

IX

Down in Flames

SQUADRON 94 had been at the front about one month when there arrived Lieut. [Paul B.] Kurtz, one of my companions of the training school days. On completion of his course at the flying school, Kurtz had been selected to make a special study of aerial gunnery in order to become an instructor to the thousands of young men who were now being drafted into Uncle Sam's aerial fleet. For this purpose he had been sent to England, and on returning to France from that country, Kurtz had received orders to report to Squadron 94 at the front in order to secure actual war experience and to make trips over the enemy's lines.

After the newcomer had asked thousands of questions and received answers to them to the best of our ability, he suggested that he should proceed to the more advanced stage of an actual combat with the enemy. As I was second in command of the squadron, being flight commander of Flight No. 1 at that time, it was my duty to arrange for him to accompany a patrol into enemy territory. No matter how much natural ability a man may possess, or how carefully he has been trained, his first experiences over enemy lines, his first contact with enemy machines, are trying to him. A moment's forgetfulness, a trifling foolhardiness, a slight miscalculation, and even a man who has been carefully and expensively trained, and who possesses all the characteristics of a successful pilot, may fall before the skill of a more experienced enemy flyer.

For this reason I always made it a practice to accompany new pilots on their first trip over the enemy's lines, and by my advice and by actual protection when aloft, assist them over that delicate period between the theory of the school and the hard practice of battle.

We were still flying the well-known Nieuport single-seater chasse or fighting machine, equipped with a Gnome *monosoupape* motor. It was then the best machine of its kind in service, although undeniably it had some faults. Having just arrived from the rear, Kurtz was not acquainted with the peculiarities of this machine. I, therefore, arranged for him to make a few short flights from our field and to practice frequent landings, so that if he ever should have sudden motor trouble he would be able to come down on any ground he found available. After a few days of this practice, he expressed himself as being capable of handling the machine under all circumstances and ready for that greatest adventure of the young pilot: that first trip over enemy's lines.

We agreed that Lieutenant Kurtz should accompany Lieutenant Chambers and me on what is familiarly known as a voluntary patrol.

Our plan of action was carefully explained to our new comrade. We were to fly in V formation; I was to lead, Chambers on my left, and Kurtz 300 feet behind and above us.[1] He was not to engage in a combat, should we meet with any enemy airmen, unless the advantage was with us. I have always made it a point to avoid a fight unless I can maneuver to get the best advantage. He was at all times to maintain his position behind and above us, playing the role of a spectator. He was instructed to try out his machine gun occasionally with a few short bursts if he had his plane pointing toward Germany. Finally, if we became scattered and he was unable to find us, he was to remember that the sun rose in the east, and, keeping it on his left, was to fly south until he felt certain that he was over French territory before making a landing.

It was decided that we should start after breakfast, promptly at eight o'clock, meet over the field at 1,500 feet, get our full altitude between Nancy and Toul, and cross over the lines at 15,000 feet. Before starting I noticed that Lieutenant Kurtz appeared rather nervous, but this was not a matter for surprise under the circumstances. Little did I understand the reason for this nervousness then, or suspect in what a tragic manner it would later be revealed to me.

Lieutenant Kurtz's machine was climbing badly, so we got up to an altitude of 14,500 feet rather slowly; at that height I decided to pass from the comparative

---

[1]See discussion in Historical Introduction of formation flying, which was designed to enhance visibility. The normal responsibility of a pilot in Kurtz's position would be to protect EVR and Chambers from an enemy who might otherwise attack them from a blind spot in their rear.

safety of our own side of the line to the hazard and adventure of the German positions. The enemy was abroad, for I caught sight of the shimmer of what I believed to be a photo-plane six miles inside our lines and very high up—probably 19,000 feet. As this enemy was certainly beyond our reach, I decided to keep the nose of my machine headed toward Germany and to continue to gain altitude as steadily as possible.

Suddenly, little fleecy white puffs appeared in the clear atmosphere ahead and above us. This antiaircraft activity of ours[2] meant that more enemy planes were abroad in our vicinity. A few minutes more and we had spotted them; three powerful single-seaters of the Albatros type, 1,500 feet above us, and about half a mile ahead. As a signal to the others I wigwagged my wings, which is the aviator's way of saying "Look out, and keep your eye on the leader." I had time to look back and see that Lieutenant Kurtz was well in the rear, and a little higher than the enemy then appeared to be.

Keeping a close watch on our opponents, I rapidly analyzed the situation. The enemy had the advantage in height; they were three, probably all experienced men, while we were two fighters and one novice, who was catching sight of a German plane for the first time in his life. But the enemy pilots were inside our lines. Down below, several hundreds of men in the trenches were watching what to them appeared to be a fight among

[2]Because of differences in the chemical composition of the ammunition they used, smoke from Allied antiaircraft shells was white and the cloud made by German shells was black.

equals—three Americans against three Germans.

In the minds of the Germans there appeared to be no element of doubt or hesitation. Having the advantage of height, they suddenly, all three, swooped down on us; first one, then the second and third dived down and sprayed us with bullets from their machine guns. I had time to notice that Lieutenant Chambers banked up on a wing tip and dived down; I did a half-*vrille,* and in less time than it takes to tell, we were both out of range. The Germans, in their diving attack, had not only failed to get any of us, but had also lost their advantage of height. The tables were turned.

We gave chase, and in a few minutes I had succeeded in separating one of the planes from the formation. It was either his life or mine! Perhaps I should get in the fatal shot, or maybe luck would be on his side; in either case, I was determined that it should be a fight to the death. Occupied as I was with my own enemy, I yet had time to notice that Lieutenant Kurtz was doing well. He and Lieutenant Chambers were in full cry after the two remaining Albatros planes; the whole show was proceeding in the direction of St. Mihiel.

Mine was a running fight until we arrived over Thiaucourt, the little city about six miles inside the German lines. Here my enemy decided that conditions were in his favor, for he swung around and headed straight for me. But I was satisfied to accept the challenge, for I was 100 yards behind and about 200 yards above my opponent, and this gave me a distinct advantage. Nearer and nearer he came, right toward me in a climbing *virage,* and working both his machine guns furiously. It is a sensation that almost defies description: there we were, only a few yards apart sparring around one another like two prize-fighters in a celestial ring. His incendiary explosive bullets were cracking all around me, and any one of them, if it touched a vital spot, was capable of putting an end to the fight. With a quick half-turn of a *vrille,* I secured a position on the tail of my enemy. It was my chance, a chance that probably would be lost in the next fraction of a second. But I had no intention of losing it and, with a pull on both triggers, a hail of bullets swept toward the German plane.

Down he swooped. Apparently he was out of control. Would he crash, or would he be able, after that giddy dive, to pull out and make a safe landing? That I could not tell, for while the spinning nosedive of an enemy looks like certain destruction, it is often, in the hands of an artful pilot, the only highway to safety.

But I was well inside enemy territory and only 10,000 feet above ground. It was quite possible that while I had been occupied in this fight other enemy planes had gathered overhead and were preparing to wreak vengeance. Personal safety and the elementary rules of aerial fighting require the pilot in such circumstances to "regain altitude, or get back to the lines as soon as possible."[3]

[3]EVR's caution in this case was typical of his ability to remain calm and his policy of observing the rules, which in turn helps

My only hope of safety lay in speed. Often on the race track, with wide-open throttle, every nerve taut, every pent-up ounce of energy concentrated in my arms, have I wished that I could infuse just a little more power into my engine.

But this case was even more crucial. Speed now meant safety, speed here meant life. My motor was flung wide open, the nose of my machine was turned down, and I raced as I had never raced before, for the prize was life itself. But, do what I could, it was impossible to shake off one of my opponents. Now I was directly over the lines; a few minutes more and I should be in our own territory and in a position either to land or get away from my persistent rival. But, the advantage the other fellow had in height was too much, and I realized that it was best for me to turn around and fight. In a flash I had kicked my tail around and was heading toward my opponent. He swooped down, reserving his fire, while I kept my fingers on the triggers of my guns. I had him in range, but I hesitated; perhaps in three seconds more I should be able to shoot with more deadly effect.[4]

Now I had my sights on him; now was the time to release both guns. At that very moment his machine

explain why he came through the war unscathed.

[4] It was axiomatic among pilots of EVR's ability that "height, speed, and a close approach" were the three main variables in successful air combat. Here again one can see how EVR's getting as close as possible to an opponent (though in this case really a friend) before firing helps explain the phenomenal record he achieved.

banked up one wing tip, and there under the lower wing I saw the concentric red, blue, and white wings of the Unites States Air Service. The supposed German was friend Chambers, who was returning from chasing the enemy, and the second plane was that of Lieutenant Kurtz, back from his first aerial scrap. God only knows why I held my fire for that brief fraction of a second.

It is not often that a man rises to the degree of joy I felt as we headed for home, the fight over, and all three safe. I had every reason to believe my German was down, possibly Chambers had gotten another, and Kurtz had deported himself wonderfully.

I searched around for the pilot Kurtz, whom I regarded as being in my care, but to my surprise was unable to find him. I cruised around for a few minutes searching in every direction, but not one plane could I see in the sky. I argued to myself that he must have gone home, and in consequence I turned my machine toward our aerodrome, hoping to pick him up at any moment. Just as I got sight of our landing ground my anxiety was relieved, for there, ahead of and below us was Lieutenant Kurtz making rings above our field, exactly as I had advised him to do.

Lieutenant Kurtz was evidently on his last turn over an adjoining field prior to landing when to unspeakable horror I saw his Nieuport drop into a *vrille* and crash straight to earth, after which bursts of angry flame shot up all around him. What could possibly have happened?

If help could be gotten to him without a moment's delay he might be pulled out of that wreckage before the flames consumed him. But I could not get to him, for the place where his machine had crashed was among barbed wire entanglements and trench works so thick that a safe landing was impossible. Below was a road, only fifty yards from the burning machine, and on the road was a French camion.[5] I speeded down, shut off my motor, and by signs and voice urged the driver to go to the rescue. The man stood still and watched. I realized later that he understood it was a hopeless task, for all the ammunition in the wrecked plane was exploding.

Unable to land close by, I sped on to our own field, jumped out of my plane almost before it had stopped rolling, vaulted into the saddle of a motorcycle, and raced towards the scene of the disaster with a vague, wild hope that I might yet be able to do some good. Could I live for a million years, I should not forget that awful sight of the charred remains of the man who had been my companion in the schools, and who only one brief hour before had set out with me full of life and hope.

A few hours later the mystery of that crash was revealed. As has already been mentioned, I had noticed before starting that Lieutenant Kurtz appeared nervous, but had not given the matter any great consideration. The explanation was given by a brother officer who had come with Lieutenant Kurtz to the squadron.

[5]"Camion": a motor truck.

Before starting on his last flight, Lieutenant Kurtz had confided to him that he was subject to fainting spells when exposed to high altitudes, and the only thing he was afraid of was that he might be seized with such a fit while in the air. Alas, his fear had been only too well founded. But what a pity it was he had not confided this fear to me, his flight commander!

The next morning a simple funeral procession wound its way down the leafy lanes, while shells passed overhead with an incongruous whine. Awaiting me at the camp on my return from this very sad ceremony was an official notice from the French commander. It stated, briefly, that an infantry officer on outpost duty in No-Man's-Land had observed that the German I had fought with had crashed to the ground, a total wreck. I had gotten my enemy; but I had lost a friend, and he had perished in the manner most dreaded of all aviators, for he had gone down in flames.[6]

[6]The crash in which Kurtz was killed occurred 22 May 1918, four days after he had joined the squadron. The victory Rickenbacker won was the third for which he received credit up to this point. For unexplained reasons, this chapter is not in proper chronological sequence, because the events recorded in the chapter that follows had actually occurred two days earlier.

X

Lufbery is Killed

Lieutenant Walter Smythe, of New York, came to me on the morning of 10 May 1918, and said: "Rick, where do you find all these Boches of yours over the lines?"

I asked him what he meant by "all."

"Why," he said, "I've been over the lines two or three times and I haven't had a single look at an enemy machine. I would like to go across with someone like you who always gets into some fun. Will you take me with you on a voluntary patrol?"

This was the spirit I liked to see in a pilot, and I immediately told Smythe I would take him over at nine o'clock this very morning if he could get ready. My regular patrol was not on until late in the afternoon, so I had all the morning to myself. Smythe was delighted with the invitation and immediately made himself ready.

We left the field together and sped quickly toward St. Mihiel. Our altimeters indicated 17,000 feet as we finished our first patrol, and found ourselves over the city of Pont-à-Mousson. No enemy machines had been encountered.

Considering it more than probable that a Rumpler[1]

---

[1] The Rumpler C-IIIA, a two-seater observation plane with a

might be coming out for photographs on such a nice morning as this, I determined to cut a slice off the German territory on our next patrol and run directly from Pont-à-Mousson to Verdun. Accordingly I set off with Smythe close by my right wing. A slight northerly course brought us directly over Mars-la-Tour, where I knew was located a fighting squadron of Germans. We should satisfy Smythe's curiosity even if we had to descend onto the enemy aerodrome.

As we crossed the little town of Mars-la-Tour, I detected a German two-seater making off toward Verdun almost directly ahead of us. It was an Albatros and was several thousand feet below us, and about two miles ahead.[2] We were in an excellent position, for not only was our presence entirely unsuspected so far in his rear, but once discovered, we had the sun at our backs and had the advantage of height and in numbers. I felt certain of the outcome of the fight and was warmly congratulating Smythe upon his good judgment in picking me as his leader in today's expedition as I dipped him a signal and began setting our course into the sun. By the time we reached Conflans I was just above the enemy's tail and in an excellent position. As yet we had remained unperceived.

---

supercharged engine that enabled it to fly at an extremely high altitude, normally beyond the range of a Nieuport's guns. The only hope of bringing down such a plane would be to intercept it during its climb, the strategy implied in the discussion that follows.

[2] Probably an Albatros C-X or C-XII reconnaissance plane, both of which had a ceiling of 16,405 feet—significantly lower than that of a Rumpler.

I stuck down my Nieuport and began my dive. My tracer bullets sped by the startled observer and gave him the first intimation he had of my proximity. The German pilot must have seen them flash past, too. For the next thing I knew was that in some way or other I had passed the Albatros and was still wildly firing into vacancy, while the two-seater enemy machine by one masterful maneuver had given me the go-by and was now on top of me. Clearly he was an old hand at this game and it behooved me to be careful.

I zoomed up again and got the upper berth. But this time I found it extremely difficult to get into a position for shooting. The pilot kicked around his tail so adroitly that every time I prepared to dive upon him I found the observer coolly sighting a brace of machine guns full into my face. Moreover, I found that at this high altitude the Albatros could maneuver as well or just a little better than could my lighter Nieuport. Once I tried to make a sharp bank to the right. I had quite forgotten the rarity of the air and, instead of a *virage,* I found I had thrown my machine into a *vrille.* Two complete revolutions were made before I could get myself straightened out. Then looking about me for my enemy, I found the Albatros nearly a mile away from me making a fast spurt for home. Smythe was composedly sailing along above me, appearing to be quite enchanted with the entertainment. I had encountered an expert pair of air fighters on the Albatros and I looked after their departing shadow with some admiration salving my disappointment. Then much of my self-satisfied abandon evaporated instantly when I began to realize that Smythe and I were over twenty-five miles inside Germany. I decided to retreat while retreating was good, fully satisfied that I had given Smythe his money's worth in the shape of a "first show."

As we passed over St. Mihiel on our way home I perceived white Archies bursting, back in the direction of Verdun. Closer scrutiny disclosed the same Albatros two-seater quietly riding the air bumps and making steadfastly for our side of the lines. The pilots thought they had me bluffed and were going on with their work in full view of Smythe and myself.

I wiggled a signal to Smythe and started again in the pursuit of the foxy Albatros. But immediately the enemy made an about-face and reentering the barrage of Archy set out at a stiff gait for Mars-la-Tour and home. I swerved a bit to the right to cut him off and glanced about me as I did so to ascertain the exact position of Smythe. He was nowhere in sight!

Below me was Etain. I was at least ten miles back of the lines. When had Smythe left me, and in what direction had he gone? Feeling more than a little uncomfortable in my thoughts at having neglected to look out for him in the last few minutes, I made a half-bank and set my course straight for home. As I learned late that afternoon, Smythe had landed inside our lines with motor troubles and was unable to reach our aerodrome until near nightfall.

As I neared the aerodrome, I saw a large crowd

gathered together on the center of the field. It was just ten-fifty in the morning when I landed beside them and hastened up to learn what calamity had overtaken my poor friend Smythe. If, through my carelessness, Smythe had become engaged in an unequal combat and had been wounded or had crashed upon landing, I could not escape the responsibility for his loss. I hurried over to the hangars, filled with apprehension.

The exclamations I heard only bewildered me the more. Major Lufbery's name was on everybody's lips. I asked if anyone had seen Lieutenant Smythe come in. The boys only looked at me vacantly and made no reply. I demanded the reason for this gathering. The answer left me dumb with dismay and horror.

Our beloved Luf was no more! Major Raoul Lufbery, the American Ace of Aces, the most revered American aviator in France had just been shot down in flames not six miles away from our field!

At about ten o'clock the antiaircraft guns on top of Mt. Mihiel began belching great white puffs of smoke overhead at a very high altitude. An alert came that a German photographing machine was coming our way and was at that moment almost directly over our field.

Major Lufbery, who had been watching the whole show from his barracks, jumped on a motorcycle that was standing in the road and rushed to the hangars. His own plane was out of commission. Another Nieuport was standing on the field, apparently ready for use. Lufbery jumped into the machine and immediately took off.

With all his long string of victories, Lufbery had never brought down an enemy aeroplane within the Allied lines. All seventeen of his early successes with the Lafayette Escadrille and his last success—when he had gone out to avenge Jimmy Hall—all had been won across the German lines. He had never seen the wreckage of a single one of his victories. Undoubtedly he seized this opportunity of engaging in a combat almost within sight of our field with abandon.

With far greater speed than his heavier antagonist, Major Lufbery climbed in pursuit. In approximately five minutes after leaving the ground he had reached 2,000 feet and had arrived within range of the Albatros six miles away.

Luf fired several short bursts as he dived in to the attack. Then he swerved away and appeared to busy himself with his gun, which evidently had jammed. Another circle over their heads and he had cleared the jam. Again he rushed the enemy from their rear, when suddenly old Luf's machine was seen to burst into roaring flames. He passed the Albatros and proceeded for three or four seconds on a straight course. Then to the horrified watchers below there appeared the figure of their gallant hero emerging in a headlong leap from the midst of the fiery furnace! Lufbery had preferred to leap to certain death rather than endure the slow torture of burning to a crisp. His body fell in the garden of a peasant woman's house in a little town just north of Nancy. A small stream ran by at about 100 yards distant and it was thought later that poor Lufbery seeing this small chance for life had jumped with the intention of striking this water. He had leaped from a height of 200 feet and his machine was carrying him at a speed of 120 miles per hour!

We were informed by a French officer of the exact spot upon which our late hero had fallen. Jumping into a motor we sped across the intervening miles at a prodigious rate and arrived at the scene of the tragedy less than thirty minutes after Luf had fallen. But already loving hands had removed his body. The towns-folk had carried all that remained of poor Raoul Lufbery to their little town hall and there we found him, his charred figure entirely covered with flowers from the nearby gardens.

I remember a conversation we had had with Major Lufbery on the subject of catching afire in the air a few days previous to this melancholy accident. I had asked Luf what he would do in a case of this kind—jump or stay with the machine? All of us had a vast respect for Major Lufbery's experience and we all leaned forward to hear his response to this question.

"I should always stay with the machine," Luf responded. "If you jump you certainly haven't got a chance. On the other hand, there is always a good chance of sideslipping your aeroplane down in such a way that you fan the flames away from yourself and the wings. Perhaps you can even put the fire out before you reach the ground."

What an irony now to recall old Luf's instructions! His machine had received a flaming bullet in the fuel tank. The next instant the little craft was but one mass of flame, from which there was no means of escape.

The following day, 20 May, the last remains of our beloved hero were laid away in our little "Airman's Cemetery." Already the small plot bore his name, and quite half a dozen of our fellows lay side by side in this foreign clay, so far distant from the land and dear ones they loved.

General Gerard, commander of the Eighth Army, arrived with his entire staff at one o'clock. General [Hunter] Liggett, commanding the 26th Division, came with Colonel William Mitchell, commanding the Air Forces of America. All bore with them quantities of beautiful flowers. Hundreds of officers from all branches of the service came to pay their last act of respect to America's most famous aviator.

I had one last flight to make in conjunction with my comrade of so many patrols. The pilots of Flight No. 1 were strapped in seats and awaiting me. Our mechanics silently handed us our baskets of flowers. Leaving the field in flight formation we circled over the hospital plot.

I flew my formation twice across the mass of uncovered heads below, then glided with closed engine down to fifty feet above the open grave. As his body was being slowly lowered, I dropped my flowers, every pilot behind me following in my wake, one by one. Returning then to our vacant aerodrome, we sorrowfully faced the realization that America's greatest aviator and Ace of Aces had been laid away for his last rest.

XI

Squadron Activities

DOUGLAS CAMPBELL, who was running neck and neck with me for the squadron record, won a celebrated victory [on 27 May]. He went out on a little private expedition of his own and while in the vicinity of Pont-à-Mousson he saw a formation of the British Independent Air Force coming home from a bombing raid on Thionville, an important railway town some thirty miles north of Metz. Some of these British bombing squadrons occupied an aerodrome only a few miles south of our own, and we frequently met them going or coming across the lines. They flew DeHavilland two-seaters with the Liberty motor, and each machine carried almost a ton of bombs. About twenty of these bombing squadrons were under the command of General Hugh Trenchard, the greatest authority on war aviation in the world, in my opinion, and they were designated as the Independent Air Force because they were not subject to any army orders. Their one function was to drop bombs on German cities.[1]

[1]The Independent Air Force (IAF), sometimes called "an air force within an air force," was a separate unit of the Royal Air Force (RAF) that was based in France under the command of Hugh Trenchard, a pioneering advocate of strategic bombing. The

Lieutenant Campbell noticed one of the British machines had dropped back almost a mile behind the others as they were returning homeward from their expedition. No fighting machines ever accompanied these bombers. They relied solely upon their close flying formation to beat off all attackers. Evidently this straggler had motor trouble for he could not keep his altitude and was slowly dropping farther and farther behind his formation. To make his situation more desperate he was at that moment being attacked simultaneously by three Pfalz fighting planes. Without hesitation Doug dived down to his rescue.

Keeping the eastern sun at his back, Campbell executed a long but rapid circle which brought him onto the rear of the enemy formation without being seen. He aimed for the nearest Pfalz and neatly shot him down with his first burst. Turning savagely upon the other two Pfalz machines, he gave them burst after burst. Both turned tail and began diving for safety.

Chasing the two Germans back for a few miles until he was satisfied they would not check their speed this side of their aerodrome, the American turned back and quickly overtook the crippled British DeHavilland. Escorting the pilot and observer to their destination, Campbell waved good-bye and made for home.

---

planes were DeHavilland DH-9 bombers with American-designed 12-cylinder "Liberty" engines. Like Billy Mitchell and other high-ranking officers in the USAS, EVR enthusiastically supported Trenchard's ideas, foreshadowing the commitment of American air doctrine to strategic bombing in the interwar years and beyond.

An hour later the commanding officer of the English squadron telephoned us, asking for the name of our plucky pilot who had downed one enemy and driven away from their intended victim two others. He stated that the British pilot and the observer had both been wounded by the Pfalz attackers and had it not been for the timely arrival of Lieutenant Campbell both would undoubtedly have been killed.

The next morning Lieutenant Campbell and I started out together on a voluntary patrol to see if we couldn't bag a few enemy planes. It was 28 May. We set out from the aerodrome at about nine o'clock under a beautiful clear sky and drove straight for the lines in the direction of Pont-à-Mousson and St. Mihiel. We were careful to keep inside our own lines so that the German Archy would not betray our presence to the enemy aeroplanes. Four or five patrols were made, back and forth, back and forth, between Pont-à-Mousson and St. Mihiel.

About an hour after we had left home I noticed a formation of machines approaching us from the vicinity of Mars-la-Tour. It was evident that they must be enemy machines since they came from that direction and were attracting no bursts of Archy from the German gunners of that locality. I dropped a signal to Campbell and began a southerly climb for greater altitude.

Reaching 18,000 feet I turned and headed back toward the enemy's lines. Now the members of the advancing formation were quite distinguishable and I made out two Albatros two-seater fighting machines coming toward us at about 16,000 feet, and above them four Pfalz single-seater fighting machines were accompanying them as protectors. Undoubtedly the expedition was planned for taking important photographs, and a strong defense had come along to enable the Albatros to accomplish their missions despite any attacks from our side.

We had about 2,000 feet altitude over them, but we needed all the advantage we could possibly get against such odds. So I withdrew, still into the sun, and waited until the whole formation had crossed the lines and were well on our side before turning for the attack.

As soon as we began our dive we were observed. The two Albatros immediately turned tail and started for the lines. The four fighting planes drew closer their formation and also turned back, keeping themselves between us and the machines they were protecting. Although the long range was hopeless, Campbell and I both fired occasional bursts as we continued after them, always preserving our advantage in altitude and never permitting them a shot at us. In this fashion we all crossed the lines again and soon were above the city of Thiaucourt, Campbell and I still holding the upper floor.

Apparently the Germans began to tire of this humiliating game, for at this juncture we suddenly noticed a breaking up of their formation; the two Albatros machines began circling back of Thiaucourt, while the four Pfalz struck off for the east and began climbing toward the Moselle valley. We watched this neat little maneuver for a few moments. Then to test the crafty trap that was so evidently being laid for us, we suddenly dived, or made a feint at a dive, upon the two abandoned Albatros machines. Then Campbell went straight down upon the nearest one while I stayed above him and kept an eye on the other four enemy fighting machines.

Instantly they reversed direction and came hurrying back. Douglas zoomed craftily back to just below me, and we continued a slow retreat toward our lines. The Pfalz maintained a safe position well in our rear.

Again the Germans undertook a fancy maneuver. We saw one of the Albatros suddenly draw away to the west, flying directly toward St. Mihiel, while the other ceased its circling and hastened to overtake the four fighting planes just ahead of him. They waited until he had overtaken them; then all five turned to the east toward the Moselle, leaving the lone Albatros an attractive bait for us still some two miles in their rear.

With extreme care we estimated the exact distances that now separated us. Fully aware of the new trap that was laid for us, it was only a question of our ability to get down at the bait and dispose of him and then regain our altitude before the superior enemy formation could descend upon us. Our judgment was as good as theirs. Our position was a little better, for we could estimate better than they the distance from our point in the sky to the slow-moving Albatros left as a decoy in the west. Better still, we knew to an inch the capabilities of our Nieuports, and perhaps the Germans would underestimate our speed. A fraction of an instant was all the mistake they need make. And they made it!

Like a flash we turned our aeroplanes and side by side dived swiftly down at the lone Albatros with our throttles full open. The Pfalz machines instantly turned to the pursuit. But even as they did so they must have realized the futility of the chase, for not only did we have a mile or more handicap, but we rapidly increased this distance between us. As we neared our target we nursed our machines until our gun sights were directly upon the enemy Albatros. About 100 shots each we fired before we eased off our machines and began to climb away to regain our altitude. Looking back we saw we had done a complete job with our Albatros. It swooped one way and then the other, and finally falling into a last *vrille*, we saw it crash at the edge of the town of Flirey just inside the Ratta Woods.

The Archy batteries below us began target practice. They had had time to calculate our position and they got in some creditable work. I sheered off toward home, but Campbell, who comes from the same breed as Jimmy Hall, made me wait for him while he returned into the barrage and captivated the German gunners below with his American aerial contortions; the barrage of shrapnel in the meantime getting very much like an Iowa hailstorm. After satisfying himself that they understood his contempt for them, Doug consented to come along home with me. We crossed the lines without suffering a hit and soon were taxiing our victorious little Nieuports across the field to the doors of our hangar.

We had scarcely gotten out of our seats when Douglas received news that completely dissipated the joy of his victory. Lieutenant John A. Mitchell, brother of our colonel and dear chum of Douglas Campbell, had been killed that morning in landing his machine at Columbey-les-Belles. Campbell and Mitchell were college chums, had entered aviation together, and had sailed for France from New York on the same steamer. They were inseparable and all their friends thought of them as two brothers. Poor Doug was inconsolable.

Friendships in flying squadrons are curious affairs. Where it is only one's daily business to go out looking for trouble, it is plainly imperative that one keep oneself always fit and clear-minded. It would never do to so occupy one's mind with emotions of love or friendship that one's fighting perceptions are dulled.

Hence I had steeled my heart against that intimate kind of friendship with my comrades that prostrates one upon the death of a friend. When Jim Miller went down I learned that necessary stoicism. Later Jimmy Hall went, and Lufbery. Many others were to follow and well I knew it. Close as our friendships were, living and working side by side with common purposes and mutual interdependence, all the pilots of 94, I believe, eventually came to look with a callous indifference on the sudden death of their dearest chum. This necessity is to my mind one of the greatest horrors of the war.

Lieutenant Smythe used to talk to me about his old mother in New York. She was a widow, and he an only son. She was in ill health, and he was haunted with the belief that a visit from him would do much to bring her back to good health and spirits.

I liked Smythe immensely from the beginning, possibly at first, because he had so flattered me with his request to go with me on voluntary patrols, but subsequently because I found that he had the ability and character of a wonderful pilot, and he was a reliable companion in a fight. Various men in my squadron appealed to me in various ways, but Smythe got so close to me by some attractive quality in his nature that I sometimes dreamed of him at night, picturing him battling against desperate odds in the air or being shot down in flames.[2]

Smythe had an unfailing fund of good nature and humor. One morning shortly after my last exploit with Douglas Campbell, Lieutenant Smythe again came to me and asked me to take him on a second expedition. We agreed to go on the following morning at four o'clock.

I might say for the benefit of those who have never been out of bed at four o'clock that it is always raw and chilly at that hour in the morning. And when one climbs up 20,000 feet in the air and cruises about for

[2]This paragraph foreshadows Smythe's death later in the book.

an hour or so with nothing more than a cup of coffee under one's belt, it requires some little enthusiasm in one's nature to derive unmixed pleasure out of it.

On this morning in question Smythe and I got up to 22,000 feet over Pont-à-Mousson and Flirey. The temperature at this altitude was probably close to fifty degrees below zero. We expected to find some early bird of the Germans coming over the lines to take their customary photographs, and it was necessary for us to have the topmost ceiling to escape his attention.

After an hour of fruitless searching, I led off again to the west, this time a little deeper within the German lines. To my surprise I noticed Smythe suddenly turn toward home and soon disappear from my sight. Supposing he had been let down by a faulty motor, I continued my patrol for another hour, saw one enemy plane that also saw me and escaped me without a combat, until finally despairing of finding any game before my fuel was completely exhausted, I returned to the field after almost two and one-half hours in the air.

Lieutenant Smythe came up to my machine as I shut off the motor.

"Hello! Eskimo!" he greeted me with some savageness. "Why didn't you stay up all day?"

I asked him why he had come down. He looked at me a moment and then began to laugh.

"Rick!" he said, "I am frozen so stiff yet that if I laugh out loud I will break in two. I don't know just how high up we were but I'll swear that I saw the sun rising for tomorrow morning!"

The Nieuport is a cold berth in high altitudes and one must dress for the part. When I learned that Smythe had worn only his ordinary clothing I could easily fancy that today's sun might look to him like the one due a week hence.

XII

Jimmy Meissner Again[1]

Such was the liaison between the Allied forces in our sector of the front in the spring of 1918 that we were frequently called upon to act in concert with the infantry or the air forces of the French and British. Thus on Decoration Day [Memorial Day, 30 May 1918], when all the thoughts from our aerodrome were directed toward the significance of the celebration that our people back home were planning for this occasion, a call came from the British that an important expedition was being carried out that morning at eight o'clock against the German railroad station at Conflans, and it would be appreciated if we Americans could furnish them some protection on their homeward journey.

Accordingly, Lieutenant Meissner was given charge of a formation of six Nieuports from Squadron 94 and Lieutenant John L. Mitchell (not to be confused with John A. Mitchell, who was killed, as already stated, at Columbey-les-Belles) led a similar formation of six

[1]In the original text, this chapter was entitled "My Fifth Victory," which was appropriate in that the win scored by EVR on 30 May 1918, described below, made him officially an Ace when it was later confirmed. The reason for the substitution of a new title is important, as will be explained later.

machines from 95, all of which left our aerodrome on this mission. They were to rendezvous over Thiau-court, which was halfway to Conflans from the front.

Thinking the chances good for a little private scrap of my own, I got my machine ready and left the aero-drome at seven-thirty. The two large flights were just fading away in the distance as I left the ground.

By the time I reached Flirey, I had attained an alti-tude of 15,000 feet and was in a splendid position to witness the whole show. There were the English squadrons returning from this expedition against the supply depots of Conflans. They had evidently dropped all their bombs and had quite as evidently aroused a hornets' nest in so doing. A large formation of enemy planes was following them hotfoot, and our fighting machines were climbing up to intercept them. Ahead of the British aeroplanes a furious storm of shrapnel indicated that Archy was not caught nap-ping. The German shells burst below and ahead of the bombing squadron but ceased as soon as the pursu-ing German machines approached that area. Those German batteries were putting up a beautiful perfor-mance but they couldn't hit the target.

Our own formations were at that moment passing over Thiaucourt and were dashing forward with all speed to the rescue of the approaching Englishmen. It looked like a regular dogfight that was preparing be-fore my very eyes. The Americans should reach the Englishmen at about the same time that the enemy overtook them from their rear.

Suddenly I noticed something going wrong with the American formation below me. Evidently another enemy flight had come up from the west and had started a free-for-all fight to prevent the Nieuports from giving aid to the bombers. As I watched this encounter I noticed one of our Nieuports, probably 3,000 feet below me and a little to the west, first flutter and then begin to fall out of control. Ever since the beginning of the stage setting I had been edging my way toward the center of the field where the opposing forces must meet. Now they were fairly under me.

The stricken Nieuport had no sooner begun its uncontrollable spin than I noted two Albatros fighting machines set themselves on his tail. Instantly I descended pell-mell onto one of them, firing at long range and continuing my fire until, to my great relief, I saw my target falling steeply to earth, quite beyond control.[2] The other Albatros hastened away.

I did not know who was the hapless pilot of the Nieuport and could not tell in what condition he was. I started swiftly down beside him to ascertain whether he was beyond further help or whether his whole performance was simply a ruse to get away from an overwhelming force. Before I had reached him I saw the Nieuport come gracefully out of the spin and with one

---

[2]Unlike the British, who awarded credit for "out of control" victories, the French did not, requiring at least one competent witness to certify that the plane in question had actually been destroyed. Because American rules followed the French practice, EVR did not receive official credit for this likely victory.

long bank begin again its upward climb. It was only a ruse! The boy was coming back to the fight!

Climbing above him, I again turned my attention to the thickest of the fray. The attacking Fokkers had been met by the remaining strength of the Americans by now and the English bombers were nearing the Allied lines. A number of individual combats were waging in various parts of the heavens. I ran about from one to the other with a savage sort of elation urging me on. It is a glorious feeling to down an enemy in combat, and the sweetness of such a victory is more than doubled if it includes saving a comrade from a fall. Who this comrade was I did not know, but I saw that he was following me along as we searched the sky from place to place for a favorable opening. Finally it came!

About five kilometers away in the direction of Pont-à-Mousson I saw a running fight that had passed quite through the rest of the combatants. I had been flying in almost the opposite direction and had not noticed their passing us. My recent protégé had left me and was already streaking in their direction. I pulled over and started in pursuit. A glance at the lines told me that the British squadron was well away and unpursued.

The little Nieuport ahead of me continued straight on, and while I was still half a mile away I saw him dart in to the attack. There were four or five Nieuports against the same number of Albatros machines; the whole show was drifting east toward the Moselle River. I slightly increased my altitude and prepared to select the most favorable door for my entrance. But whilst I was in the very act of entering it, a sudden change in the situation attracted my attention. The same little Nieuport that had been in trouble so recently over Thiaucourt, and which had again gone in red-headed against these Albatros, was diving down on the tail of one enemy while a second Albatros perceiving his advantage had gotten into a similar position on *his* tail. Even while I was starting down to make the fourth in this headlong procession, I saw the leading Albatros suddenly zoom sharply up and loop over onto his back. The Nieuport went under him at headlong pace.

Both Albatros were now on the Nieuport's tail and I was firing intermittently at each of them, hoping to divert their attention for the fraction of a second necessary to relieve the pilot in the Nieuport. With a careful aim I settled a long burst of bullets into the Albatros ahead of me. I saw at once that he was finished. The machine continued straight ahead until it crashed full into the forest that lines the east bank of the Moselle.[3]

In the midst of this diving battle the pilot in the Nieuport had tried the same maneuver that the enemy Albatros had so recently achieved. Pulling back his joystick with great suddenness, the Nieuport rose and let the two machines, one a pursuer, the other my victim, and now pilotless, pass beneath him. But at the

---

[3]When later confirmed, this victory became Rickenbacker's fifth official win, qualifying him as an Ace. Because one of his earlier victories was not credited to him until many years later, however (see Chapter VI) the one described here was really his sixth and is so officially listed today.

same instant came the sound of that sinister crackling that indicated to me that the strain had again been too much for the strength of the Nieuport's wings. The whole surface of the canvas on the right wing was torn off with the first wrench! It was the same familiar old accident that had so nearly claimed Jimmy Meissner a fortnight previously—that had indeed landed Jimmy Hall a prisoner in German lines and that had so terrified me a few days before. And here we were again at least four miles north of No-Man's-Land! Would he disintegrate here or would he be able to make some sort of landing in the forest-covered mountains below? It was a pitiable choice.

Fortunately we were left alone with our problem—the pilot of the other Nieuport and myself. The two Albatros had evidently decided to call it a day. They may never have known the catastrophe that overtook their coveted victim. I took a rapid survey of the heavens before turning my helpless attention to the ugly situation in which my protégé now found himself. Truly, if he gets out of this alive, I thought to myself, he will certainly survive the war!

"The boy who can pilot a machine without any fabric on it, as that chap is doing, is certainly something of an artist," I again said to myself as I put on the sauce and hastened to overtake my wobbly companion, who was staggering toward our lines much like a drunken man. But at any rate he *was* getting there. I came up to within twenty feet of him and looked curiously into the pilot's seat.

There was Jimmy Meissner again, turning a cheery grin toward me and taking his ease while he waved a hand to me! Jimmy Meissner indeed! No wonder he could fly a machine without canvas. With the practice he was getting he would soon be flying without wings. This was the second time he had gone through with practically this same experience, and I had saved him from attack on both occasions.

I stayed close beside Jimmy all the way in. When he finally settled down on our field for his final little crash he came wobbling over to me from the wreck as blithe and merry as ever.

While we were congratulating Jimmy upon his second miraculous escape on a collapsed machine, John L. Mitchell of Squadron 95 settled upon the field beside us. And he had another interesting story of the day's adventure.

He had noticed an enemy two-seater and two protecting fighting planes of the enemy accompanying it just east of the British bombers who were returning. His entire formation dived down to the attack and a brisk little battle took place at only 3,000 feet above ground. One after another Mitchell's formation of six machines *piquéd* down at the two-seater and let go a burst. At the last swoop, the enemy plane burst into flames and crashed.

Then they took up the pursuit of the two defending planes and Mitchell chased one of them as far north as Vigneulles, which is halfway to Metz from the front-line trenches. At this point the fleeing German evidently decided that he was no match for the American who dared to follow him so deep within his own territory, for he dived suddenly to earth and attempted to land in a large open field just outside the town. Mitchell followed him all the way down, firing continuously as he attempted to land. The pilot made a miscalculation of his distance, being probably scared out of his wits, he ran full into a fence and turned a double somersault before ending in a total smash.

Just how the pilot came out of this misadventure Mitchell had no way of ascertaining, but as long as the wreckage remained in his sight no person attempted to emerge therefrom.

It was a glorious day for Squadrons 94 and 95. We had brought down in combat four aeroplanes of the enemy without the loss of a single one of our own. We lost one machine through accident in this fight, but there were so many amusing incidents connected with this accident that none of us took it seriously. It happened in this way:

The comedian and life of Squadron 95 was Lieutenant [Wilfrid V.] Casgrain of Detroit, Michigan. Lieutenant Mitchell took him on this expedition although it was his first trip over the lines. Casgrain took a gallant part in the attack on the two-seater machine, that ended in its destruction in air.

But in recovering from the downward dive, Casgrain made the same mistake that so many of us had made in pulling up the Nieuport too quickly. He lost his canvas, just as Meissner had done.

A view of No-Man's-Land

Courtesy Corbis—Bettmann

139

Being unaware that proper manipulation would permit him to fly home in that condition, Casgrain put his nose down immediately and began a long glide to earth. Evidently he thought he was much nearer home than he was. For as we were told later by an artillery observer who had seen him land, Casgrain floated blandly halfway across No-Man's-Land, which is about a mile wide at this point, selected a smooth piece of ground, and landed with the ease of an eagle.

He stepped out of his machine with a nonchalant manner, map in hand, and set about quietly perusing it as much as to say, "Well, here I am! Now just where am I?"

At this moment several rifle balls dug up the dirt at his heels. He dropped his map and made a jump for some nearby trees. After a short consideration of his position he was seen to leave the trees and advance straight toward the German trenches, his hands held up in the air!

Poor old Casgrain evidently thought he was well behind the German lines, after his first rude awakening. As a matter of fact, he might just as well have walked in the other direction and passed through into our own lines, if only he had known that he was in No-Man's-Land.

The officers' mess at Squadron 95 does not tire of repeating this story to the present day. A few days after the cessation of hostilities, they learned from released prisoners with great satisfaction that their star comedian had been well cared for in German prisons, where he had been the wit of the camp. A fortnight after his capture he was caught hoarding his food in order to have a supply on hand when an opportunity came for an escape. For this offense Casgrain was sent north to Prussia just before the Armistice was signed.

The American gunners who witnessed Casgrain's landing in No-Man's-Land brought their 75s to bear upon his aeroplane as soon as they discovered he had abandoned it.[4] It lay somewhat nearer the German trenches than our own. All the rest of the day they hammered away at it without scoring a single hit. Presumably the novices in this battery were experimenting at some range-finding, for they shot away much ammunition without damaging the machine. This particular battery evidently had not had much practice before they left the United States.

That night the humorous Germans in the trenches went out and secured the little machine. The next morning the American gunners saw the top plane[5] of the Nieuport standing upright in the German front-line trench. The bulls-eye cocarde, which was brightly painted with red and blue circles around the big white center, stood directly facing them as much as to say:

"Now! Here is the target! Take another try at it!"

[4]It was the duty of a pilot brought down behind enemy lines to set fire to his plane if at all possible so that it would not fall into hostile hands. Because Casgrain had not destroyed his aircraft, the American batteries were trying to do it for him. "75s": 75-millimeter French field guns that were famed for their mobility and accuracy.

[5]"Top plane": the top wing.

XIII

America's First Ace

At the close of the war, Squadron 94 not only held first place among all American squadrons in length of service at the front,[1] but we held the record in number of enemy planes brought down, and the record number of Aces for any one squadron as well. I believe no single squadron in the world has won similarly so many victories as the American 94 Hat-in-the-Ring Squadron had credited to it during the first six months of its existence. Our victories, which were confirmed, totaled sixty-nine, ending with the last aerial victory of the war—that of Major [Maxwell] Kirby, who shot down his first and last enemy machine just to the northeast of Verdun at about noon on Sunday, 10 November 1918.

Many of the pilots who had gone out on their first patrols with me counted themselves later among the American Aces. While many Americans had secured five or more victories in the air before the pilots of 94

[1] As previously noted, the 95th was the first American squadron to arrive at the front but had to be sent to Cazeau for training in aerial gunnery, giving the 94th the greatest length of service in action. Counting airmen who had become Aces in the Lafayette Flying Corps, ten Aces served in the 94th. The 139th ranked second with nine. The 94th had first place in total victories, having actually downed sixty-four confirmed enemy planes.

began their full strides, these early Aces, such as Lufbery, [Frank L.] Baylies, and [David E.] Putnam of
French escadrilles, and [Clive W.] Warman, [Freder-
ick] Libby, and [Francis P.] Magoun, who were en-
rolled with the British, all were trained under foreign
methods and flew foreign machines. The first official
American Ace is therefore claimed by our squadron.
This Simon-pure American air fighter, who entered
the war with Americans and did all his fighting with
the Americans, was Lieutenant Douglas Campbell, of
San Jose, California.[2]

Douglas Campbell was twenty-two years of age
when he made his first trip over the lines. His father was
the head of the Lick Observatory on Mount Hamilton,
California. Douglas had received an unusually good
schooling before he entered the war, being an old boy
of Hotchkiss, and later graduating from Harvard with
the class of 1917. The outbreak of the war caught him
traveling in Austria with his family. They avoided the
active theater of war by going through Russia and getting thence from Denmark to England.

After finishing his college course, Doug began
preparing for aviation by entering the ground school

[2]"Official" should be read with the realization that EVR had
already won his fifth victory, which was not yet confirmed, on 30
May—one day earlier than Campbell had scored his own fifth win.
"Simon-pure American" is used because EVR was trained by
French instructors. The care with which such words were put into
the text is another indication that EVR was well aware that his
claim to being the first American Ace was at least as good as
Campbell's.

Lieutenant Douglas Campbell, America's First Ace

Courtesy Auburn University Archives

work at Cornell University. He was among the first cadets to be sent to France, arriving in Paris in August 1917. He had not as yet received any training in flying but was thoroughly familiar with wireless operation, aerial navigation, and aeroplane motors.

Made adjutant under Captain Miller, who was then in command of the American Flying School at Issoudun, Lieutenant Campbell had great difficulty in extricating himself from this indoors work, where every day's stay made him more and more valuable to his superiors. He was determined to learn to fly, with the expectation that, once possessed of his wings, he might find his transfer to an active service at the front more quickly obtainable.

There were no beginners' training machines at Issoudun. Only the 23 Model Nieuports were there. Pilots were supposed to receive initial training on the slower Curtiss machines, or the Caudrons, before attempting to fly the fast Nieuports.[3] But Campbell feared he would never get necessary permission to take this preliminary training, so he determined to get through without the beginner's course.

Little by little he edged his way into the advanced

[3]The Nieuport 23, which entered service early in 1917, was almost identical with the more heavily used Nieuport 17 except that it had a modified gun installation. Both planes were obsolete by 1918. The single-engine Caudron G-3 and twin-engine G-4 were even more outmoded, dating to 1914–1915. The Curtiss J-N-4, an American-built trainer known as the "Jenny," later became famous in stunt flying but was considerably slower than combat planes used in 1918.

training school. He finally considered himself well-enough schooled in the principles of flying to make his first essay on a solo flight. He went up all right, flew away all right, landed all right. In other words Lieutenant Campbell learned to fly alone on a fast scout machine—a feat I do not remember any other American pilot having duplicated.

Douglas Campbell was always a silent and self-possessed fellow. He was popular among his fellows from his first appearance in Squadron 94. Quiet and thoughtful in manner and gentle in speech when on the ground, Lieutenant Campbell in the air was quite a different character. He went after an enemy pilot like a tornado, often exposing himself to deadly openings. His very impetuosity usually saved him from danger unless his opponent was an old hand at the game and knew how to measure up the proper amount of defensive and offensive tactics in the same maneuver.

On 31 May, Lieutenant Campbell went out on a voluntary patrol alone—i.e., Doug went out looking for trouble. He made quite a long flight inside the German lines at a great altitude, but discovering too many enemy aeroplanes aloft he decided to return to the lines. When still three or four miles behind the German front, he discerned a German Rumpler machine evidently taking photographs of our advanced positions just south of Flirey.[4] Flirey lies just inside our

[4]The plane was either a Rumpler C-IIIA or C-IV. Because of its ample defensive armament, supercharged engine, and 21,000–22,000-foot ceiling, it was one of the war's best observation aircraft.

lines about halfway between Pont-à-Mousson and St. Mihiel.

The Rumpler aeroplane was the machine used by the enemy for observation and photographing. It was a two-seater and both the pilot and the observer who sat behind had machine guns so mounted that they covered both the front and the rear. The pilot's gun was fixed, that is, it lay flat on top of the engine hood and could not be raised or lowered. The pilot must raise or lower the nose of the aeroplane itself to bring his sights upon a target. The bullets shoot straight through the revolving propeller, and the trigger of the gun is so connected with the propeller shaft by a synchronizing gear that the hammer of the gun falls only when the propeller blade is out of the way of the issuing bullets.

The observer in the rear seat, however, is able to move his twin guns about and point them in any direction. An attack is, therefore, usually made upon such a machine from a position under its tail. If an attack comes from below, the observer cannot shoot without cutting holes through his very own tail. The forward pilot cannot use his guns at all. The only defense against such an attack is a quick swing to the left or right so that the observer can see the attacking

---

When flying at maximum altitude, it was invulnerable to Allied antiaircraft guns and pursuit planes. The Rumpler, whose pilots and observers often suffered severe anoxia despite carrying oxygen bottles on their missions, foreshadowed the development of such later spy planes as the famous Lockheed U-2.

enemy and bring his guns into action. This move the attacking aeroplane must anticipate.

Campbell was coming into the enemy's range from a very favorable direction. He had the sun at his back and moreover, he was coming from Germany into France. His presence in that direction would not be suspected.[5]

Maneuvering until he was sure of his position, Lieutenant Campbell first tried a diving attack from above and behind the Rumpler. He had an excellent chance of killing the observer with the first burst long before the latter would swing his guns around and aim them. But no such easy victory awaited him.

As he began his dive he began firing. Six or seven shots issued from the Nieuport's single gun, and then it jammed. The observer turned around and saw the diving Nieuport almost upon him. He quickly seized his own gun mount and got to work. Campbell was compelled to fly a wide circle away out of range while he worked the breechblock of the Vickers[6] and freed the jam. Now it must be a contest between a one-man scout and a two-man fighting 'bus. The best pilotage and the coolest nerve must win.

As Doug returned to the attack he discovered at once that he had a veteran pilot against him. The Rum-

[5]The Rumpler had to be flying well below its maximum altitude for Campbell to carry out the attack described here.
[6]"Vickers": a rifle-caliber machine gun invented by Hudson Maxim, an American, and manufactured under license in several countries by firms including Vickers, a British armsmaker.

pler crew showed no sign of panic or fear. The Germans did not even propose to retreat!

Campbell approached somewhat warily and began a study of the enemy's tactics. The Nieuport could turn and twist with much greater agility than the heavier machine. It had greater speed and a faster dive. Underneath the Rumpler was a safe position from which the American could keep out of view and occasionally point up his nose and let go a burst of bullets through the enemy's floor. Campbell darted in, braving a few hurried shots, and secured his position. But he didn't keep it long!

With a skill that won from Campbell still greater respect for his pilotage, the German pilot suddenly banked over, giving his observer an excellent shot at the Nieuport below. It was no place to linger, and Douglas quickly vacated. He dived again and came away at a safe distance. Again he turned the proposition over in his mind. These fellows were evidently desirous of a real battle. Well, thought Campbell to himself, let the best man win. Here goes!

Circling the enemy again and again at such speed that no careful aim at him was possible, Campbell smiled grimly to himself as he saw the observer frantically continue his firing. At this rate he must soon exhaust his ammunition and then Campbell's turn would come. Doug continued his maneuvers, at times firing a shot or two to tempt his opponent into still greater activity. Round and round they went, the German pilot attempting to kick his tail around to keep pace with the quicker circles of the flitting Nieuport.

The pilot was surely a wonder. The observer, however, was not in the same class as an air fighter.

For fifteen minutes Campbell continued these maneuvers. So far as he knew not a single bullet had entered his plane. Then suddenly he noticed that the pilot had changed his tactics. Instead of trying to keep the Nieuport within range of the observer, the German pilot was now keeping his tail behind him and sought always to get a shot himself with his forward gun. Campbell flew in closer to the tail to get a look at his situation.

Coming in toward the observer from a diagonal direction, Campbell approached to within fifty feet of the enemy and saw a curious sight. The observer was standing proudly upright and his arms were folded! From the edge of his cockpit the empty ammunition belt floated overboard and flapped in the wind. He had indeed exhausted his ammunition and now stood awaiting his doom without a thought of asking for mercy. He wore a haughty expression on his face as he watched the American approach. As Doug said later, he was so impressed with the bravery of the action that he felt he could not continue the combat against an unarmed enemy. The Prussian's expression seemed to say: "Go ahead and shoot me! I know you have won."

Upon second thought Lieutenant Campbell realized this was not a game in which he was engaged. It was war. These men had photographs of our positions within their cameras that might be the death of hundreds of our boys. They had done their best to kill him and he had endured their bullets in order to ob-

tain just this opportunity. And the pilot was still continuing his effort to outwit the American and get him
beneath his guns.

With his next maneuver Campbell began firing.
With almost his first burst he saw that he had won.
The machine of the enemy suddenly descended very
rapidly, the next second it began falling out of control,
and a few minutes later Lieutenant Campbell saw its
last crash in our lines, a few hundred yards north of
the little village of Ménil-le-Tours.

Campbell returned to the field and immediately
jumped into a car and drove over to the scene of the
crash. Here he quickly found the mangled Rumpler
and in the midst of the débris were the bodies of the
two late occupants with whom he had had such a prolonged duel. Both had been killed by the fall.

The brave observer whose demeanor had so aroused
Campbell's admiration was in truth a Prussian lieutenant. The pilot held the same rank. Both were subsequently given a military funeral and their personal effects
were sent back to Germany in their names.[7]

Lieutenant Campbell detached from the conquered
Rumpler the black crosses that decorated its wings
and brought them home with him as first evidence of
his well-won victory. As the machine crashed within

[7]Following a code of chivalry akin to that of medieval times,
combatant air services in WWI buried fallen enemy airmen with
great pomp in military funerals and took pains to notify their units
about their death. Enemy pilots often dropped flowers on the
graves of opposing airmen as a token of esteem.

our lines it required but a few more hours in which to have Lieutenant Campbell's victory officially confirmed. It was his fifth! He had been the first American pilot to win five official confirmations. Douglas Campbell that night received the heartiest congratulations from all the boys in the squadron as the first American Ace. Almost self-taught and equipped with not the safest machine at the front, Campbell had within six weeks of his first flight over the lines fought five successful duels with the boasted air fighters of the Germans.[8]

During the early hours of the same day in which Campbell was bringing this distinguished honor to Squadron 94, an episode occurred that illustrates the great aid that aeroplanes give to the land forces in warfare. Sadly enough this illustration is negative rather than affirmative, for it shows the misfortune that resulted from the failure of our ground troops to always use our aeroplanes before a contemplated advance.

---

[8]The account of Campbell's victory given in this chapter is a study in magnanimity. Despite having downed his fifth (actually his sixth) enemy plane the previous day, EVR did not gain confirmation of this victory until 12 June 1918 and was not officially credited with one of his previous wins until 1960 (see Chapter VI). Official listings show that EVR had six wins by 30 May, whereas Campbell had only five by 31 May. A careful reading of chapters XII and XIII in both the published and original forms shows that EVR was well aware of these facts; he knew that he had a valid claim to the honor Campbell had received but chose not to make an issue of the matter. It was for this reason that the title of Chapter XII, which was originally "My Fifth Victory," was changed to "Jimmy Meissner Again" before the book was published.

Trench warfare, France, 1917

Courtesy Col. Robert R. McCormick Research Center of the First Division Museum at Cantigny, Illinois

Northwest of Seicheprey a small offensive movement had been planned by the American infantry. By some means or other the enemy had received advanced information of this attack and had prepared a trap for them.

According to the prearrangements, our artillery began the show with a terrific bombardment of shells along the German trenches. Something like 20,000 shells were poured into a small area of ground inside of one hour. Then the doughboys[9] got the word and went over the top.

They raced along across No-Man's-Land, dropped into the first-line trenches of the Germans, crawled out of them, and went on to the second. All the way on to the third-line trenches of the Germans they continued their victorious course. When they arrived there they counted up their prisoners and found that the whole bag consisted of but one sick soldier, whom the Germans had been unable to remove!

While they were scratching their heads over this extraordinary puzzle, German gas shells began to drop among them. The enemy had calculated to an inch the exact positions they had just evacuated, and they quickly filled the trench lines with deadly fumes. Over 300 of our boys were gassed more or less seriously before they had time to meet the devilish menace. Then

---

[9]"Doughboys": American infantrymen, from a nickname given to foot soldiers in Texas who were powdered white with the dust of adobe soil. Thus, they were often referred to as "adobes," which was shortened to "dobies" and then "doughboys."

they realized they had wasted their ammunition on vacant trenches, and had blindly walked into a carefully prepared trap!

One single preliminary aeroplane flight over this area before beginning the offensive would have disclosed to our troops the whole situation. In fact, I believe this function of "seeing for the army" is the most important one that belongs to the aviation arm in warfare.[10] Bombing, patrolling, and bringing down enemy aeroplanes are but trivial compared to the vast importance of knowing the exact positions of the enemy's forces and "looking before you leap."

[10]The point that EVR makes here is the central thesis of an important book that appeared while this edition of *Fighting the Flying Circus* was being prepared. See James J. Cooke, *The U.S. Air Service in the Great War, 1917-1919* (Westport, Conn.: Praeger, 1996).

XIV

Rumpler No. 16

L IEUTENANT SMYTHE went out with me again on 4 June 1918. He had now become a valuable companion, and I placed the utmost dependence upon his reliability and good judgment. We crossed the lines near Pont-à-Mousson to take a look into the enemy territory and see if any inquisitive aeroplane might be coming over for photographs.

Within a dozen minutes after passing the trenches I picked up the distant silhouette of two enemy machines approaching us from the direction of Metz. I saw at first glance that these fellows had more than a 1,000-foot advantage over us in the matter of altitude. Without waiting to discover whether or not they had any friends behind them, I turned sharply about and began climbing for a greater height. We could neither attack the enemy nor defend ourselves advantageously so far below them.

While flying south and climbing steeply I noticed ahead of us, in the direction of our own aerodrome, an enormous number of white shellbursts dotting the heavens at about our altitude. These were American antiaircraft shells and they told me clearly that an enemy aeroplane was operating over Toul; likewise they indicated that no American planes were in the sky there, or else our gunners would be much more cautious in firing.

Up to this time I had downed five German aeroplanes, every one of them behind their own lines. Confirmation for my last victory, won on 30 May had not yet come in, so officially I was not yet an Ace. That was of little consequence, but the matter of dropping a German plane within our own territory where I might land beside him and have the satisfaction of seeing what sort of prize I had bagged—this was a pleasure that I rather ardently desired. Consequently, I forgot all about the late object of our attack, who presumably was still coasting along five or six miles behind us. I wigwagged my wings to attract Smythe's attention, pointed the nose of my Nieuport toward the city of Toul, and forged with all possible speed ahead in that direction. Smythe well understood and followed close behind.

As we drew nearer, we easily distinguished the outline of a two-seater photographing machine tranquilly pursuing its way amidst the angry bursts of shrapnel. I wouldn't have taken a million dollars for my opportunity at that moment. The enemy was in our very front lawn and would drop within a few kilometers of my own hangar. He hadn't even noticed my approach but was lazily circling about, no doubt photographing everything of interest in the vicinity with calm indifference to the frantic efforts of our Archy batteries.

It was a Rumpler, just as I had thought. I had him in a tight position. He couldn't see me, as I was exactly in the middle of the sun. I had just the right amount of elevation for a leisurely direct attack. Smythe stayed above me as I pushed down my joystick and began my slide.

Painted in big black letters on the side of his fuselage was the number "16." The outline of the "16" was beautifully shaded from black into orange color. Just ahead of the "16" were the ornate insignia, also in orange representing a rising sun.[1] I pictured the spot on the wall over my sleeping cot where those insignia would hang this evening after dinner as I directed the sights of my machine gun past the rising sun, past the observer's seat, raised them a trifle, and finally settled them dead into the pilot's seat only 100 yards ahead of me. Absolutely certain of my aim, I went ahead and pressed the trigger.

Words cannot describe my chagrin and rage as I realized that my gun had jammed after the first two or three shots. I dashed on by my easy target at the rate of 200 miles per hour, cursing madly at my gun, my ammunition, and at the armorer at the aerodrome who had been careless in selecting and fitting my cartridges. The two or three bullets that I had fired merely served to give the alarm to the Germans in the machine. They would turn at once for home while I withdrew to repair my miserable firearms.

It was too true. Already they were headed for Germany and were moving away at top speed. I directed

[1] The rising sun was probably a personal marking and not a unit insignia. Leonard E. Opdycke offered advice on this point.

my swifter-climbing machine upon a parallel course that would soon distance them as well as regain me my former superior height; and as we flew along I disengaged the faulty cartridge from the chamber of the Vickers and fired a few rounds to see that the mechanism was in good firing order. All again arranged to my satisfaction, I looked below to see how far my craft had carried me.

I had crossed over the lines! There lay Thiaucourt below me, not more than a mile away. The enemy machine had been steadily diving for home all this time and I had a very few seconds left me for an attack of any kind. All hopes of getting a victory inside of my own lines had now disappeared. I should be lucky if I got confirmation for a victory at all, since we were now so far inside Germany and so near to the ground. I dived on to the attack.

Most of one's trouble in this world comes from something wrong inside one's self. If I hadn't been so stupidly optimistic at the outset of this engagement, I should have been more cautious, and my first disappointment would not have made me forget to keep an eye out for other enemy machines. I had forgotten even Smythe in my rage at losing the best chance for a brilliant shot that had ever come my way. I had been flying for five minutes with almost no thoughts except angry disappointment. Now I had a rude awakening.

Even as I began my last dive upon the Rumpler I heard, saw, and felt living streaks of fire pass my head. They crackled and sparkled around me like a dozen popcorn roasters, except that they had a far more consistent and regular rhythm. I saw a number of these tracer bullets go streaming past my face before I realized what a blessed idiot I had been. Almost scared out of my wits with the dreadful situation in which I now found myself, I did not even stop to look around and count the number of enemy machines on my tail. I imagined there were at least 1,000 from the streaks of fire that their tracer bullets and incendiary ammunition cut through my wings. I kicked my rudder with my right foot and shoved my joystick to the right with a single spasmodic jerk. My machine fell over onto its wings and slid sideways for a few hundred feet and then, seeing a clear country between me and dear old France, I pulled her back into line and fed in the gas. The suddenness of my maneuver must have caught the Germans quite by surprise, for as I straightened out, I looked behind me and saw the two fighting single-seaters that had been on my tail still on their downward dive. I had gotten away so quickly they did not even yet know I had gone.

No. 16 and the orange-colored Rising Sun that I fancied would be decorating the walls over my sleeping cot were still leering at me from the fat sides of the Rumpler as it descended leisurely to the ground.

As I took my melancholy, yet grateful, way homeward I reviewed and checked up the events of the morning. I resolved then and there never again to permit premature elation or circumstances of any kind, good or bad, to rile my temper and affect me as they had this morning. Fate had been extraordinarily good to me and I had escaped miraculously with only a few bullet holes through my wings, but I could never expect to be so fortunate again.

It was with a chastened spirit that I confronted our armorer a few minutes later and told him about my jam. Instead of bringing a severe punishment to the careless mechanics who had tested my gun and ammunition, I mildly suggested that they make a more stringent examination of my cartridges hereafter.

At this time I was second in command of Squadron 94 and, as one of the privileges of the office, I could go off on voluntary patrols at any time I desired so long as such proceedings did not interfere with my required duties. I naturally preferred going by myself, for I felt no responsibility for other pilots under such circumstances, and I had a much better chance of stealing up close to enemy aeroplanes without discovery. In formation flying, the whole flight is limited to the speed and altitude of its weakest member. Formation flying is very valuable to an inexperienced pilot; but after one has learned to take care of oneself, one prefers to go out with a roving commission.

The morning following my disappointing encounter with No. 16 of the Rising Sun Squadron, I went over to my hangar at an early hour to see that all was right with my machine. Inside the shed I found the mechanics busy with my Nieuport. The gun had been dismounted and was still in the repair shop. Some defect had been discovered in the mechanism, they told

me, and it had been necessary to take it to the gun repair shops for examination. My machine was out of
commission for that day.

Looking over the available machines I found that
Lieutenant Smythe's Nieuport was in good condition,
although the guns were not correctly aligned, according to Smythe's judgment.[2] He readily consented to
my using it for a little patrol, though this necessitated
his remaining behind. I knew nothing of the capabilities of his machine, yet I was pleased to try the effi-
cacy of his twin-gun mounting. My own Nieuport
carried but one gun.[3]

Flying high over Nancy, Toul, and Commercy, I
tried to learn the topmost ceiling of Smythe's machine.
The highest altitude, it should be explained, to which
any machine can climb, is controlled by the steadily increasing rarity of the atmosphere. The higher one
rises, the greater speed is required, to enable the thin-
ner air to sustain the weight of the aeroplane. Consequently, the limit of altitude for any given machine
depends on two factors: its horsepower and weight. In
order to climb an extra 1,000 feet, you must apprecia-
bly increase the horsepower or diminish the weight.
To resume: I reached 20,000 feet and found that
Smythe's machine would go no higher. I fired a few

[2] The original text states that both Smythe's plane and its guns
were "brand new," explaining why the guns had not yet been properly aligned.

[3] The original text clarifies this detail by stating that EVR was
carrying only one machine gun to lighten his plane and thus make
it more maneuverable.

bursts from each gun and found that they operated smoothly. Everything appeared to be all right. I headed for Germany and began to scour the hostile skies. For a time nothing appeared. Then, coming from the direction of Metz, I observed a photographing two-seater, accompanied by scouts acting as protectors.

Acting upon the same tactics that had appealed to me yesterday, I turned back into the sun and awaited their passing over our lines. To my delight I saw the two fighting machines escort the Rumpler fairly across our lines and then themselves turn back into Germany. They had not seen me and evidently considered their protection no longer necessary. I hugged the sun closely and let the Rumpler sail by below me. Imagine my extravagant joy when I again made out the painted Rising Sun in orange colors along the side of the Rumpler's fuselage, and the big black numerals "16" following it! My escaped prize of yesterday was again within my clutches. It would never escape again.

The barren walls of my sleeping quarters again rose before my eyes. Manfully, I choked down all unwonted feelings of optimism as I thought of yesterday's mishaps, but still I felt confidence in the outcome of today's encounter. This was too good to be true.

Compelling myself to patience, I followed my enemy along as he made his way still further to the south. He had some special mission to perform, of this I was sure. I wanted to know just what this mission was. At the same time, the farther back he ventured, the better would be my chances for dropping him within our territory. He was now almost over Commercy. My sole fear was that some careless move of mine would disclose me to the attention of the observer.

As he left Commercy behind him and approached, I made up my mind to delay no longer. I suddenly left my position in the sun and darted out to the rear to intercept his retreat. It was to be a straightforward battle in the open. Let the best man win!

Again my luck was with me, for I reached a point directly behind him and had turned toward him for my first shots before they were aware of my presence. I had decided upon my tactics. Diving upon him from a diagonal direction, my first bursts would doubtless cause him to put his machine into a *vrille*. I would anticipate this and zoom up over him and catch him dead under my next diving attack. As I neared the Rumpler's tail from a three-quarters direction, I saw the observer suddenly straighten himself up and look around at me. He had been down in the bottom of his office, probably taking photographs of the scenery below.[4] The pilot had seen my machine in his mirror and had just given the warning to the rear gunner. As he faced me I began firing.

Two unexpected things happened immediately.

Instead of falling into a *vrille*, as any intelligent pilot

---

[4] "Office": slang for cockpit; see glossary at the beginning of the book. The camera on a plane of this type was usually set to take pictures automatically at a speed timed with that of the aircraft, but the observer may have been adjusting his equipment.

would certainly have done, this German zoomed sharply up and let me go under him. In fact I had about the thousandth part of a second in which to decide to go under rather than ram the monster. Thus my clever plans were all upset by the refusal of my antagonist to do the maneuver that I had assigned to him. Our positions were reversed. Instead of my being on top and firing at him, he was on top and by some extraordinary miracle, he was firing at me.

I circled away and looked back to unravel this mystery. I quickly solved it. From out of the belly of the Rumpler a wicked-looking machine gun was pumping tracer bullets at me as fast as any gun ever fired! It was a new and hitherto unheard of method of defense—this shooting through the floor. No wonder he had climbed instead of trying to escape.[5]

To add to my discomfiture I jammed both my guns on my next attack. There appeared to be no justice in

[5]Several authorities on German aircraft in WWI have stated that this section of the text cannot be accurate, because no plane of this type had belly guns. Only armored trench-strafing aircraft that flew at lower altitudes, such as the A.E.G. J-1 and J-2, had this feature. To have put a belly gun and its extra ammunition in an observation plane would have increased its weight and thus decreased its speed, its ceiling, and its maneuverability. Such an encumbrance would have been both self-defeating and unnecessary in a plane that was designed to be normally out of range of attacking aircraft. It is possible that the observer in the Rumpler had swiveled his machine gun into such a position alongside the fuselage that it was firing directly downward, making it seem from a distance that it was protruding from the plane's belly. Dan Abbott, James Davilla, and Leonard E. Opdycke offered advice in this matter.

the world! I circled away out of range and moodily cleared the jam in one of my guns. The other absolutely refused to operate further.

In the meantime I had not failed to keep an occasional eye upon the movements of my adversary and another swift glance at intervals to see that no other enemy machines were coming to interrupt the little duel that was to ensue. I sobered up completely and considered the exact chances of getting in one swift deathblow with my more adroit Nieuport before the more heavily armed Rumpler could bring its armament to bear upon me. The enemy machine was flying homeward now, and straight in the direction of St. Mihiel.

Coming at him again from below, I got in two or three good bursts that should have made an impression upon him—but didn't. The lower berth I found altogether too hot a position to hold, owing to the floor guns of the enemy, so I zoomed suddenly up overhead and circled back to try to catch the observer unprepared to receive me. Several times I tried this dodge but I found one of the most agile acrobats in the German army on duty in that back seat. He would be lying face-downward in the tail of his machine one second, firing at me. I would zoom up and come alongside and over him within two seconds, yet I always found him standing on his feet and ready for me. We exchanged burst after burst, that observer and I, and soon came to know all about each other's idiosyncrasies. I do not know what he thinks of me; I know that he was the very nimblest airman I ever saw.

We had been at this game for forty minutes, and the Rumpler pilot had not fired a shot. I had long ago given up hope of their ever exhausting their ammunition. They must have had a week's supply for the rear guns alone. And now we were well back of the German lines again. I continued to circle in and fire a short burst of half a dozen shots, but found it impossible to break through their defensive tactics long enough to get a true aim upon any vital part of their machine.

We were getting lower and lower. They were preparing to land. I fired a farewell burst, and in the middle of it my gun again jammed. The pilot waved his hand "good-by-ee" to me, the observer fired a last cheery burst from his *tournelle* guns,[6] and the show was over for the day. My coveted "16" would not decorate my bedroom walls this night.

I flew thoughtfully homeward, wondering at the curious coincidence that had brought No. 16 and me together for two days running, and the strange fate that seemed to protect it. It was unbelievable that a heavy two-seater could escape a fighting machine with all the circumstances in favor of the latter. It must have been something wrong with me, I concluded.

Just then my motor gave an expiring "chug" and I began to drop. I leveled out as flat as possible and looked ahead. I should be able to glide across the

[6]Machine guns in the rear cockpit that were mounted on a circular track so that they could be swiveled into a number of positions.

trenches from here if Smythe's machine was any good at all. So fed up with disappointment was I that I did not much care whether I reached the American lines or not. What could have happened to the fool motor anyway?

I glanced at my wristwatch and found the answer. I had been so absorbed in my pursuit of No. 16 that I had forgotten all about the passing of time. It had been two hours and thirty-five minutes since I had left the ground, and the Nieuport was supposed to carry oil for but two and a quarter hours' flight. The oil completely exhausted, my motor was frozen stiff and a forced landing in some nearby shellhole was an imminent certainty.

The continued favors of Providence in keeping enemy planes away from me in that homeward glide served to restore my faith in Justice. I crossed the lines and even made the vicinity of Ménil-la-Tours before it became necessary to look for a smooth landing ground. There was little choice, and each choice there was appeared to be worse than the others. Barbed wire stretched across every field in close formation. Selecting the most favorable spaces, I settled down, just cleared the top of the wire with my wheels and landed without crashing in a narrow field.

As I climbed out of my machine, several doughboys came running up and inquired as to whether I was wounded. A few minutes later a Major Miller drove up the road in a touring car, having seen my forced landing from a nearby town. I left a guard in charge of the stranded aeroplane and drove away with the major to telephone my aerodrome for the aeroplane ambulance and to report that I had landed without injury. As it proved impossible to "get through" by telephone, the major very kindly offered to drive me home in his car. In half an hour I was back with my squadron, none the worse for the day's adventures, but, on the other hand, none the better save for a little more of that eternal fund of experience that seemed to be forever waiting for me over the enemy's lines.[7]

But as soon as I stepped out of the car I learned of an occurrence that dispelled all thoughts of my own adventures. Douglas Campbell had just landed and was dangerously wounded!

[7]I have been unable to identify the "Major Miller" mentioned in this passage.

XV

Campbell's Last Fight

SHORTLY AFTER I had left the aerodrome that morning for my second rendezvous with my *bête noire*, Jimmy Meissner and Doug Campbell had followed me on a little expedition of their own. They had chosen the vicinity to the east of Pont-à-Mousson.

Doug and Jimmy were two of the best pals in the world. Indeed it would be a very difficult matter for anybody to be in Jimmy Meissner's company for more than an hour without becoming his pal. Both these boys had companionable natures. They were constantly in each other's company, Jimmy and Douglas, and very frequently they went off on these special hunting parties together.

On this occasion it appears that after a short tour together back of the lines they became separated. Jimmy went off on a wild-goose chase of his own, leaving Lieutenant Campbell reconnoitering back and forth over the same locality to the east of Pont-à-Mousson. Upon one of his patient tacks Campbell discovered a Rumpler coming from Germany and evidently aiming toward the vicinity of Nancy. He hid himself in the sun and awaited its approach.

The actual encounter took place at about the same time I was fighting my No. 16 some twenty miles to the west of them. Douglas began his battle with everything in his favor. He caught the Germans completely by surprise and put enough bullets into the enemy craft to sink an ordinary 'bus. But he wouldn't drop. He simply sailed along and continued to pot Doug's Nieuport every time he swung in for an attack. They had very much the same sort of a running fight I was having with my antagonist, No. 16.

Finally Meissner saw something going on over the Nancy sky, and came speeding back in to take a hand in the combat. Just as Jimmy drew near to the scene of the scrap, he saw that he was diverting some of the pilot's attention to himself. Campbell saw this, too, and immediately took advantage of the opportunity.

Coming diagonally in toward the observer from behind, Doug suddenly changed his course and swerved around to the front for a shot at the preoccupied pilot. He got in a fairly long burst before he was compelled to turn aside to avoid a collision. Though he had not touched the pilot, he had the good fortune to shower the motor with bullets; to his great joy he saw that the machine was really out of control. The pilot, unable to maintain headway and maneuver at the same time, had put down his nose and was gliding northward for his lines.

At this juncture, Jimmy took a hand in the scrap, and both the pilot and observer had their hands full to prevent a surprise attack from one of the two circling Nieuports.

But the Americans' time was short. The lines were

but half a dozen miles away. With his present height the German pilot could glide his machine well behind his own lines. The *coup-de-grace* must be delivered at once if the Americans were to prevent the morning's photographs from falling into the hands of the enemy.

There was no way of communicating a plan of simultaneous attack between the two Nieuports. But both pilots had the same intention and watched each other jockeying around the Rumpler until a favorable opening presented itself. Suddenly both Meissner and Campbell came in upon the enemy from opposite sides. Campbell got a faster start, and braving the fire from the observer, dived below for 200 feet, only to zoom suddenly upward and direct another long burst through the floor of the Rumpler. Swerving then off to the right he again came by the side of the observer. The latter unfortunately had changed his position to fire at Meissner after Campbell had darted below him on the other side. As Doug now reappeared from below the Rumpler, he came full into range of the observer's guns.

Doug was just coming out of his zoom and was beginning a flat circle to the front when a loud explosion at the small of his back told him that he had been hit. He felt a burning pain run up the length of his spine. He was still some two miles above Mother Earth, and his first thought was to retain his senses until he could bring his machine safely to the ground. He immediately flew for home, leaving the outcome of the battle to his comrade.

Meissner saw Campbell draw away and immediately jumped to the conclusion that he had been wounded. He had not seen the bullets strike him, however, and there was always a chance that merely an engine failure had compelled Doug to withdraw. No matter what was the cause, Jimmy's duty was to prevent the safe return of the enemy machine to its own lines. He could be of no help to his companion anyway. He continued his harassing of the pilot, and so occupied that gentleman with maneuvers that by the time the trenches were reached, Jimmy had the satisfaction of seeing that the Rumpler could not possibly get to a safe zone for landing.

Just 100 yards beyond the German first-line trench the Rumpler crashed. Both the pilot and observer scrambled from their seats and ran for their lives. Our doughboys gave them a shower of bullets that greatly accelerated their speed. The enemy soldiers in their trenches stood up and leveled a machine-gun fire at our men to protect their aviators' foot race for safety. The next moment the American artillery directed a heavy shellfire of high explosive against the abandoned Rumpler. These were better marksmen than the last I mentioned. After half a dozen shots, nothing but fragments remained.

All this spectacle Jimmy gleefully observed before he turned his machine homeward and hastened to find out what had happened to Douglas Campbell. He reached the aerodrome just about the same time I did. Doug was safely landed and had climbed out of the machine without assistance. Although suffering much pain, he would not leave the field until he had learned just how he had been hit. A short inspection disclosed the whole story.

An explosive bullet fired by the observer had come through the floor of Campbell's machine just at the instant he was making a turn. It had penetrated the bottom of the fuselage, gone through the bottom of his seat, and then had struck a wire that had exploded the missile not three inches from Campbell's back.

The fragments had scattered backward and to the side, riddling the framework and fabric that covered the fuselage behind the seat. Very few of the fragments had gone forward. This miraculous circumstance had undoubtedly saved Doug's life.

Jimmy and I gazed with stupefaction at the smiling and imperturbable Doug. He stood beside us refusing all aid, and appeared more deeply interested in the condition of his machine than in his own wounds. In the back of his Teddy-Bear suit a long, jagged tear showed us where the missile had entered his body. Frightful blood stains covered his back. Yet he was deaf to all our entreaties and refused to let us lead him away.

I asked what had been done about getting an ambulance down and found that Campbell had sent for a motorcycle! I could not help laughing at this childish desire to avoid making a scene, which I very well knew had actuated Doug's request for a motorcycle. I immediately commandeered an automobile, and, putting Douglas carefully in it, several of us accompanied him to the hospital.

With continued fortitude, Doug refused an anaesthetic while the surgeon was removing the bullet.[1] It was found that the steel nose itself had been deflected by the wire into Doug's back. By some miracle it had not touched his spinal column but had traveled up alongside it for five or six inches and finally buried itself in the muscles under the shoulder! This little memento Doug now preserves as his most cherished souvenir of the war.

With splendid grit Doug smiled and talked while the doctor proceeded with the operation. He drew all the details of the finish of the Rumpler from Jimmy and learned with great satisfaction that this was his sixth official victory. In reality, Douglas Campbell's victories total seven, but for one that was downed, to my certain knowledge, he never received official confirmation.

Had it not been for this unfortunate accident, Lieutenant Douglas Campbell would undoubtedly have one of the highest scores of victories claimed by any air fighter, for he was just entering upon his full stride. As it was, he never fought again. Upon his return in November from America, where he was sent to recover his strength after leaving the hospital, Doug rejoined his old squadron, only to find that its days of fighting were over.

The subject of my encounter with Rising Sun No.

---

[1] That is, he refused to be completely anaesthetized. The original text states that Campbell was given a local anesthetic.

16 occasioned no end of amusement about the mess, and many bets were laid as to the outcome. I dreamed about No. 16 at night and was up bright and early on the lookout for him every morning. I took a few of the bets myself, naturally enough. I never in my life wanted anything so much as those orange-colored insignia decorations for my quarters. I planned to build a house some day suitably designed to set off those works of art to the best advantage.

The fates were surely laughing at me all this time. My further adventures with No. 16 would have appeared comic to me if they had not been so infuriating.

The very next day I went up in my own machine with just the one resolve burning in my brain. I saw nothing else in the sky and searched for nothing else. In fact, I had scarcely gained my very topmost altitude and set forth in the direction of what I now knew was the favorite path of this daily visitor before I saw him coming to meet me. It was almost as though we had met by appointment.

As I have said, I reached my very highest altitude before going forth to this tryst. Some Nieuports have a higher ceiling than others. It depends on the quality and natural fitness of the motor. My 'bus reached 18,000 feet that morning. It had just been fitted with two Vickers guns instead of the one it formerly carried. This additional weight of thirty or forty pounds lowered my ceiling by at least 500 feet.

Try as I would, I could get no higher. As we approached each other, No. 16 and I, the Rumpler was at 20,000 feet and was still climbing. My German friends knew perfectly well they could climb higher than any Nieuport. It might make their photographs a little indistinct, but even those were better than our own taken from 12,000 feet. They came steadily on; I turned as they passed me and continued a parallel course some 2,000 feet below them.

The railroad stations at Nancy and Toul were their objectives this morning. Without deigning to pay any attention to me, they proceeded over their course and deliberately snapped their pictures.

So we continued along all over the northeast of France. I suppose most of the films they developed that afternoon showed the wings of my Nieuport below them.

My one chance was to keep below them and follow them until they came down. As there is no record of any German machine not coming down finally, I determined to follow them back to Berlin, if necessary, in order to get a shot at them when they passed my level. Thus we crossed the lines and proceeded steadily northward. I could outfly the Rumpler and outdive him, but his superior engine power and greater wing spread gave him a much higher ceiling.

After seeing mile after mile slip away beneath my wings, and still no evidence of change of heart in my antagonists, I began to speculate upon the quantity of gasoline the Rumpler carried. I knew too well the limits of the Nieuport's fuel supply. And the disadvantage again lay with me. For, if we both became exhausted at the same time, the Rumpler would be in his own territory, while I would be many hostile miles from my own.

With savage realization that I was again defeated, I turned around and took my way homeward. I could imagine my two adversaries laughing at me as I gave up the chase. They began to glide downward as soon as I turned my back. I sheered back at them just to have the satisfaction of showing them I was still their master. Obediently they climbed for their superior ceiling.

When I reached the camp I scoured the hangars for information of the highest climbing machine on the aerodrome. My comrades followed me about, supplying me with much gratuitous information and advice. They advised me to leave off both guns next day, which might permit me to reach 20,000 feet. Or, if I took no fuel along, I might go to 30,000 feet. Uncomplimentary references to the weight of my shoes and heaviness of my grouch aided me considerably.

The result of my researches indicated that Captain [Kenneth] Marr's machine had the best reputation for climbing and I immediately set off to obtain his consent for the loan of his Nieuport on the morrow.[2]

Considerably discouraged over the prospects of securing my bedroom trophies from Rising Sun No. 16, I nevertheless climbed into Captain Marr's machine the next morning at exactly 8:15 and amid the cheers

[2]Marr had other things on his mind. On 7 June 1918, the same day that EVR used his borrowed Nieuport in his last attempt to shoot down the Rumpler, Marr replaced Huffer as commander of the 94th.

and the boys who gathered to see me off, I bade the mechanics to pull away the chocks. I made a direct path to our rendezvous of yesterday.

I put Captain Marr's Nieuport up to a little over 19,000 feet that morning, and there she hung. Every artifice that ever moved an engine was experimented in, but without increasing her capacities an inch. Just as I had satisfied myself that I had exhausted her possibilities, I discovered my old friend, No. 16, winging his way calmly toward me.

Just as yesterday, the Rumpler was some 2,000 feet above my highest possible elevation. With rare magnanimity, my old friends kindly came down a few hundred feet to keep me company. I joined in the procession as of yore, and the two machines made another grand tour of the northeasterly cities of France where we photographed all the railroad lines and canals, surveyed the charming landscape in all directions, and finally decided to call it a day and go home. My presence served to prevent our batteries from firing noisy shells at my friends, and they must have appreciated this act of courtesy.

I accompanied them to their aerodrome, maintaining the proper distance between us. Seeing they wanted to alight, and mindful of their courtesy throughout the day, I turned about and made for home.

That night I came down with the fever and was immediately sent to Paris on leave.

XVI

Becoming an Ace

Pᴀʀɪs in wartime is well enough known to millions
of my fellow countrymen, but the scene that presented itself to my astonished eyes as I alighted at the
Gare de l'Est on the morning of 8 June 1918 merits a
description. That date, it will be remembered, marked
probably the lowest ebb in the spirits of the Parisian
populace.

The Germans were along the Marne and only thirty
miles from the capital. Château-Thierry was in their
hands. The villagers in that vicinity who had braved
four years of adjacent warfare were now swept away
from their homes. Thousands of these poor refugees
were arriving in Paris on the morning I entered it.

Used as I was to the various horrors of war, there
was a terror in the countenances of these homeless
people that made a new impression on me. Old
women, young women, all clothed in wretched gar-
ments and disheveled headgear wandered blindly
through the streets adjoining the stations, with swarms
of crying children clinging to their skirts. Pathetic as
this scene was, it had its comic features in the extraordinary articles that these fleeing peasants had chosen to carry with them.

Umbrellas seemed to be the most precious thing

that they had tried to save. A little bundle, probably containing a loaf of bread and a few articles of clothing, was carried by each woman. The children were loaded down with such strange treasures as axes, parrot cages, wooden buckets, and farm implements. The few old men who accompanied them hobbled along empty-handed, with the utmost patience and abandon. Evidently the whole care of the migration was left to the energetic women of France.

They had all been walking for many miles; this was very evident. Their clothing was dusty, worn, and crumpled. Their faces were pinched and wretched, and an indescribable look of misery and suffering filled every face. The pathos of this scene will never leave my memory.

After a good night's sleep far away from the roar of artillery, I woke up to find the sun shining and a fine day well progressed. After breakfast, I took a stroll along the Champs-Elysées under the Arc de Triomphe, and through the beautiful walks of the Bois de Boulogne. It was easy to read upon the faces of the people one met the deadly fear that gripped them. Thousands had already fled from Paris. The authorities were that morning considering again moving the seat of the government to more distant city of Bordeaux. The capture of Paris before the American aid could arrive was a possibility that worried every Parisian.

I tried to fancy the exulting German officers walking down these same beautiful avenues, driving their motor cars through these splendid woods, and occupying such of these magnificent palaces as happened to tempt their cupidity. Then I thought of the "Spirit of the Marne" that had so strengthened the French people in those cruel days of 1914. Studying the set faces of these passers-by I could discover that the same indomitable spirit still held them.

After a few days in Paris,[1] I returned to my aerodrome by way of Army headquarters, then situated in Chaumont just south of Toul. Good news awaited me at my mess. I learned that General [Benjamin D.] Foulois[2] had been out to see us, and after hearing the repeated stories of the narrow escapes we had had with the fragile Nieuports, he had promised to secure Spad [XIII] aeroplanes for our whole squadron. They were to be driven with the 220-horsepower Hispano-Suiza motor and would serve to equip us second to none of the squadrons in France.

Furthermore, confirmations had been secured for my fifth victory and several cablegrams from America were handed me, congratulating me on becoming the second American Ace. The news had reached the States before it had found me in Paris!

We had another victory too. Jimmy Meissner, Alan Winslow, and Thorne Taylor had met with a Hannover

[1]The original text and EVR's *Diary* show that EVR, who was on a 48-hour leave, spent only two days in Paris, leaving for Chaumont on 10 June 1918 and arriving at Toul the following day.

[2]Foulois was chief officer of the USAS from November 1917 until May 1918, when he was replaced by Billy Mitchell and became assistant chief.

two-seater on 13 June 1918, and after a ten-minute combat had the satisfaction of seeing the enemy go down in flames and crash just north of Thiaucourt. The boys were very much elated over the additional news of our contemplated removal to a busier sector of the front. Hunting had become very poor along our old sector. The enemy machines were infrequently met and almost no fighting machines of the Germans were now opposing us. An occasional observing machine came our way, but he usually fled long before we had an opportunity for an attack.

We had been for two months on this sector and had received all the preliminary practice fighting that we desired. All the boys were restless and were anxious to get to the thick of the battle down on the Marne where the "Big Push" was now taking place.[3] Fresh from the rumors of Paris, I naturally inflamed their appetite for the contest by picturing to them the state of affairs as I had seen it in the capital.

At this period we began to notice that the German air tactics seemed to pin all hopes for success upon formation flying. Larger and still larger numbers of enemy aeroplanes clung together when they ventured into hostile skies. From flights of three to five machines in one formation, their offensive patrols now included

[3]The Battle of Belleau Wood, one of the bloodiest engagements of the war for American troops, was in progress. Germany enjoyed air superiority in that sector as of 14 June, explaining why moving the 94th and other units of the 1st Pursuit Group there was being considered.

whole squadrons of some twenty or more machines.

Certain advantages undoubtedly accrue to such formations. Mere numbers serve to scare away the more cautious air fighters, and even the most daring find themselves confronted with such a bewildering and formidable number of antagonists that to attack, one must necessarily include defending oneself against several.

Squadron 94 therefore began sedulously to practice flying in similar large formations. Day after day we called together all our available machines and took the sky together, met at a designated altitude, and forming a compact group, we circled about, executed the various maneuvers that must attend an offensive or defensive movement, and strove always to keep all our aeroplanes in such a position that no single one could ever be cut out and subjected to an attack by an enemy formation. This was a valuable lesson to all of us, and later on we accumulated quite a respectable number of victories by reason of our familiarity with this method of squadron formation flying. Especially valuable is formation flying to the inexperienced pilot. One illustration will serve to demonstrate my meaning.

On the evening of 18 June 1918, a few days after I had returned to the command of my Flight No. 1 in Squadron 94, we were notified by the British bombing squadrons that they were undertaking a raid on the railroad yards of Thionville that evening at 7:30. Thionville, or Diderhofen as it is called by the Germans, lies west of Metz and is the favorite gateway to the front from the German interior in the direction of Coblenz and Cologne. Huge supplies were kept there. and several squadrons of enemy machines were always on the alert to repel these bombing raids.

Calling the boys together, I asked for volunteers to go with me on this protective mission for the British. Six pilots stepped forward and we immediately prepared our plans.

Lieutenant Hamilton Coolidge had just joined our group and had not yet made his first trip over the lines. He asked permission to accompany us, and, thinking this would be a good opportunity to keep an eye upon him, I consented to his going. We were to meet the bombing machines over Thionville at 7:30 sharp, and at an altitude of 16,000 feet. We circled about at 2,000 feet until all were ready, then formed our positions and flew over in close formation.

As we were getting off the field I noticed that Squadron 95 was likewise sending up a number of machines.

In ten minutes more I realized that there would be a hopeless tangle of the two formations if I persisted in collecting my followers at the prearranged rendezvous. All the machines were circling at about the same position and collisions would be inevitable. I accordingly flew about in a wide circle, signaling to my pilots to draw away and follow me. Time was pressing and we must get to Pont-à-Mousson by 7:30, even if we were not in our best formation.

Arriving over the Moselle River at Pont-à-Mousson

exactly on the minute, I saw in the direction of Metz heavy Archy fire. This meant that Allied machines were there and were attracting German fire. I flew in to see what it was all about and found a single Salmson machine,[4] belonging to the American Squadron 91,[5] falling in a sharp *vrille.* At 4,000 feet he picked himself up, and regaining control of his machine, he leveled off for home. I accompanied him back over the lines and saw him safely off for his aerodrome and then turned my attention again to the British bombing machines. Near St. Mihiel then, I found that part of my formation was following Lieutenant [William F.] Loomis. Coolidge had attached himself to this party.

We cruised about together until dusk began to gather, and still there was no sign of the British machines. Suddenly Loomis left me with Coolidge in his wake. I decided one or both of them had experienced motor trouble and watched them disappear with no misgivings. I dropped down over Pont-à-Mousson, and getting fairly into the twilight, turned my machine toward home.

Arriving in the vicinity of my landing field, I was suddenly surprised to see a Nieuport flash past me going in exactly the opposite direction. I didn't know who it could be. It was now so dark that longer flying

[4]The Salmson 2A2, a heavily armed French-built reconnaissance aircraft that was one of the best observation planes of the war. Nine American observation squadrons were equipped with it.

[5]The 91st Observation Squadron, operational only since 7 June, was suffering heavy losses in its early missions because of its inexperience.

would be almost suicidal. Feeling instinctively that it might be one of the new pilots, I started in pursuit. A mile or so this side of the lines I overtook him.

Swerving in closely ahead of the stranger, I wig-wagged my wings and circled back. To my great relief, I saw that he understood me and was following. We soon made our way back to the Toul aerodrome and landed without accident. I went over to ascertain the identity of my companion. It was Coolidge.

After a question or two, Ham admitted that he had become confused in the darkness and had lost sight of Lieutenant Loomis, and for some reason or other became convinced that he was flying in the wrong direction. He had reversed directions and was flying straight into the enemy's lines when I had so fortunately passed nearby and had intercepted him.

Formation flying then has its uses in other ways than in combat fighting. We had made a confused mess of our formation on this occasion; but for a miracle it would have ended in the loss of a new pilot who later was to become one of the strongest of our men.[6]

The next morning I was awakened at three o'clock by an orderly who told me Major Atkinson wished to talk to me over the telephone. Even as I stood by the telephone I could hear a tremendous barrage of artillery from the German lines. Something big was on.

[6]As EVR indicates, the rescue operation he performed at this time had important future consequences. Coolidge went on to become an Ace with eight confirmed victories before being killed by antiaircraft fire on 27 October 1918 during an action for which he posthumously received the Distinguished Service Cross.

XVII

A Perplexing Bank of Fog

T HE HEAVY FIRING that was now so apparent to me
had awakened Major [Bert M.] Atkinson[1] in his
bed at headquarters, which was in a building adjoining us. He had immediately called to order us to take
a patrol over the lines at the first break of day and ascertain what this unusual demonstration could mean.
I looked at my watch. It was then just five minutes
past three. In another hour it would be light enough
to leave the field.

Running over to Lieutenant Meissner's billet, I
roused him out and then went on to waken the three
or four pilots in his flight. In ten minutes all five of us
were in the kitchen stirring up the cooks to faster efforts in the heating of coffee and toast. I had already
telephoned the hangars and ordered all our machines
out on the field in full readiness.

At a quarter of four we were in our machines and
were leaving the field. Two other pilots had joined us.
It was just beginning to grow light enough to make out
the tails of our machines ahead of us.

[1]An extremely capable officer soon to be promoted from major
to lieutenant colonel and put in charge of the 1st Pursuit Wing,
Atkinson was at this time commander of the 1st Pursuit Group in-
clusive of the 95th, 94th, 27th, and 147th Pursuit Squadrons.

I directed Lieutenant Meissner to have three of his pilots fly at an altitude of 5,000 feet, and for him to take the other two pilots in his formation and fly below them at 1,500 feet. I, myself, was to keep as close above the contour of the ground as possible and see what the Germans were doing in their first- and second-line trenches.

With all the details of our mission fully understood, we set off and made directly for the north, where the heaviest shooting seemed to be going on. As we neared the lines I could see the constant flashing of the German guns in the darkness. The greatest activity appeared to be just halfway between Pont-à-Mousson and St. Mihiel. Here in the vicinity of Seicheprey the country lies comparatively flat between the mountains that border the Moselle on the one hand and the Meuse on the other. I knew this locality well and could fly at only 100 feet from the ground without fear of striking against some mountainside in the darkness.

The Germans were doing most of the firing. This was plainly evident from the continuous flashes. The noise of the exploding shells was deadened by the roaring of my aeroplane motor. As I neared the center of all this excitement, I sheered off to the north and flew down low enough over the German trenches to permit the tornado of German shells to pass well over my head. Along this course I followed the entire length of the trenches, back and forth, back and forth, until I was sure there were no enemy troops waiting for the barrage to cease before pouring over the top.

Major Bert Atkinson, commander of the 1st Pursuit Group
and later commander of the 1st Pursuit Wing

The more I studied the situation the more puzzled I became. I saw the German shells bursting close behind our lines. From the nature of the bursts I knew they were high-explosive shells. This was the usual preliminary to a sudden rush over the top, yet no German troops were there waiting.

The whole vicinity of the German front was covered with a dense fog. The intermittent gunflashes showed dimly through this mist. Off to the east and the west, where the Meuse and Moselle rivers might be supposed to emit a fog of this sort, the landscape was clear. It was all very puzzling to me.

On each of my excursions back and forth over the German trenches I *piquéd* down from my low level and fired long bursts into their lines with my two machine guns. I could see my flaming tracer bullets cutting through the night and burying themselves within the enemy's trenches. It was still too dark to distinguish the ground at any distance from the trenches, but I was positive that if any considerable number of men were there they were well under cover.

At last I ran out of ammunition. I decided to fly home, make a report of what I had seen, and replenish with fuel and cartridges.

I telephoned my report to Major Atkinson while the mechanics were looking after my 'bus, and in ten minutes I was back again for the region of Seicheprey. By this time the first streaks of dawn were lighting up the ground. While still a great distance away, I noticed the strange clinging bank of fog that began at the German line and covered a space about three miles east and west, and half a mile deep.

As I again approached the German trenches I saw more activity there. I dived upon them, letting go long bursts from my guns. Instantly they disappeared from view. It was a very enjoyable game I had as long as any heads remained in view, but after one or two dashes along this front, I could find no more targets. They had retired to their underground dugouts.

Many a German fled in terror before my approach that morning. I found myself chuckling with delight over the consternation I single-handedly was spreading throughout that German camp. Coming down immediately over the trenches, I would observe a group of soldiers standing outside a dugout, all leveling their rifles at me. With a sudden swerve, I would bring them before my sights, and long before they could all cram themselves within the opening I would have 100 bullets inside their group and be beyond their reach.

One particular battery of 77s[2] lay a mile back of the lines and seemed to be having a particularly jolly party. Their flashes almost doubled the other batteries in rapidity. I determined to fly over and pay them a visit.

As I neared them, I saw six or eight three-inch guns standing side by side in a little clearing, the line of gunners all rushing swiftly to and fro, picking up and passing forward the fifteen-pound shells. The guns were firing at the rate of almost one shot each second.

[2]"77s": refers to a 77-millimeter artillery piece that was the standard German light field gun of World War I.

A continuous flash could be seen from this little battery, so rapidly did the gunners work. In a twinkling after my first shot, the whole battery became silent.

Pointing my nose directly at the end of the line, I pressed my triggers and raked the whole line before straightening my aeroplane. Then with a quick bank I came about and repeated the performance. Before I had started back, every man had fled for shelter again.

One more dash at the next battery and my ammunition was again exhausted. I returned to the aerodrome, where I found that Lieutenant Meissner and his pilots had returned without anything new to report. At 7:30 we all reassembled for breakfast.

We were still discussing the extraordinary episode of the morning and none of us had arrived at any reasonable explanation for the enemy artillery activity when a visitor was announced for breakfast. He came in and introduced himself as Frank [J.] Taylor, representing the United Press Association.[3]

He told us he was out of touch with events lately himself, for he had been up all night with the American Gas Organization, which had just been experimenting with their first gas attack on the German trenches north of Seicheprey! Then we all shouted! The whole circus became as clear as daylight to us.

[3]A California newspaperman, Taylor became a war correspondent with the American Expeditionary Force in France for the United Press in 1918 after being an ambulance driver in the Balkans in 1917. He later became a noted journalist with Scripps-Howard and other newspaper chains.

The attack had not been announced generally, and Major Atkinson himself was in ignorance as to its hour for demonstration. The Germans, awakened by the fumes at three o'clock this morning, had very naturally imagined that it would precede a sudden attack by our troops. Consequently they ordered out all their available artillery to shell the advanced positions of the Americans, thinking they would destroy our masses of troops in waiting.

The fact was that none of our troops were there, but were soundly sleeping in their beds until the terrible uproar of the German guns compelled them to stay awake. The whole gas attack was but an experiment by our forces, and so far as I have learned, was the first time gas was used in war by our American troops.[4]

Mr. Taylor invited me to accompany him to Baccarat, a small metropolis of that region of France, lying between Lunéville and Dijon. As we passed Lunéville and proceeded eastward I again noticed the unusual tranquillity of this sector of the war zone. The British Independent Air Force had its hangars of large Handley-Page Bombing Machines along this road. These huge aeroplanes carried bombs of high explosives weighing 1,650 pounds each. Nightly, these squadrons flew over to the Rhine cities and laid their

---

[4]Gas warfare, first used by the Germans in April 1915, was employed on an experimental basis by the American forces in the summer of 1918 despite a lack of enthusiasm by Pershing and his staff. According to one scholar, 3,400 American soldiers were operating gas cylinders during this phase of the war.

eggs in and about these railroad centers and factory lo-
calities. To my amazement I discovered that this
British aerodrome was but twelve miles behind the
lines. The German Rumplers came overhead every
morning and photographed the field, but no attempts
were made to destroy the Handley-Page machines by
either shelling from the lines or by aeroplane raids.

As Mr. Taylor and I were scudding along over these
smooth roads through the forests of the Vosges, we noticed a family of wild boar rooting in the edge of a
field. We backed up the car and I asked Mr. Taylor to
be good enough to wait for me a minute while I went
over and picked up one of the little pigs for a mascot
for our squadron. He very kindly complied. I did not
notice the expression on his face until I returned a
few minutes later.

Armed with my walking stick I made a detour, so
as to come upon the enemy and surprise them from
their rear. My plans were to make a sudden attack and
divert one of the youngsters from the formation, then
close in upon him and complete the capture. My tactics were unusually successful, and I bore down upon
my prize and was just stooping over to pick him up
when I heard a rush from the rear.

I hesitated for the fraction of a second. Old Mother
Boar was about ten yards abaft my stern and was
piquéing upon me at some sixty miles per hour. Further delay on my part would have been a mistake. I performed a *renversement,* put on the sauce, and zoomed
for the roadway at sixty-one miles per hour. Amid the

enthusiastic cheers of Mr. Taylor, I escaped the charge of the enraged enemy by putting myself through two or three *virages* en route to the car. The beast rushed by me, snorting fire from both forward guns and covering me with a shower of dirt from her hoofs.

I finally made a leap for the runningboard of the car, minus my walking stick and a good deal of breath.

"What's the trouble, Rick?" inquired Taylor enthusiastically. "Did you come back to tell me something?"

"Yes," I panted. "I looked them over and decided they were too young to be torn from their mother. Let's go on."

"But you forgot your stick," retorted Taylor. "I'll wait for you while you go back and get it."

"Oh, never mind the stick," I answered. "It didn't belong to me anyway."

A few weeks later I had an opportunity to see how the French sportsmen proceed in their wild boar hunts. The mayor of a little French village invited several of us to come over one Sunday morning and take part in the hunt.

By nine o'clock there were fully 100 persons gathered together in the little plaza facing the village church. About twenty carried guns; the balance were duly sworn in by the mayor to act as beaters-up. It was a very impressive ceremony and the whole village stood by to witness the scene.

After walking a mile or two through the woods, we were halted. The mayor addressed us and gave explicit orders for further proceedings. There was one old boar in these woods, he informed us, who had now three dum-dum bullets[5] inside his anatomy. He was a very tough and very dangerous customer. The mayor strongly advised us to first pick out a convenient tree and take our positions in its immediate vicinity. If the boar came along we could take a shot at him, or not, just as we individually happened to view the situation. Personally, he advised us to climb the tree and let some other fellow do the shooting.

The beaters-up, who were all standing at attention, thereupon saluted and disappeared within the forest. We lighted our pipes and measured the distance to the adjacent overhanging limbs. For an hour nothing happened to relieve the monotony.

At last we heard hoots and yells from the forest. The party of beaters-up was advancing toward us, beating the saplings with their sticks and uttering strange cries. I took a last glance at my tree overhead and then crouched down to have a look between the tree trunks at the approaching enemy. It was a strange sight.

There, not fifty feet in front of me, I saw a motley gathering of animals of all descriptions. Red foxes, black foxes, wildcats, two or three innocent-eyed deer, a number of partridge and grouse, and quite a flock of wild boar stood stock-still, gazing back at me. Not fifty feet in their rear came the village boys, hooting and

[5]Hollow-pointed bullets that expand upon hitting their target.

yelling to let us know where not to shoot. They were bringing us our game along ahead of them like a flock of barnyard fowls!

It seemed quite impossible to fire in that direction without inflicting casualties among the beaters-up. I therefore continued staring at the animals, until they tired of posing for me and turned their procession *en masse* toward the south.

One of the Frenchmen shot a fox that Sunday morning, and we all returned to the village tavern for a glass of wine, highly delighted with the successful day's sport.

Upon my suggesting to His Honor that his beaters-up had occupied a somewhat dangerous position at the crucial moment for firing, he shook his head sorrowfully and replied:

"Yes, it is too true! They are unfortunately wounded at times." Then, with a gleam of pride, he added: "But they are good boys. They have accustomed themselves to the danger and they do not shrink."

And thus is the great national sport of the Vosges carried on. Upon the occasional victory over the toothsome wild boar of the forest, a triumphant procession follows behind the champion, who strides gallantly through the village street with his trophy hanging, head down, over his back. If the village is not too densely populated, every inhabitant within it dines upon a delicious meat that night.

XVIII

Strafing the Drachen

OBSERVATION BALLOONS, or *Drachen*[1] as the Germans call them, constitute a most valuable method of espionage on the movements of an enemy, and at the same time are a most tempting bait to pilots of the opposing fighting squadrons.

They are huge in size, forming an elongated sausage some 200 feet in length and perhaps fifty feet in diameter. They hang swinging in the sky at a low elevation—some 2,000 feet or under, and are prevented from making any rapid movements of escape from aeroplane attack by reason of the long cable which attaches them to their mothertruck on the highway.

These trucks that attend the balloons are of ordinary size—a three-ton motor truck that steers and travels quite like any big lorry one meets on the streets. On the truckbed is fastened a winch that lets out the cable to any desired length. In case of an attack by shellfire, the truck simply runs up the road a short distance without drawing down the balloon. When it is observed that the enemy gunners have again calculated its range, another move is made, perhaps back to a point near its former position.

[1]*Drachen*: German for "dragons."

Large as is its bulk and as favorable and steady a target as it must present to the enemy gunners three miles away, it is seldom indeed that a hit from bursting shrapnel is recorded.

These balloons are placed along the lines some two miles back of the front-line trenches. From his elevated perch 2,000 feet above the ground, the observer can study the ground and pick up every detail over a radius of ten miles on every side. Clamped over his ears are telephone receivers. With his telescope to his eye he observes and talks to the officers on the truck below him. They, in turn, inform him of any especial object about which information is desired. If our battery is firing upon a certain enemy position, the observer watches for the dropping of shells and corrects the faults in aim. If a certain roadway is being dug up by our artillery, the observer notifies the battery when sufficient damage has been done to render that road impassable.

Observation balloons are thus a constant menace to contemplated movements of forces, and considered as a factor of warfare, they are of immense importance. Every fifteen or twenty miles along the front, both sides station their balloons, and when one chances to be shot down by an enemy aeroplane, another immediately runs up to take its place.

Shelling by artillery fire being so ineffective, it naturally occurs to every aeroplane pilot that such a huge and unwieldy target must be easy to destroy from the air. Their cost is many times greater than the value of an aeroplane. They cannot fight back with any hope of success. All that seems to be required is a sudden dash by a swift fighting aeroplane, a few shots with flaming bullets—and the big gasbag bursts into the flames. What could be more simple?

I had been victorious over five or six[2] enemy aeroplanes at this time and had never received a wound in return. This balloon business puzzled me, and I was determined to solve the mystery attending their continued service in the face of so many hostile aeroplanes flying constantly in their vicinity.

Accordingly, I lay awake many nights pondering over the stories I had heard about attacking these *Drachen*, planning just how I should dive in and let them have a quick burst, sheer off and climb away from their machine-gun fire, hang about for another dive, and continue these tactics until a sure hit could be obtained.

After discussing the matter with our commanding officer, Major Atkinson, who readily gave me his approval, I sought out Reed Chambers, Jimmy Meissner, Thorne Taylor, and Lieutenant Loomis. These four with me would make an ideal team to investigate this proposition.

First we obtained photographs of five German balloons in their lairs from the French Observation Squadron. Then we studied the map and ascertained the precise position each occupied: the nature of the land, the relative position of the mountains and rivers,

[2]The sixth being the German plane that EVR had brought down on 7 May 1918, for which he did not receive official credit until 1960; see Chapter VI.

the trees and villages in the vicinity of each, and all the details of their environment.

One by one we visited these balloons, studying from above the nature of the roadway upon which their mothertrucks must operate, the height of the trees above this roadway, and where the antiaircraft defenses had been posted around each *Drachen*. We knew the reputation of these defenses, and they were not to be ignored.

Since they alone were responsible for the defense of the balloons, we very well knew that they were unusually numerous and accurate. They would undoubtedly put up such a thick barrage of bullets around the suspended *Drachen* that an aeroplane must actually pass through a steady hailstorm of bullets both on coming in and on going out.[3]

Willy Coppens, the Belgian Ace, had made the greatest success of this balloon strafing. He had shot down over a score of German *Drachen* and had never received a wound.[4] I knew he armed his aeroplane

[3]Because of the defensive firepower with which balloons were surrounded and the close presence of fighter planes ready to defend them at a moment's notice, "balloon busting" was regarded as the most hazardous type of mission a pilot could undertake. Airmen willing to attempt such missions were held in special esteem by their comrades and were regarded with awe if they were consistently successful.

[4]Coppens, the leading Belgian Ace of WWI, shot down thirty-seven enemy aircraft, of which twenty-eight were balloons. The statement that he "had never received a wound" was no longer true by the end of the war; shot down by German antiaircraft fire in October 1918, he was badly injured and saw no further action.

with flaming rockets[5] that penetrated the envelope of the gasbag and burned there until it was ignited. This method had its advantages and its disadvantages. But another trick that was devised by Coppens met with my full approval.

This was to make the attack early in the morning or late in the evening, when visibility was poor and the approach of the buzzing motor could not be definitely located. Furthermore, he made his attack from a low level, flying so close to the ground that he could not be readily picked up from above. As he approached the vicinity of his balloon he zoomed quickly up and began his attack. If the balloon was being hauled down he met it halfway. All depended on the quickness of his attack and the sureness of his aim.

On 25 June 1918 my alarm clock buzzed me awake at 2:30 sharp. As I was the instigator of this little expedition, I leaped out of bed with no reluctant regrets and leaned out of my window to get a glimpse of the sky. It promised to be a fine day!

Rousing out the other four of my party, I telephoned to the hangars and ordered out the machines. The guns had been thoroughly overhauled during the night, and incendiary bullets had been placed in the magazines. Everything was ready for our first attack; we sat down to a hurried breakfast.

[5]Some Nieuports were equipped with up to eight LePrieur incendiary rockets fired from tubes mounted to the wing struts. Electrical wires connected to the tubes set off the rockets, which looked like oversized Chinese firecrackers.

The whole squadron got up and accompanied us to the hangars. We were soon in our flying suits and strapped in our seats. The motors began humming and then I felt my elation suddenly begin to leak out of me. My motor was stubborn and would not keep up its steady revolutions. Upon investigation, I found that one magneto[6] absolutely refused to function, leaving me with but one on which I could rely!

At 4:30 we left the ground and headed straight into Germany. I had decided to fly eight or ten miles behind the lines and then turn and come back at the balloon line from an unexpected quarter, trusting to the systematic discipline of the German army to have its balloons just beginning to ascend as we reached them. Each pilot in my party had his own balloon marked out. Each was to follow the same tactics. We separated as soon as we left the field, each man following the direction of his own course.

Passing high over Nancy, I proceeded northward and soon saw the irregular lines of the trenches below me. It was a mild morning and very little activity was discernible on either side. Not a gun was flashing in the twilight that covered the ground and as far as my eye could reach nothing was stirring. It was the precise time of day when weary fighters would prefer to catch their last wink of sleep.

[6]Like early automobile engines, aircraft engines received ignition from current supplied by alternators with permanent magnets known as magnetos. The Nieuport 28 had two magnetos, explaining why EVR was concerned about flying with only one.

Cutting off my motor at 15,000 feet over the lines,[7] I prayed once more that when the time came to switch on again, my one magneto would prove faithful. It alone stood between me and certain capture. I could not go roaring along over the sleeping heads of the whole German army and expect to preserve my secret. By gliding quietly along with silent engine as I passed deeper and deeper within their territory, I could gradually lose my altitude and then turn and gain the balloon line with comparatively little noise.

"Keep your Spunk Up—Magneto, Boy!"—I sang to my engine as I began the fateful glide. I had a mental vision of the precise spot behind the enemy balloon where I should turn on my switch and there discover— liberty or death! I would gladly have given my kingdom that moment for just one more little magneto!

At that moment I was passing swiftly over the little village of Goin. It was exactly five o'clock. The black outlines of the Bois de Face lay to my left, nestled along the two arms of the Moselle River. I might possibly reach those woods with a long glide if my motor failed me at the ultimate moment. I could crash in the treetops, hide in the forest until dark, and possibly

[7]As the original text explains, rotary engines of the type that powered a Nieuport 28 made so much noise that to achieve surprise it was necessary in a balloon attack to cut them off at an altitude of about 5,000 meters, glide toward the target, and cut the engine on again just before reaching the objective so as to climb rapidly out of danger just before the balloon was hit by the incendiary bullets. This explains why EVR was concerned about whether or not his engine would restart with only one magneto.

make my way back through the lines with a little luck.

And then I saw my balloon! Conscientious and reliable men these Germans were! Up and ready for the day's work at the exact hour I had planned for them! I flattened out my glide a trifle more, so as to pass their post with the minimum noise of singing wires.[8] A mile or two beyond them I began a wide circle with my nose well down.

Finding the earth rapidly nearing me, I *viraged* sharply to the left and looked ahead. There was my target floating blandly and unsuspiciously in the first rays of the sun. The men below were undoubtedly drinking their coffee and drawing up orders for the day's work that would never be executed. I headed directly for the swinging target and set my sights dead on its center. There facing me with rare arrogance in the middle of the balloon was a huge Maltese Cross—the emblem of the German balloons. I shifted my rudder a bit and pointed my sights exactly at the center of the cross. Then I deliberately pressed both triggers with my right hand, while with my left I snapped on the switch.

There must be some compartment in one's brain for equalizing the conflicting emotions that crowd simultaneously upon one at such moments as this. I realized instantly that I was saved myself, for the motor picked up with a whole-souled roar the very first in-

[8]The wires with which aircraft were braced during this period made a unique "singing" noise in the wind when a plane was flying at high speed, particularly during a dive.

stant after I made the contact. With this lifesaving realization came the simultaneous impression that my
whole morning's work and anguish were wasted.

I saw three or four streaks of flame flash ahead of me
and enter the huge bulk of the balloon ahead. Then the
flames abruptly ceased.

Flashing bullets were cutting a living circle all
around me, too, I noticed. Notwithstanding the sub-
tlety of my stalking approach, the balloon's defenders
had discovered my identity and were all waiting for
me. My guns had both jammed. This, too, I realized
at the same instant. I had had my chance, had shot my
bolt, was in the very midst of a fiery furnace that beg-
gars description and thanks to a benignant providence, was behind a lusty motor to carry me home.

Automatically I had swerved to the right of the suspended gasbag and grazed helplessly by the distended
sides of the enemy *Drachen*. I might almost have ex-
tended my hand and cut a hole in its sleek envelope,
it occurred to me, as I swept by. The wind had been
from the east, so I knew that the balloon would stretch
away from its supporting cable and leave it to the right.
More than one balloon strafer has rushed below his
balloon and crashed headlong into the inconspicuous wire cable that anchors it to the ground.

I had planned out every detail with the utmost success. The only thing I had failed in was the expected
result. Either the Germans had some material over
their *Drachen* that extinguished my flaming bullets, or
else the gas that was contained within them was not as

highly inflammable as I had been led to believe. Some three or four bullets had entered the sides of the balloon. Why had they failed to set fire to it?

Later on I was to discover that flaming bullets very frequently puncture observation balloons without producing the expected blaze. The very rapidity of their flight leaves no time for the ignition of the gas. Often in the early dawn the accumulated dew and moisture in the air serve so to dampen the balloon's envelope that hundreds of incendiary bullets penetrate the envelope without doing more damage than can be repaired with a few strips of adhesive plaster.

As I doggedly flew through the fiery curtain of German bullets and set my nose for home, I was conscious of a distinct feeling of admiration for the Belgian, Willy Coppens. And since he had demonstrated that balloon strafing had, in fact, a possibility of success, I was determined to continue my investigation.

Then I began to laugh to myself at an occurrence that until then I had had no time to consider. As I began firing at the sausage, the German observer who had been standing in his basket under the balloon with his eyes glued to his telescope, had evidently been taken entirely by surprise. The first intimation he had of my approach was the bullets that preceded me. At that instant he dropped his telescope and dived headlong over the side of his basket with his parachute. He did not even pause to look around to see what danger threatened him.[9]

[9]Balloon observers were equipped with small parachutes that

Evidently the mothertruck began winding up the cable at the same time, for as the observer jumped for his life, the balloon began to descend upon him. I caught the merest glimpse of his face as I swept past him, and there was a mingled look of terror and surprise upon his features.

On my way homeward I flew directly toward a French observation balloon that swung on the end of its cable in my path. Without considering the consequences of my act, I sheered in and passed quite close to the Frenchman who was staring at me from his suspended basket.

Suddenly the Frenchman leaped headlong from his perch, and clutching his parachute rope with his two hands, began a rapid descent to earth. And not until then did I realize that coming directly at him, head on from Germany as I did, he had no way of reading my cocardes that were painted underneath my wings. He had decided that I was the enemy and did not care to take any chances at a jump with a blazing gasbag about his ears.

Fortunately for me, the French gunners below could read my bright insignia from the ground and they suffered me to pass without taking any revenge for the trick I had played upon their unsuspecting comrade.

---

opened automatically when an observer jumped from the basket. This technique worked so well that only one American observer, Lieut. Cleo Ross, lost his life jumping from a flaming balloon.

Arriving at the aerodrome at 5:45, I found that I was the last of my little party of balloon strafers to land. The other four were standing together, looking rather sheepishly in my direction as I walked toward them.

"Well, what luck?" I inquired as I came up to them. Nobody spoke. "I thought I saw a big blaze over in your direction, Jimmy!" I went on addressing myself to Lieutenant Meissner. "Did you get him?"

"No!" replied Jimmy disgustedly. "The balloon was not up in the air at all. I didn't get a sight of it. I didn't even see where they had hidden it!

"Did you get yours, Reed?" I asked, turning to Chambers.

"H—, no!" retorted Lieutenant Chambers emphatically. "I shot the thing full of holes, but she wouldn't drop."

The other pilots had much the same stories. One had failed to find his balloon, and the other had made an attack but it had brought no results. All had been subjected to a defensive fire that had quite reversed their opinions of the Archibald family.

"I suppose you burned yours all right, Rick?" said Reed Chambers rather enviously as we walked up to the mess together. "What do you think of us."

"I think, Reed," replied I, "that we are the rottenest lot of balloonatical fakers that ever got up at two-thirty in the morning. But I am happy to discover," I added, thinking of my one puny magneto, "that none of us had to land in Germany."

XIX

The Château-Thierry Salient

THE SCENE of Squadron 94's operation would now change from the Toul sector to the Château-Thierry region. On 27 June 1918, all four American fighting squadrons were ordered to Château-Thierry. We were now four in number, for Squadron 27, commanded by Major Harold E. Hartney, and Squadron 147, commanded by Major [Geoffrey H.] Bonnell, had recently completed training and had moved in alongside 95 Squadron and our little Hat-in-the-Ring Squadron.

Toul is a city of some 20,000 inhabitants and would be quite the metropolis of its region were it not for the larger city of Nancy that lies but fifteen miles east. It has certain quaint and interesting aspects, including a well-preserved and ancient moat and battlements that surround the old city, a picturesque plaza in the center of the town, and several venerable old buildings dating well back into ancient history. Moreover, Toul had shops and busy streets where overtired aviators could stroll about and gaze on the shifting crowds.

Our new surroundings were of rather a different character. We settled on an old French aerodrome at Touquin, a small and miserable village some twenty-five miles south of Château-Thierry and the Marne

River. The aerodrome was large and smooth and abundantly equipped with the famous French hangars that consist of steel girders with walls and roofs of canvas. They were very spacious, quite cool in summer, and camouflaged admirably with the surrounding scenery.[1]

But no provision had been made at Touquin for the pilots and officers.

All of our aeroplanes flew from Toul to Touquin, while the rest of the aerodrome impedimenta was carted rapidly away to the new quarters in lorries, trucks, and trailers. The pilots of Squadrons 27 and 147 were rather new at that time, and it was thought wise to assign some of the older pilots of Squadrons 94 and 95 to the task of leading them through the air to the new field.

Lieutenant [Edward] Buford [Jr.] of Squadron 95 had a reputation of scorning the use of a map in flying over France. He had been selected to lead the pilots of Squadron 27 to Touquin on that morning. I saw him leave the ground with his twenty-odd machines and disappear in the distance. When I arrived at Touquin I learned that none of Lieutenant Buford's flight had yet put in an appearance. Late that night they all arrived safely. Upon being questioned as to their day's joyride, they told us that Buford's celebrated sense of direction had taken the entire squadron directly south instead of west. After flying until their fuel had given out, they all landed at an aerodrome that at that mo-

[1]Known as Bessoneau hangars, such buildings had a standardized design.

ment fortunately appeared below them. Here they learned they were at Lyon, in the south of France, instead of Touquin! After filling up with petrol and securing maps, they again set off and eventually arrived at their proper destination.

We found delightful quarters for Squadron 94's officers in an old abandoned château a few miles south of the field. It had been evacuated by its owners in 1914, when the Germans had made their first rapid advance beyond the Marne. Gorgeously furnished and surrounded by wonderful scenery, it was by far the finest habitation a body of pilots ever found.

On the day of our moving from Toul I had felt a return of the fever. Upon landing at Touquin I realized that I had a serious chill. It was only after I had arranged for the squadron's operations and general necessities, that I realized how badly I felt, and upon getting permission from Major Atkinson, drove to Coulommiers and was put to bed immediately by the surgeon commanding an early established evacuation hospital. It was not until 2 July that I left the hospital, after having narrowly averted a serious case of pneumonia, and returned to my squadron.

During my absence the [1st Pursuit] Group had suffered two losses and had won three victories. Lieutenant [Walter B.] Wanamaker of the 27th Squadron was from my home city of Columbus, Ohio. He, I learned, had gone out on patrol on 3 July and had been shot down above Chateâu-Thierry. For weeks we feared he had been killed, but finally we received

word from the Red Cross in Switzerland that Wanamaker had merely been forced down within enemy
territory and had been captured unhurt.

On 4 July, the Americans intended to celebrate in
Paris with much magnificence. I obtained permission
to visit the capital. Captain Kenneth Marr and several
of our pilots went in with me to see the celebration.
They returned early the following day, leaving me to
take my own time in rejoining the squadron.

Hardly had they gone when the impulse came to me
to go down to Orly, where the American Experimental Aerodrome was located,[2] and see for myself just
what the situation was in regard to our Spad aeroplanes. I called on the major in charge [Huffer] of the
supply depot, and learned to my delight that he had
actually begun arrangements for the immediate equipment of the Hat-in-the-Ring Squadron with the long-
deferred Spads. At that moment, he told me, there
were three Spads on the field for our use.

I hastened to the field, and there I found three of the
coveted flying machines that I knew had many accomplishments superior to the rival Fokkers. The
nearest machine to me had the initial figure "1,"
painted on its sides. I asked the mechanics in charge
if this machine had been tested.

"Yes sir! All ready to go to the front!" was the reply.

[2]The facility, located just outside Paris, was a depot where
French-made aircraft for American use were inspected and
equipped with machine guns and other accessories before being
flown to the front.

Rickenbacker in a Spad
Courtesy Auburn University Archives

"Is this one of the machines belonging to Squadron 94?" I inquired.

"Yes, sir. There are two more over there. The others will be in here in a few days."

"Well, I am down here from Squadron 94, myself," I continued, a sudden wild hope entering my brain. "Is there any reason why this machine should not go to the squadron today?"

"None that I know of, sir!" the mechanic answered, thereby forming a resolution in my mind that I very well knew might lead me to a court-martial, provided my superior officers chose to take a military view of my offense.

Inside ten minutes I was strapped in the seat of the finest little Spad that ever flew French skies. Without seeking further permission or considering stopping to collect my articles at my hotel, I gave the signal to pull away the blocks, sped swiftly across the smooth field, and with a feeling of tremendous satisfaction, I headed directly away for the Touquin aerodrome.

Not until I had landed and had begun to answer the questions of my comrades as to how I got possession of the new machine, did I begin to realize the enormity of the offense I had committed.

But to my joy, no censure was given me. On the contrary, I was given this first Spad to use as my own! Within an hour, my mechanics were fitting on the guns and truing up the wings.

It was at this period of the American offensive, it will be remembered, that the final German retreat began at Château-Thierry. Our aerodrome at Touquin was located so far behind the lines that we were limited to very short patrols over enemy territory. As the enemy continued to withdraw farther and farther back, it was evident that we must abandon our magnificent château at Touquin and move nearer the front. Every day the German Rumplers came over our field and blandly photographed us while our Archy batteries poured up a frantic lot of useless shells. I doubt if the enemy remained in ignorance of our change of location a single day. For as soon as we began settling at the Saints aerodrome a few miles nearer the lines, we again noticed the visits of the high-flying Rumplers.

In fact, one of our squadron pilots, who was captured at this period, told me, after his release, that the German intelligence officer exhibited to him a full list of the names of all of our pilots. The officer kindly inquired after the health of Major Hartney, who had seen distinguished service with the British before joining the American Air Service, and then he asked if Rickenbacker had been formulating any new balloon plans!

XX

The Death of Quentin Roosevelt

THE GERMAN ADVANCE, beginning in late June, had resulted in forcing a deep salient in the lines between Soissons and Reims. These two cities lie on an east and west line, both are situated on the Vesle River, and only twenty-odd miles separate them. Reims, to the east, had withstood the assaults of the enemy, but Soissons and the important highways and railroads centering there were now held by the Germans.

Straight south from Soissons the trenches now ran south for twenty miles, until the banks of the Marne River were reached; then they curved northward and east, the belligerents facing each other from opposite sides of the river almost to Epernay—a city almost directly south of Reims.

Thus, the salient that now most threatened Paris and the region south of the Marne was approximately twenty miles deep and twenty miles wide. It included Château-Thierry, which lay on the north bank of the Marne. Our aerodrome at Touquin lay south another twenty miles from Château-Thierry. In that position we were then also south of the city of Paris itself.

With full knowledge of the increasing strength of the American army in France, and having decided to stake all on one last effort before the arrival of our troops in their entirety, the German commanders had then even stripped the able-bodied men from their munitions factories throughout Germany in order to secure a victory at the front before it became too late. The loss of these factory workers spelled an ultimate failure in the supply of munitions of war necessary to a long campaign. If this last desperate thrust failed, the Germans must admit themselves defeated.

The subsequent breakdown of the German army was the natural climax to this desperate strategy. This final drive for Paris and Amiens must be the last. Every ounce of energy was therefore expended. Every division and every squadron of aviators that could be spared from other sections of the front were hurriedly concentrated on these two districts—that of Château-Thierry and the St. Quentin-to-Amiens district.

When the orders came to Squadron 94 to shift from Toul to this new Château-Thierry sector, the German fighting squadrons had already left the vicinity of Verdun–St. Mihiel–Pont-à-Mousson. Only the regular photographing and observing machines were still abroad there for our entertainment. Arrived at our new quarters, we found a very different situation. Our entertainment here promised to be fast and furious enough to suit the most ambitious airman.

It was quickly discovered by our own intelligence officers that the best of the German fighting squadrons were now patrolling our skies. Captured prisoners, the markings on the planes we shot down, the photographs and observations of our airmen, and other

Lieutenant Quentin Roosevelt

Dedication of Roosevelt's Grave, France, 1918

Courtesy United States Air Force, 1st Fighter Wing History Office

sources that are employed to gain this information—all told the same story.

At the aerodrome at Coincy, a large field just north of Château-Thierry, was located the distinguished von Richthofen Squadron, then commanded by Captain Reinhard. Its machines were distinguishable by their scarlet noses and by the extraordinary skillfulness of their pilots. It was now included in Jagdstaffel No. 1, which was comprised of four flights of some seven machines each.[1]

The Jagdstaffel No. 2 was a scarcely inferior aggregation of German Aces, which was under command of Captain [Bruno] Loerzer,[2] himself a victor over forty-two aerial antagonists. The aeroplanes of his squadron were also Fokkers. Instead of the scarlet markings on nose and wings, Jagdstaffel No. 2 had the belly of each fuselage painted a bright yellow.[3] These machines occupied the same field with the von Richthofen Circus.

The third famous fighting squadron of the Germans, Jagdstaffel No. 3, was then under command of

[1] Manfred von Richthofen, the most famous of all German pursuit pilots, was killed in action on 21 April 1918. At that time he commanded a fighter wing (Jagdgeschwader), not a squadron (Jagdstaffel) as stated in the text. He was succeeded as leader of Jagdgeschwader No. 1 by Wilhelm Reinhard, a veteran flyer who ultimately scored twenty wins.

[2] Loerzer actually commanded Jagdgeschwader III, which included Jastas 2, 26, 27, and 36.

[3] Jasta 2 used black and white markings. Jasta 27, a part of Jagdgeschwader III, used yellow markings and may be the unit to which Driggs is referring in this passage.

Captain Bettenge,[4] an air fighter celebrated in Germany not only for his twenty-five victories but for his great success as a trainer of adroit air fighters.

This squadron occupied an aerodrome back of St. Quentin. While usually engaged with British antagonists further north, this squadron frequently made its appearance opposite us during the hottest fighting.

Thus it became evident to us that we American aviators were at last to meet the very choicest personnel of the enemy air forces. Not only would these experienced pilots be mounted on superior machines, but they had been trained to fly in such close formation that they need fear no attack until they themselves were ready to accept combat. And they had consolidated here in such numbers that every time we crossed the lines we found the sky full of them. Squadron 94 at that time had seventeen pilots and twenty-four aeroplanes available. Squadrons 95, 27, and 147 had approximately the same number of planes each. No other American fighting squadrons were then assisting us in the defense of this sector.

The losses in our group during the four weeks we occupied this sector at Château-Thierry amounted to thirty-six pilots, who were either captured or killed. Among the latter class was Quentin Roosevelt, who fell in flames on 14 July 1918. Our victories during this

---

[4]Possibly Lieutenant (not Captain) Gerhard Bassenge, who returned to Jasta 2 (part of Jagdgeschwader III) in July 1918 after being wounded the previous November. Bassenge ultimately won seven victories (not twenty-five), and did not command a unit.

same period were thirty-eight, two more than the number we had lost.

Quentin Roosevelt's death was a sad blow to the whole group. As President Roosevelt's son, he had rather a difficult task to fit himself in with the democratic style of living necessary in the intimate life of an aviation camp.[5] Every one who met him for the first time expected him to have the airs and superciliousness of a spoiled boy. This notion was quickly lost after the first glimpse one had of Quentin. Gay, hearty, and absolutely square in everything he said or did, Quentin Roosevelt was one of the most popular in the group. We loved him purely for his own natural self.

He was reckless to such a degree that his commanding officers had to caution him repeatedly about the senselessness of his lack of caution. His bravery was so notorious that we all knew he would either achieve some great spectacular success or be killed in the attempt. Even the pilots in his own flight would beg him to conserve himself and wait for a more fair opportunity for victory. But Quentin would merely laugh

[5]Quentin Roosevelt was the fifth and last child of Theodore Roosevelt and his second wife, Edith Carow Roosevelt. As stated here, Quentin had difficulty fitting into the USAS because of his status as the son of an ex-president. His superiors tried not to assign him to combat duty but finally acquiesced to his wishes by posting him to the 95th PS. When made a flight leader over his protests, he turned control of the group over to another officer, Lt. Edward Buford, Jr. His subsequent death was partly due to the recklessness he displayed. Roosevelt's famous father was grief-stricken and died only a few months later on 6 January 1919.

away all this serious, well-meaning, and good advice.

A few days before his death Quentin Roosevelt went over the lines with his formation, and they came home without him. Later he arrived and laughingly announced that he had shot down his first enemy machine. Upon being questioned about the combat, he admitted that he had been lost striking off by himself to investigate a large formation of enemy machines, which he had discovered in the distance. Resolving to be prudent in the matter, he reversed his direction after discovering they numbered over twenty to his one. He flew about alone for a while, then discovering, as he supposed, his own formation ahead of him, he overtook them, dropped in behind and waited patiently for something to turn up.

It came about fifteen minutes later.

His formation continued almost straight ahead during all this time, he following quietly along in the last position. Quentin had no idea where they were headed and didn't care. He had violated his duty once by leaving them and now he intended blindly to follow the leader. Meditating thus, he failed to notice that the leader had dipped a signal and had begun to *virage* to the left. Quentin awoke just in time to see the aeroplane ahead of him suddenly stick his nose up and begin a *virage*. Then to his horror he discovered that he had been following an enemy patrol all the time! Every machine ahead of him wore a huge black Maltese cross on its wings and tail! They were as unconscious of his identity as he had been of theirs.

Quentin fired one long burst as he in turn completed the *virage* and rejoined the formation. The aeroplane immediately preceding him dropped at once, and within a second or two burst into flames. Quentin put down his nose and streaked it for home before the astonished Germans had time to notice what had happened. He was not even pursued!

Roosevelt met his death during an unusually severe dogfight in the air. He left the aerodrome with his formation of five planes and proceeded across the lines east of Château-Thierry. The sky was thick with enemy formations as usual. Both our own and the enemy's aeroplanes were largely engaged at that time in strafing trenches and the main highways on which columns of troops were continually advancing to occupy the lines. One did not have to seek far to find a fight.

Within ten minutes after crossing the trenches, the little formation from Squadron 95 took on a Fokker formation of seven machines. They were both at a low altitude and evidently both were intent on discovering a favorable ground target covered with marching men. The five Americans accepted the German challenge for a combat and dropped all other business for the time being.

During the rapid circling about, in which both groups were endeavoring to break up the formation of the antagonist, Quentin discovered the approach of another flight of red-nosed Fokkers coming from above and behind. He withdrew by himself and flew ahead to meet the newcomers, climbing as he flew. The others were utterly unconscious of his departure, since Quentin flew in the last rear position on one of the wings.

It was a cloudy day and the aeroplanes were up near to and occasionally lost in the obscurity of the clouds. Suddenly Lieutenant Buford, the leader of Quentin's formation, saw a Nieuport falling through the clouds from above him. It was out of control as it swept by him. Without realizing whose machine it was, Buford knew that an enemy force was above him. He already had more than his hands full in the present company. Signaling his pilots to follow him, he broke off the contest and recrossed the lines. Then he discovered the absence of Quentin Roosevelt!

That same night a wireless message came from the Germans saying that Quentin had been shot down by Sergeant [Karl] Thom of the von Richthofen Circus. Thom at that time had a record of twenty-four planes to his credit. The additional information was received that Quentin had been buried with military honors. No honors, however, could have compensated our group for the loss of that boy. The news was flashed throughout the world that Quentin Roosevelt was dead!

During all this time, I had been practically out of the fighting at the front. I had made but two flights over the lines at Château-Thierry, one on my old Nieuport and the second on my Spad. On neither expedition did I meet an enemy aeroplane, nor was I anxious to do so until I had quite mastered the tricks and wiles of my new Spad.

On 10 July I became suddenly aware of a sharp pain in my right ear. It grew worse and I decided to have the squadron doctor look me over. He sent me to Paris by the next train to have the eardrum lanced. An abscess had formed that might prove dangerous.

Thus, I was again forced to fret and turn on a hospital bed for several days while my squadron was going through with the most severe trials in its short experience. Doug Campbell was away, leaving Jimmy Meissner, Reed Chambers, Alan Winslow, and Thorne Taylor the principal stars of our organization. I used to lie in my bed and wonder how many of these old comrades would greet me when I returned to my aerodrome!

On 15 July, while lying half asleep on my bed in the hospital, I was suddenly startled by a tremendous explosion outside my windows. The nurses soon came by with frightened expressions on their faces. I asked one what it was.

"It was one of the long-distance shells the Boches are again firing into Paris!" she said. "They began that when they were about to start their great offensive of March twenty-first. For some time they have not been shooting into Paris. Now that it begins again, it is certain that they are commencing another drive!"

The young French woman was right. The very next day we heard that the anticipated drive from Château-Thierry had begun. The heavy artillery barrage started at midnight and the offensive on which the Germans were founding all their hopes was now on.

It was, in fact, the beginning of the end of the war! Nobody then realized it, of course, but General Foch, who possessed exact information of just when and where the enemy would strike, had prepared for it by crowding in huge quantities of artillery from Château-Thierry to Reims, from Reims on eastward to the Argonne Forest. Just two hours in advance of the first German shell, he began such a terrific barrage over the lines that the enemy forces were completely disorganized. They were never again to threaten Paris or the Allied armies!

And then the Second Division of the American Army began their great drive at the top of the Château-Thierry salient at Soissons while the French began to pinch in the line at Reims. All that great area of twenty-by-twenty miles was crammed with German troops, German artillery, German supplies. It must be moved at express speed to the rear or all would be captured.

Our squadrons at this great period did tremendous work in strafing the main highways leading to the Germans' rear. One of the pilots of Squadron 27, [Zenos R.] "Red" Miller, of Baltimore, who was shot down and captured while on one of these highway-strafing expeditions, later described to me the extraordinary scenes he passed through while being taken to the rear under guard.

In his march to the prison camps that night, Miller was conducted up the main highway from Château-

Thierry to the north. Two German cavalrymen rode on horeseback and he trotted along on foot between them. American shells were falling thick on this road and at every burst Miller and his conductors expected to be hurled among the dead and dying who filled the ditches.

The road was literally jammed with horses, lorries, guns, and men. All were hurrying northward. Along the sides of the roads hundreds of soldiers were detailed to drag from the roadway those men, trucks, horses, and guns that had been struck by American shrapnel and that lay there obstructing the traffic. Ropes were hastily attached to these obstructions and they were pulled out of the way and dumped by the roadside.

Another gang of soldiers worked side by side with these men, filling as quickly as possible the holes in the highway made by these exploding shells. Everything was hurry, noise, dust, and confusion.

Red was so mortified by his capture, so exhausted by his continuous trot between his two captors, and so scared by the constant shelling of the road over which they were passing that he resolved to break away from his two captors and risk their bullets rather than continue indefinitely in his present plight.

It was getting dark as they passed a small piece of woods to the right. Red suddenly stopped and bent over to lace up his boots. The two horsemen cast a glance at him, then seeing he was innocently engaged, drew up their horses and waited for him. As soon as the right-hand horse had passed him, Red straightened up and jumped for the nearest trees. He dashed through the brush in the darkness, scratching his face and tearing his clothes, but did not hear that a single shot had been fired at him.

He stopped and was peering about for a suitable tree in which to spend the night, hoping that by morning the country would be cleared of Germans, when an electric torch was flashed into his face! He threw up his hands and surrendered, finding that he had stumbled full into a camp of German artillery!

When his captors again recovered him, Red fully expected to be shot for attempting to escape. Imagine his surprise when they begged him not to tell anybody about his escapade! They feared they would receive a worse punishment than he because of their carelessness in permitting him to escape!

XXI

The Flying Circus Scores Heavily

IT WAS NOT until 31 July that I was able to mount my Spad and again take my place in fighting formations. Even then I started out with much apprehension, for the doctors had told me that it was highly improbable that I should ever be able to fly again, owing to the condition of my ear.

To my delight I found that no ill resulted from this trial flight; and I put my machine through all sorts of acrobatics and landed with the satisfaction of knowing that I was as good as new.

That was the day of terrible losses to our group. Every squadron lost heavily, but the severest loss to the group was borne by Squadron 27.

Lieutenant John McArthur of Buffalo, New York, had up to that date destroyed five enemy machines in combat and promised to be one of the greatest fighting airmen in the American army. Everyone who knew him admired him immensely. The pilots who had flown over the lines with him looked on Jack McArthur almost with reverence. He was cautious, quick, a clever pilot, and a dead shot.

Early in the morning of 31 July, McArthur led out his crack formation of six planes to try a strafing expedition on the aerodrome and hangars of the von

Richthofen Circus, which occupied the aerodrome north of Fismes.

From this expedition, only one from the formation ever returned.

Not until weeks later did we hear any news of this missing five. Then came a letter from one of them telling us what had occurred. They had reached their objective without mishap, and had strafed the hangar and billets of the von Richthofen crowd.

Whether or not any of the enemy machines came up to fight them, we did not learn. But the Richthofen aerodrome was twenty miles inside the lines and our aerodrome was thirty miles this side of the lines. When the strafers turned their noses homeward they found a forty-mile wind against them. They had already been out over an hour and could hardly hope to reach the home field against this gale before their fuel would be exhausted. They might easily reach some nearer aerodrome on our side of the lines, however, and toward this object they set their minds.

Halfway to the lines they encountered several formations of enemy planes who were fully aware of their predicament and were waiting for them to come out. Up and down, back and forth, McArthur led his little formation, seeking for a place to break through the enemy's ranks. Finding the German pilots too adroit for him, he finally resolved to break through, regardless of the tremendous odds against him.

McArthur led the attack, and like Horatius of old, he embraced all the spears in his own breast, to enable his comrades to pass through them. He fell, killed in the air, and one of his pilots fell beside him. But even this heroic sacrifice was in vain.

The remaining three pilots of his formation passed the encircling enemy machines only to find that this protracted maneuvering had quite exhausted their fuel. One by one their motors spluttered and died. The entire formation dropped to earth, some landing safely, others crashing in shellholes, all of them finding themselves behind the German lines.

Squadron 94's greatest loss on that fatal day was Alan Winslow, the Chicago boy who had the honor of bringing down the first enemy machine conquered by the pilots of the Hat-in-the-Ring Squadron.

Late that evening he was seen by another member of his flight diving down on a Fokker with which he had taken on a combat. The two machines continued downward until the dusky ground swallowed both of them from view. The rest of Winslow's flight returned home and long did we sit up waiting for news of Alan.

The pilots stood about under the stars pooping up Very lights[1] into the clear sky, hoping that he might see the signal from afar and come roaring in. To every war pilot there is an extraordinary pathos about the flashes of these distant signal lights at night. I never see these bright balls of fire cut through the night sky without feeling a clutch at my heart—without remembering

[1] "Pooping up": a nautical term meaning "to break over the stern of a ship." "Very lights": brilliant balls of light shot from a special pistol as pyrotechnic signals.

the anguish with which I have watched and waited and hoped for the return of some dear comrade.

They rush from the mouth of the pistol with a noise like that of a child's popgun. The silvery ball climbs upward 200 or 300 feet with a soft roar; there it gracefully curves in its trajectory and begins slowly to fall downward, shedding a powerful light on the surrounding landscape and casting its beckoning signal for a score of miles around. On any fine night as one flies homeward from the lines, these Very lights strike the eye from every aerodrome, both friendly and hostile. To a member of the mess they denote a warm welcome from his comrades. To a stranger comes the significant intimation that yonder some member of an expectant family is still missing!

A month later one of the members of our squadron, while in London, met Alan Winslow's brother, Paul Winslow, a member of the most famous of Great Britain's fighting squadrons, No. 56. Asked if any news had been received of Alan, Paul Winslow replied simply, "He went west!"

Upon returning to the squadron, however, a letter was found awaiting him from Alan Winslow himself! He wrote from a German hospital, stating that he had been wounded in the combat, and had received a bullet that had shattered the left arm. Following amputation above the elbow, he was quite contented to find himself so well out of the occurrence!

The sorrows, the surprises—the joys of war-flying are legion!

XXII

Our Spads Arrive

By 8 August 1918 our whole squadron was fitted out with the machines that we had so long coveted. The delight of the pilots can be imagined. In the meantime we had lost a number of pilots while on the flimsy Nieuports, not by reason of their breaking up in air but because the pilots who handled them feared to put them into essential maneuvers that they were unable to stand. Consequently our pilots on Nieuports could not always obtain a favorable position over an enemy nor safely escape from a dangerous situation. The Spads were staunch and strong and could easily outdive the Nieuports. And our antagonists opposite the Château-Thierry sector were, as I have indicated, the very best of the German airmen. How greatly our new Spads increased our efficiency will be seen from the results that followed.

By 8 August our victorious doughboys had pushed back the Germans from the deep Château-Thierry salient of twenty miles square, and the lines now ran along the Vesle River, directly from Soissons to Reims. This long advance left our aerodrome at Touquin far in the rear. So far, in fact, that it was necessary for our aeroplanes to come down near the lines and refill with gasoline before continuing our two hours' patrol.

The old Richthofen aerodrome at Coincy was now in our hands. We established our filling station on this aerodrome. It lay then but eight miles south of the German front trenches.

At lunchtime on 10 August we received orders for all hands to get aloft at once and form an aerial barrier in front of a small piece of woods that lay just back of our lines northwest of Fère-en-Tardenois. This wood was scarcely two miles from the enemy trenches, and our natural supposition was that our generals were filling this area with troops or guns and desired to conceal the fact from enemy espionage.

Upon landing at the Coincy field for refilling with gasoline, we found that our surmises were correct. Long convoys of motorlorries, all cleverly camouflaged to merge with the roads and fields, were rapidly passing northward, and all were packed full of our doughboys. The road kept humming with these convoys all the afternoon. Evidently there was to be a big push on the morrow directed against Fismes from this very advantageous position so close to their front.

Just as we were getting away, Lieutenant [Edward P.] Curtis of Squadron 1 came running up to me and told me that he was ordered to select a flight of our machines to protect him in a photographing mission north. The army authorities desired to have the fullest information as to just what the enemy was doing before completing arrangements for the morrow's attack. He asked me if I would pick out a few pilots from my squadron and be ready to go up with him.

Rickenbacker in his Spad, showing the mounted guns

Courtesy National Air and Space Museum, Smithsonian Institution

243

I asked for volunteers, as this was purely a voluntary mission. Five pilots immediately asked for the job and we drew our machines apart from the others.

Being in command of this expedition, I determined to see to it that a complete understanding existed between our Spad pilots and the pilots of the Salmson machines of Squadron 1 who were to do the photographing. The region to be photographed was a large one, covering several towns lying between the Vesle and the Aisne rivers and all the highways running between them. It would take some time to thoroughly cover this territory, and we were certain to be attacked before completing the excursion.

I talked to the pilots for five minutes and made everybody understand that when they saw me make a *virage,* or circle on one wing, just ahead of them, they must immediately make a dive for our lines without any delay, photographs or no photographs. With our experience of the strength of the enemy Fokkers in this sector, it would be senseless suicide for our five machines to attempt to parley with overwhelming numbers of the enemy. It would be useless to get the photographs if we could not return with them.

At 5:30 sharp we left the ground and flew away over Fismes. At that time Fismes was directly on the line. American troops held the southern half of the city and German troops occupied the northern half. Fismes lay just halfway between Reims and Soissons.

We were directly over Fismes when I detected a formation of eight red-nosed Fokkers stealing around

on our left. They had evidently just left their aerodrome and were coming over to patrol the lines. Their
present maneuver was as clear as crystal to me. They
hoped to get behind us at a superior altitude and then
come in on our rear with the sun at their backs. It was
precisely the maneuver I should have attempted in
their place.

We had the advantage of them in one particular—
they did not know how deeply we intended going into
their territory. I saw by their actions that they intended
to overlook us until we were well within their grasp,
and then they would suddenly discover us.

"Very well!" I said to myself, "we will go ahead and
photograph until you are ready to attack!"

Affecting ignorance of their presence, I continued
straight toward Germany. We made a short cut from
southeast to northwest and came back in the contrary
direction. A few discreet circles enabled the photographers to cover fairly well the territory they wanted
without taking us more than six miles within the German lines.

As we began our second circuit, the Fokkers determined to start something. They had made up their
minds that we were not playing fair with them. Five of
their machines came darting down on us from a great
altitude, while the remainder continued cruising the
lines between us and home. I saw the attack coming
and put my Spad in motion at the same instant.

Diving down behind my little formation, which was
tranquilly pursuing its way northward, I passed be-

hind the tails of the rear machines and immediately zoomed up directly in front of them, turning sharply back to the right so that they could not help seeing me. Without further thought of their possible misunderstanding of this prearranged signal, I began climbing for altitude directly toward the approaching Fokkers. The five enemy machines had their sharp-edged wings cutting the air directly toward me. It is a thrilling and a somewhat fearful sight to see the outline of a Fokker biplane descending on one.[1] I see them in my dreams very frequently after too hearty a supper late at night.

Beginning firing at a comparatively long range, I held the Spad on its steepest course and waited to discover which side of me the Fokkers would choose to pass. Soon they began firing, too, and the swift streaks of fire formed a living path along which we both traveled. I felt deep down in my heart that they would not stop to take me on. Their object was to get the two-seater that had the damaging photographs. They would swerve to my right at the last instant in order to place me between them and my formation. My Spads must be well together and headed downward toward the lines by now. I had no time to look around, for I was lying back, half on my back, the earth well under my tail, and the sun under my engine, which prevented it from shining full into my eyes. Almost instinctively I prepared to flatten out and immediately swing over

[1]The German aircraft were Fokker D-VIIs, by common consent the best fighter planes on either side in WWI.

to the right. The enemy must move in that direction!

As we whizzed past each other I ceased firing and flattened out my course. The enemy machines had passed me and I now had the upper ceiling. They had fortunately continued on down after the Salmson, just as I had expected them to do. Now the other Spads in my flight must look after them. Evidently none of the five had been injured by my fire any more than they had injured me. We, each of us, had presented a very small target subject to injury.

As I eased off my motor I heard the crackling of machine-gun fire below me. I first cast another glance at the distant Fokker formation above me, then looked down over the sides of my office. Surely the five Fokkers could not have reached my Spads so soon! They should have been diving for the lines long ago!

As I looked down I discovered a regular dogfight[2] was in progress. Certainly those were Spad machines that were turning and twisting about the encircling Fokkers, and the Spads, in fact, seemed to outnumber the Fokkers. Something strange about the color of the Spads' wings first struck my attention, and then I dis-

---

[2]"Dogfight": a wild aerial encounter in which a great many aircraft—sometimes several dozen, and in rare cases up to 100—fight at extremely close quarters. Often more planes were lost in midair collisions in such a melee—sometimes called a "furball"—than were shot down by gunfire. Dogfights occurred in WWI because of the relatively compact areas in which fighter pilots had to maneuver because of the short range of their guns. No true dogfights occurred after WWI, but the term is still used by some writers in connection with other conflicts.

covered that this fight was between a French squadron of Spads and another formation of Fokkers that had evidently arrived at the same spot at the same time. Without my being aware of it, two different groups of aeroplanes had been watching our little party all this while and had all concentrated below me to meet the diving Fokkers!

The Salmson and my five Spads were well below me in about the position I expected to find them. The Spads had instantly obeyed my signal and had begun diving even as they headed around to the rear. They were well out of the melee.

Considerably chagrined over my lack of caution, and thanking my lucky stars again that the new arrivals that had stolen in from an unobserved quarter were part friendly instead of all hostile, I turned about and vindictively charged into the midst of the combat.

A Fokker had just zoomed up ahead of a diving Spad, letting the Frenchman proceed below him at headlong speed, when I arrived on his tail. With my first burst, the Fokker turned over and fell earthward out of control. Still too angry with myself to think of caution, I was badly scared a moment later by the spectacle of flaming bullets streaking past my face. I dropped over onto my wing, kicked my rudder crosswise, and fell 100 yards in a *vrille*. No more bullets coming in my direction, I hastily pulled my Spad into position and cleaved the air for home! I wanted to get off by myself and think this over! Never again would I venture into hostile skies without twisting my neck in all directions for almost every moment of the flight!

That night, after an examination of my machine, I called to my mechanics and directed them to bring me the painter's paints and brush. With painstaking care I took the brush and drew little circles around three holes in my wings where German bullets had passed through.

"Cover these holes as neatly as possible," I directed the mechanics, "and then have the painter put a small Maltese cross over each patch. These are little souvenirs that will remind me of something next time I am over the lines!"

---

[3]EVR's experience was common in a dogfight, even among superb air fighters like himself. As Richard P. Hallion, one of the keenest students of air combat, has noted, even the great Manfred von Richthofen lost his life partly as a result of "not checking six o'clock" (in other words, failing to look behind his back) in such a wild scramble. As EVR learned, the best course of action in a dogfight was to "dive in, get a kill or two, and keep on going." Staying in the melee for any length of time invited catastrophe. It should also be noted with regard to this passage that EVR's recurrent ear trouble made it extremely painful for him to move his neck in various directions.

XXIII

Back Close to Verdun

ONE OF the extraordinary things about life at the front is the commonplace way in which extraordinary things happen to one. And though one may wonder and be greatly perplexed over it, there are no intervals for giving due thought to the matter. Thus, a day or two after my last experiences, while I was refilling my tank at Coincy preparatory to another flip over the lines, I met two American doughboys there who told me that my brother[1] was in camp but a few miles north of me.

My brother had been at the front with the Signal Corps for three or four months, and though I had repeatedly tried to find his address, I had not been able up to this time to locate him.

I immediately obtained permission to take an afternoon off; and borrowing a motor car from one of the officers there, I set off to the north in quest of my brother's camp.

The roads to the north had but a fortnight ago been in full possession of the enemy troops. Signs along the way pointed out the next village in unmistakable fashion. The highway I was traversing led to the town

[1]Louis E. Rickenbacker, who was six years younger than EVR.

of Fère-en-Tardenois and had been badly worn by the retreating enemy artillery and wagons. American shells had landed at precise intervals along the line of their retreat. Hurried replacements of surface had evidently been made by the Germans in order to permit the continued use of this road. And now our own doughboys were busily at work repairing these same roads so that our own artillery might go on in pursuit of the fleeing Germans.

As my car approached these groups of busy workers, my chauffeur blew them a long blast of warning. They withdrew to the edge of the road and watched me pass, with an expression of mingled irony and respect. I tried to assume the haughty mien of a major general while under their brief scrutiny and was beginning to feel pleased with myself when I suddenly heard one of the doughboys call out, "Hullo, Rick!"

I looked around, stopping the car by simply cutting off the spark. An undersized doughboy had dropped his shovel and was running forward to overtake me. As he came up, I recognized him as an old friend of mine from my home town.

"Gee whiz! Rick," he said, "where the dickens are you going?"

"Oh, up the road a ways to see my brother," I replied "I just heard he was at the next village. How are you, Bob? When did you get over here?"

"About a month ago. Hell of a way to come to break rock, isn't it? Well, so long! I've got to get back on the job!" He squeezed my hand and hurried back. I never saw him again. As I proceeded onward along my way, I continued to marvel at this peculiar coincidence.

For months I had been making new friends, had been completely immersed in this new life—had seen nothing of my old friends. And now within a single hour I had found myself bumped suddenly alongside my own brother and against an old schoolboy friend!

After a very brief visit with my brother, I returned home, passing through Fère-en-Tardenois and south-ward along the same roads I had so recently traversed. Even in the short interval of my passing, a marvelous amount of work had been accomplished.

Rows on rows of three-inch shells were stacked up within convenient reach of the army lorries. Their willow and straw baskets, each containing a single German shell, formed a regular row six feet high and fifty feet long. Then came a space filled with huge twelve-inch shells all standing upright on their bases. Next were stacked boxes of machine-gun ammunition, hundreds and hundreds of them, occasionally interspersed with stray boxes of rockets, signal flares, Very lights, and huge piles of rifles, of machine guns, and of empty brass shells of various sizes. The value of an average German city lay spread along that road—all worthless to the former owners—all constructed for the purpose of killing their fellow men![2]

[2]The passage just concluded, one of the most vivid in the entire book, has no counterpart in the original text. A good example of Driggs's literary style, it typified the way in which he brought drama and verisimilitude to a manuscript that could not otherwise have been published—but the details themselves were imaginary.

This whole period of what we called the "Château-Thierry" show became somewhat chaotic to me. Briefly, it lasted from 2 July to 3 September 1918. I had missed much of it in the hospital. The little flying I had done over the lines had not been especially satisfactory. And now I began to feel a recurrence of my ear trouble. The constant twisting of my neck in air, turning my head from side to side to constantly watch all the points of the compass had affected in some mysterious way my former malady. On 18 August I suffered actual agony and was unable to get out of bed.

This was a sad day for our happy mess. Two of our pilots, one the same Lieutenant Smythe who had made so many patrols with me, the other an equally popular fellow by name of Lieutenant Alexander B. Bruce, of Lawrence, Massachusetts—these two pilots, while patrolling over the enemy's lines at a very high altitude, had collided. With wings torn asunder, both machines had dropped like plummets to the distant ground below. The news came in to us while I was in bed. I had actually just been dreaming that Smythe was up with me fighting Fokkers. And I had dreamed that he had just been shot down in flames![3]

When Captain Marr came in to see how I was getting along, he told me about this horrible catastrophe. Smythe had appealed to me in many ways. He had told

[3]In his *Autobiography,* EVR stated that Smythe's death "had happened just the way I saw it in my mind." EVR, convinced of the reality of extrasensory perception and precognitive dreams, was keenly interested in psychic phenomena throughout his life.

me that he had been in the French Ambulance Service since early in the war.

Bruce, I had not known so well, as he had been with us but a few days. But the whole frightful episode really constituted a considerable shock to the nerves of our squadron.

The fighters on the front can never understand why the authorities back home deny them necessary arms and ammunition. We air fighters cannot understand why we cannot have parachutes fitted on our aeroplanes to give the doomed pilot one possible means of escape from this terrible death.[4] Pilots sometimes laugh over the comic end of a comrade shot down in course of a combat. It is a callousness made possible by the continuous horrors of war. If he dies from an attack by an enemy, it is taken as a matter of course. But to be killed through a stupid and preventable mistake puts the matter in a very different light.

For the past six months the German airmen had been saving their lives by aeroplane parachutes. A parachute is a very cheap contrivance compared to the cost of training an aviator. Lufbery and a score of other American aviators might have been saved if this matter of aeroplane equipment had been left to experienced pilots.

[4]EVR reverted to this theme frequently in speeches after the war. It became part of his indictment of the shortsightedness of American military aviation policy when he testified at the court-martial of Billy Mitchell in 1925 and argued for the creation of an independent United States Air Force.

During the following week Paris surgeons operated on my troublesome ear at the hospital. It has never bothered me since. As soon as I was able to get about I maneuvered for my speedy return to the front, for I had heard that the Americans were about to begin a tremendous drive on the St. Mihiel salient.

On 3 September I learned that Squadron 94 had moved back to the Verdun sector. That indicated to me that plans were ripening for the St. Mihiel offensive by the Americans.[5] I obtained permission to leave the hospital as cured and hastened to our aviation head-quarters to obtain my orders to return to the front.

My squadron was already at home on the famous old highway that had saved Verdun. Located about fifteen miles south of Verdun at Rembercourt, the aerodrome covered the crest of a hill that two years before had been in the possession of the Germans. Squadron 95 was there, together with Squadrons 27 and 147. The lines of the enemy ran south from Verdun along the Meuse until they reached St. Mihiel, scarcely twelve miles straight east from us. This aerodrome, which had been constructed and used by the French escadrilles, was now to be occupied by our little group until the end of the war. During the coming month of September, I was to win four more victories in the air and then to be given the greatest honor that has ever come to any pilot—the command of the squadron that he truly believes to be the finest in the whole world, his own!

[5]This massive operation, the first American offensive of the war, began on 12 September 1918.

XXIV

The St. Mihiel Drive

Aʟᴛʜᴏᴜɢʜ we did not know it at the time, we were now on the last laps of the war. Every taxi driver or waiter in Paris could have told one just where the Americans were concentrating for their great attack on the St. Mihiel salient. The number of guns, the number of troops and just where they were located, how many aeroplanes we had, and similar topics of war interest were discussed by every man on the streets.

Consequently, I was much amused when I was arrested at the outskirts of Bar-le-Duc by a suspicious member of our Military Police and very closely questioned as to my character and identity. He informed me later that every person entering or leaving Bar-le-Duc was given the same searching examination. Spies were abroad and he was taking no chances of letting information leak out as to what was going on. I assured him that I would not tell a soul and was permitted to drive on.[1]

These extraordinary precautions always seemed

[1]Although gossip about the upcoming attack on the St. Mihiel salient was rife in Paris, General Pershing and his staff were engaged in an elaborate ruse to convince the Germans that the American attack would come on a different front. These circumstances may explain why EVR had so much difficuly trying to enter Bar-le-Duc.

more or less ridiculous to men who had been close to the firing lines during the war. The nearer one gets to the lines, the simpler appears the matter of espionage. Doubtless, scores of Germans crossed the lines every night, arrayed themselves in the uniform of dead American or French soldiers and mingled freely and unsuspected with our troops until they desired to return to their own side. As there are hundreds of our soldiers wandering about looking for their regiments, a few extra wanderers create no suspicion. Yet, if one of these should venture to Bar-le-Duc or any other city far away from the actual scene of activities— Heaven help him.

At the aerodrome I was welcomed by my old friends with a heartiness known only to flying squadrons. A peculiar and lasting friendship is created between boys who fight in the air. No other fraternity is like it.

Jimmy Meissner, I found, was now in command of Squadron 147. Al [Alfred A.] Grant of Austin, Texas, had command of 27, succeeding Major Hartney, who had been promoted to the command of the whole group at this aerodrome. Squadron 95 was still under Major [David McK.] Peterson who, with his galaxy of "stout fellows," including Bill [William H.] Taylor, Sumner Sewell, Ted [Edward P.] Curtis, Harold Buddy, Jack [John L.] Mitchell, and Benny [Lansing C.] Holden, led the four squadrons in their number of victories. This squadron rivalry led to great efforts on the part of all our fighting flyers. Later, principally through the extraordinary prowess of Frank Luke, his

Squadron 27 for a time led our group in the number of its victories. But before the end of the war the highest score came to the squadron that knew all along that they could win it—old 94, with its Hat-in-the-Ring. My squadron did a famous lot of fighting during the month of October. It surpassed the other squadrons of our group, as well as all the other American squadrons at the front.

At dinner that night—the night of my arrival—word came that the Big Show was to start in the morning.

Precisely at five o'clock I was awakened by the thundering of thousands of colossal guns. It was 12 September 1918. The St. Mihiel Drive was on!

We had received orders to be over the lines at daybreak in large formations. It was an exciting moment in my life as I realized that the great American attack was actually beginning.

Dressing with great haste, I ran through the rain to the mess hall. There I found groups of the fellows all standing about impatiently awaiting the chance to get away. But the weather was certainly too bad to attempt any flight to the lines. We were compelled to wait.

About noon, word came to us that the attack was progressing quite favorably.[2] None of our machines had been able to get up. Although it was still raining,

---

[2]The German forces had already been planning to withdraw from the salient, and were starting to do so when the American barrage began, forcing them underground. The timing of the attack thus caught the enemy by surprise, resulting in an easier victory than anticipated.

the visibility was getting better. We could see that the clouds were nearly 1,000 feet above the ground.

Taking Reed Chambers to one side, I proposed to him that despite the rain we try a short flip over the lines to see for ourselves what it was like. He agreed, and while the others were at lunch we climbed into our machines and made off. At 600 feet above ground we found that we were just under the clouds and still had quite a long view of the landscape.

Flying straight east to St. Mihiel, we crossed the Meuse River and turned down its valley toward Verdun. Many fires were burning under us, most of them well on the German side of the Meuse. Villages, haystacks, ammunition dumps, and supplies were being set ablaze by the retreating Germans.

We proceeded as far as Verdun. Then turning east we continued flying at our low altitude and passed over Fresnes and Vigneulles.

Vigneulles was the objective point of the American forces. It lies east of Verdun some fifteen miles and about the same distance north of St. Mihiel. One American army [the 5th Army Corps] was pushing toward it from a point just out of Verdun while the other attack was made [by the 1st and 4th Army Corps] from the opposite side of the salient. Like irresistible pincers, the two forces were drawing nearer and nearer to this objective point. The German troops who were still inside the salient would soon be caught inside the pincers.

As Reed and I turned south from Vigneulles we

saw that the main highway running north to Metz was black with hurrying men and vehicles. Guns, stores, and ammunition were being hauled away to safety with all possible speed. We continued on south through the very heart of the St. Mihiel salient, flying always low above the roadway that connected Vigneulles with St. Mihiel. Here, likewise, we found the Germans in full cry to the rear.

One especially attractive target presented itself to us as we flew along this road. A whole battery of German three-inch guns was coming toward us on the double. They covered fully half a mile of the roadway.

Dipping down at the head of the column I sprinkled a few bullets over the leading teams. Horses fell right and left. One driver leaped from his seat and started running for the ditch. Halfway across the road he threw up his arms and rolled over on his face. He had stepped in front of my stream of bullets!

All down the line we continued our fire—now tilting our aeroplanes down for a short burst, then zooming back up for a little altitude in which to repeat the performance. The whole column was thrown into the wildest confusion. Horses plunged and broke away. Some were killed and fell in their tracks. Most of the drivers and gunners had taken to the trees before we reached them. Our little visit must have cost them an hour's delay.

Passing over St. Mihiel, we hastened on to our aerodrome. There we immediately telephoned headquarters with information of what we had seen and particularly of the last column of artillery we had shot up in its retreat from St. Mihiel. This was evidently splendid news and exactly what G.H.Q. had been anxious to know, for they questioned us closely on this subject, inquiring whether we were convinced that the Germans were actually quitting St. Mihiel.

I assured them that there was no question about the retreat being in full swing. Thereon, they told me that they would immediately begin shelling that road with our long-range guns so as further to impede the withdrawing of the enemy's supplies along this artery.

Later observations that we made over this road indicated that our gunners had made a good job of this task. The Germans had abandoned huge quantities of guns, wagons, and supplies and had only saved their own skins by taking to the woods and covering the distance to Vigneulles on foot. The highway was utterly impassable.

That same night we were advised that the victorious Americans had taken Thiaucourt—that scene of so many of our operations back of the lines. A stout enemy squadron had always occupied the Thiaucourt aerodrome and we had had many a combat with its members. Henceforward we would miss the menace of this opposing unit. And we were also informed that at last Montsec had fallen!

Montsec was to this sector what Vimy Ridge was to the British troops about Lens. Its high crest dominated the entire landscape. From its summit the enemy could look over the whole south country. From observation posts that we later discovered on its summit, we saw that our aerodrome had been under surveillance by the German observers! Not a machine could leave our field at Toul without being seen by these watchers atop Montsec! No wonder their many photographing machines escaped us! Many and many a time we had hurried out to the lines in answer to an alert, only to find that it was a false alarm. Now we understood why we lost them. The Germans had seen our coming, and by signaling their machines had given them warning in time to evade us. They retired and landed and waited until we had returned home, then they calmly proceeded with their interrupted work!

The capture of Montsec was a remarkably fine bit of strategy, for it was neatly outflanked and pinched out with a very small loss indeed. Our infantry and Tank Corps accomplished this feat within twenty hours.

When one remembers that the French lost nearly 30,000 men killed, wounded, and missing in their attack on Montsec in fall 1916—and then held this dearly bought ground for only twenty minutes—one appreciates what a wonderful victory the American doughboys won.[3]

On our trip up this same road the following day, Reed Chambers and I saw the retreat of the enemy and the advance of our doughboys in full swing. The Germans were falling back northward with an unusually

[3]To storm the 400-foot hill, the victorious American forces used special wire-cutting and wire-scaling equipment that the French had not had at their disposal.

strong rear guard protecting their retreat. Already they
were out of reach of our guns' accurate aim, for the day
was again cloudy with occasional rains, and no aeroplanes were able to regulate the gunfire.

But closely pressing them from behind came our
eager doughboys. They scurried from cover to cover,
always crouching low as they ran. Throwing themselves flat onto the ground, they would get their rifles
into action and spray the Germans with more bullets
until they withdrew from sight. Then another running advance and another furious pumping of lead
from the Yanks.

Reed and I flew above this scene for many miles,
watching the most spectacular free show that ever man
gazed on. It was a desperate game, especially for the
Germans, but I cheered and cheered as I caught the
excitement of the chase, even high over their heads as
I was.

In the midst of my rejoicing I suddenly heard the
rat-tat-tat of a machine gun below me and felt a few
hits through my plane. I looked down in amazement
and saw there behind the shell of a ruined building
three Germans pointing a machine gun at me and
pumping away at my aeroplane. I tipped over my
machine into a sharp *virage* and grasped my triggers. Before the men could lift a hand I had my
stream of bullets going plump into their center. One
man fell dead on the spot. The other two dropped
their guns and dived for a doorway. I was over the ruined village of Apremont.

FORWARD AMERICA !

Forward America! *United States, 1917*

Courtesy Wilson Library, University of North Carolina at Chapel Hill

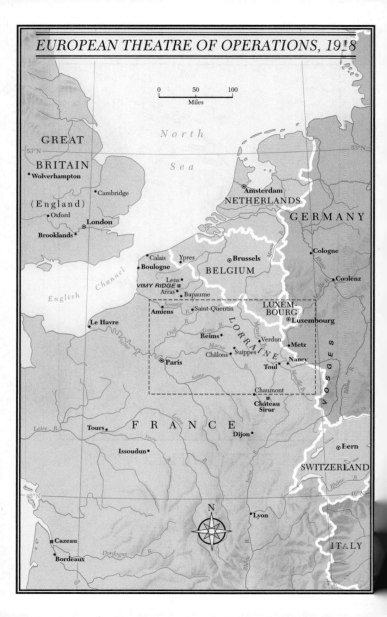

EUROPEAN THEATRE OF OPERATIONS, 1918

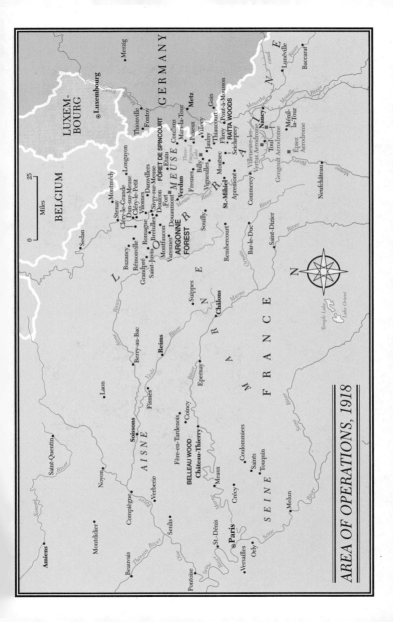

AREA OF OPERATIONS, 1918

The Air War. *Russia, 1914*

Courtesy Hoover Institution Archives, Stanford University

And You? Subscribe to the War Loan. *Germany, 1917*

Courtesy Wilson Library, University of North Carolina at Chapel Hill

Good books, good comrades. *Germany, 1916*

Courtesy Hoover Institution Archives, Stanford University

Books Wanted. *United States, 1915–1918*

Courtesy Wilson Library, University of North Carolina at Chapel Hill

Keep Him Free. *United States, 1917–1918*

Courtesy Wilson Library, University of North Carolina at Chapel Hill

Captain Edward Vernon Rickenbacker,
portrait by Howard Chandler Christy

Courtesy National Air and Space Museum, Smithsonian Institution

Emblem of the Hat-in-the-Ring Squadron

Courtesy United States Air Force,
1st Fighter Wing History Office

Coasting along some eight or ten miles further I saw that the whole country was swarming with the retreating Germans. I noted the progress of our own troops below and marked down their positions on my map. Having lost Reed during my little fracas with the machine gunners, I circled westward and covered the Verdun region without seeing anything either of him or of enemy aircraft. When I returned home I found the weather very bad south of the Meuse and was not surprised at the little air activity in that region.

Reed came in an hour or two later. He had landed at our old Toul aerodrome to see one of his old pals. And there he learned the grievous news that David Putnam, America's leading Ace, had just been shot down in combat. Since the death of Lufbery and [Frank L.] Baylies and the capture of [Paul F.] Baer, Putnam, with his twelve victories, had led all the American fighting pilots.[4] His nerve and fighting ability were well known to all of us. He had once shot down four enemy machines in one fight.

Putnam had gone up about noon today with one comrade. They encountered a Fokker formation of eight planes out on patrol and immediately attacked them. Putnam was struck almost at once and his machine crashed to the ground in flames.

---

[4]Putnam was killed in action on 12 September 1918 after winning thirteen (not twelve) confirmed victories; Baylies died while continuing to serve with a French elite unit, the Storks, on 17 June 1918 after shooting down twelve enemy planes. Baer was taken prisoner by the Germans on 22 May 1918 after scoring nine victories.

The next day was an exciting one for our group. I shot down one of the von Richthofen Circus and just escaped getting downed myself. Sumner Sewell[5] of Squadron 95 lived through one of the most extraordinary series of accidents I ever heard of, and several others had encounters that yielded more victories.

It was a clear fine day and I took off from the field alone at about eight o'clock in the morning, with the expectation of finding the sky full of aeroplanes. Anxious to see the extent of the American advance toward Vigneulles, I made for Thiaucourt and the north. Thiaucourt always gave me a shudder in former days and I usually took care to take a high path over its top. But now I spun across its abandoned aerodrome with much indifference and for the first time had a good look at its hangar arrangements.

Later, crossing the Moselle about four miles north of Pont-à-Mousson, I noticed considerable antiaircraft shelling up in the direction of Metz. I climbed higher and scanned the sky for machines.

Here they come! A large flotilla of American "Flaming Coffins," as their pilots called the Liberty machines,[6] were coming home at 12,000 feet after a bombardment of Metz. And just behind them and a lit-

[5]Sewell, who shot down seven enemy aircraft by the end of the war, ultimately became governor of Maine (1941–1945).

[6]Made in the United States under license, these DeHavilland DH-4 aircraft, equipped with American-designed Liberty engines, were called "Flaming Coffins" because the fuel tank, located just behind the cockpit, was highly vulnerable to enemy bullets and burst into flames when hit, sending crew members to their death.

tle above were four very fast-moving Fokkers. I stuck up my nose and began climbing for the sun.

I continued eastward until I had gained about 1,000 feet in altitude over the enemy machines, then I turned about. The Germans had followed the American machines to the lines and then had turned back westward in the direction of the Three-Fingered Lake. This was just the opportunity I had been hoping for. Now I had the sun at my back, and it was unusually brilliant this morning.

After a gradual *piqué* with motor half open, I descended to a position within 100 yards of the last man of their formation. The four were in diamond formation and none of them had seen my approach. At fifty yards I pressed my triggers and played my bullets straight into the pilot's seat. His machine slipped over onto its side, and after one wide swoop sideways began its last long fall to earth.

No sooner did my gun begin to crackle than the leader of the flight swung up his machine in a climbing *virage,* the other two pilots immediately following his example. And then I received one of the biggest jolts I can remember!

We had heard that the famous von Richthofen Circus had evacuated its old aerodrome in the west and had been reported in our sector. But so far none of us had met them about here. Now, as these three light Fokkers began simultaneously to come about at me, I found myself staring full into three beautiful scarlet noses headed straight in my direction. It scarcely needed their color to tell me who they were, for the skill with which they all came about so suddenly convinced me that this was no place for me. I had blundered single-handedly into the von Richthofen crowd!

I did my best to get away in a dignified manner, but a sudden spurt of fire past my nose convinced me that I would be very lucky if I got away with an unpunctured skin. The contortions I then undertook must have awakened the admiration of my three pursuers! At odd moments I would try to admire their extraordinary adroitness in handling their machines, for the heavens seemed quite crowded with those three dancing Fokkers. No matter where I turned there were always at least two of them there before me!

I need no more living proof of the flying ability of that celebrated German squadron of fighting pilots. They whipped their machines about me with incredible cleverness. I was looking for an opening for a quick getaway and they seemed only desirous of keeping me twisting my head off to follow their movements, so I had this slight advantage of them there. At last an opportunity came to try to outrun them, and with motor full open and nose straight down I looked back and saw them fading away in my rear.

I returned to my aerodrome quite elated with my first victory over this crack fighting squadron.

XXV

American Ace of Aces

O N 15 SEPTEMBER the weather was ideal for flying.
I left the aerodrome at 8:30 in the morning on a
voluntary patrol, taking the nearest air route to the
lines.

I had reached an altitude of 16,000 feet by the time
I had reached the trenches. The visibility was unusually good. I could see for miles and miles in every direction. I was flying alone, with no idea as to whether
other planes of our own were cruising about this sector or not. But barely had I reached a position over No-
Man's-Land when I noticed a formation of six enemy
Fokkers at about my altitude coming toward me from
the direction of Conflans.

I turned and began the usual tactics of climbing
into the sun. I noticed the Fokkers alter their direction
and, still climbing, move eastward toward the Moselle.
I did not see how they could help seeing me, as
scarcely half a mile separated us. However, they did
not attack nor did they indicate that they suspected my
presence beyond continuing steadily their climb for elevation. Three complete circles they made on their
side of the lines. I did the same on my side.

Just at this moment I discovered four Spad machines far below the enemy planes and some three

miles inside the German lines. I decided at once they must belong to the American Second Pursuit Group.

The leader of the Fokker formation saw the Spads at about the same moment I did. I saw him dip his wings and stick down his nose. Immediately the six Fokkers began a headlong *piqué* directly down at the Spads. Almost like one of the formation I followed suit.

Inside the first 1,000 feet I found I was rapidly overtaking the enemy machines. And by the time we had reached 5,000 feet I was in a position to open fire on the rear man. Not once had any of them looked around. Either they had forgotten me in their anxiety to get at their prey or else had considered I would not attempt to take them all on singlehandedly. At all events, I was given ample time to get my man dead into my sights before firing.

I fired one long burst. I saw my tracer bullets go straight home into the pilot's seat. Then there came a sudden burst of fire from his fuel tank and the Fokker continued onward in its mad flight—now a fiery furnace. He crashed a mile inside his own lines.

His five companions did not stay to offer battle. I still held the upper hand and even got in a few bursts at the next nearest machine before he threw himself into a *vrille* and escaped me. The sight of one of their members falling in flames evidently quite discouraged them. Abandoning all their designs on the unsuspecting Spads below, they dived away for Germany and left me the field.

I returned to my field, secured a car, and drove immediately up to the lines to our balloon section. I wanted to get my victories confirmed—both this one of today and the Fokker that I had brought down yesterday in the same sector. For no matter how many pilots may have witnessed the bringing down of an enemy plane, official confirmation of their testimony must be obtained from outside witnesses.

Upon the tragic death of Major Lufbery, who at that time was the leading American Ace with eighteen victories,[1] the title of American Ace of Aces fell to Lieutenant Paul Frank Baer of Fort Wayne, Indiana, a member of the Lafayette Escadrille 103. Baer then had nine victories and had never been wounded.[2]

Baer is a particularly modest and lovable boy, and curiously enough he is one of the few fighting pilots I have met who felt a real repugnance in his task of shooting down enemy aviators.

When Lufbery fell, Baer's commanding officer, Major William Thaw, called him into the office and talked seriously with him regarding the opportunity before him as America's leading Ace. He advised Baer

[1] Lufbery's final two victories on 12 and 27 April 1918 were unconfirmed, leaving him with sixteen official victories.

[2] Baer's unit became officially the American 103rd PS on 18 February 1918, and he won all of the nine victories mentioned here between 11 March and 22 May of that year, when he became a prisoner of war. But for the fact that he was French-trained he merited the claim of being the first American flyer to become an Ace after the United States entered WWI, which may explain why he is here associated only with the Lafayette Escadrille in order to preserve that distinction for Campbell as a member of the 94th.

to be cautious and he would go far. Two days later Baer was shot down and slightly wounded behind the German lines.

Thereafter, Lieutenant Frank Baylies of New Bedford, Massachusetts, a member of the crack French Escadrille of the Cigognes, held the American title until he was killed in action on 12 June 1918. Baylies had thirteen victories to his credit.[3] Then David Putnam, another Massachusetts boy, took the lead with twelve victories over enemy aeroplanes. Putnam, as I have said, was, like Lufbery, shot down a day or two before my last victory.[4]

Now Lieutenant [Edgar G.] Tobin of San Antonio, Texas, and a member of the Third Pursuit Group, had six official victories. He led the list. I for my part had five victories confirmed. But on receiving confirmation for the two Fokkers I had vanquished yesterday and today, I would have my seven and would lead Tobin by one. So it was with some interest and impatience that I set off to try to find ground witnesses of my last two battles above St. Mihiel.

[3]The Cigognes (Storks) was an elite French fighter group composed of five separate units that won an exceptionally high number of victories. Some of France's greatest Aces, including Georges Guynemer, Charles Nungesser, and Rene Fonck, flew for the group. Baylies refused a captaincy in the USAS to remain with the unit.

[4]As already noted, Putnam had thirteen official victories, nine of which he won flying for French units and four of which he earned after joining the American 139th in June 1918. Numerous unconfirmed victories would have brought his total to twenty-nine. He was killed in action on 12 September 1918.

Mingled with this natural desire to become the leading fighting Ace of America was a haunting superstition that did not leave my mind until the very end of the war. It was that the very possession of this title—Ace of Aces—brought with it the unavoidable doom that had overtaken all its previous holders. I wanted it and yet I feared to learn that it was mine! In later days I began to feel that this superstition was almost the heaviest burden that I carried with me into the air.

Eating my sandwiches in the car that day, I soon ran through St. Mihiel and made my way on the main road east to Apremont and then north to Thiaucourt. I knew that there had been a balloon up near there both days and felt certain that their observers must have seen my two combats overhead.

Unfortunately the road from Apremont to Thiaucourt was closed, owing to the great number of shell-holes and trenches that crisscrossed it. After being lost for some two hours in the forest that lies between St. Mihiel and Vigneulles, I was finally able to extricate myself and found I had emerged just south of Vigneulles. I was about one mile south of our trenches. And standing there with map in hand wondering where to go next, I got an unexpected clue.

A sudden flare of flames struck my sight off to the right. Running around the trees I caught a view of one of our balloons between me and Thiaucourt completely immersed in flames! Halfway down was a graceful little parachute, beneath which swung the observer as he settled slowly to Mother Earth!

And as I gazed I saw a second balloon two or three miles further east toward Pont-à-Mousson perform the same maneuver. Another of our observers was making the same perilous jump! A sly German had slipped across our lines, had made a successful attack on the two balloons, and had made a clean getaway. I saw him climbing up away from the furious gale of antiaircraft fire that our gunners were speeding after him. I am afraid my sympathies were almost entirely with the airman as I watched the murderous bursting of Archy all around his machine.

In half an hour I arrived at the balloon site and found them already preparing to go aloft with a second balloon. And at my first question they smiled and told me they had seen my Fokker of this morning's combat crash in flames. They readily signed the necessary papers to this effect, thus constituting the required confirmation of my last victory. But for the victory of yesterday that I claimed, they told me none of the officers were present who had been there on duty at that time. I must go to the Third Balloon Company just north of Pont-à-Mousson.

After watching the new balloon get safely launched with a fresh observer in the basket, a process that consumed some ten or fifteen minutes, I retraced my steps and made my way back to my motor. The observer whom I had seen descending under his parachute had in the meantime made his return to his company headquarters. He was unhurt and quite enthusiastic over the splendid landing he had made in the trees. Incidentally, I then learned that but two or three such forced descents by parachute from a flaming balloon are permitted by any one observer. These jumps are not always so simple, and frequently very serious.

On my way to the Third Balloon Company, I stopped to inquire the road from a group of infantry officers whom I met just north of Pont-à-Mousson. As soon as I stated my business, they unanimously exclaimed that they had seen my victim crash near them. After getting them to describe the exact time and place and some of the incidents of the fight I found that it was indeed my combat they had witnessed. This was a piece of real luck for me. It ended my researches on the spot. As they were very kindly signing their confirmation, I was thinking to myself, "Eddie! You are the American Ace of Aces!" And so I was for the minute.

Returning home, I lost no time in putting in my reports. Reed Chambers came up to me and hit me a thump on the back.

"Well, Rick!" he said, "how does it feel?"

"Very fine for the moment, Reed," I replied seriously, "but any other fellow can have the title any time he wants it, so far as I am concerned."

I really meant what I was saying. A fortnight later when Frank Luke began his marvelous balloon strafing he passed my score in a single jump. Luke, as I have said, was on the same aerodrome with me, being a member of Squadron 27. His rapid success even brought Squadron 27 ahead of Squadron 95 briefly.

The following day I witnessed a typical expedition

of Luke's from our own aerodrome. Just about dusk on 16 September Luke left the major's headquarters and walked over to his machine. As he came out of the door he pointed out the two German observation balloons to the east of our field, both of which could be plainly seen with the naked eye. They were suspended in the sky about two miles back of the enemy lines and were perhaps four miles apart.

"Keep your eyes on these two balloons," said Frank as he passed us. "You will see that first one there go up in flames exactly at 7:15 and the other will do likewise at 7:19."

We had little idea he would really get either of them, but we all gathered together out in the open as the time grew near and kept our eyes glued to the distant specks in the sky. Suddenly Major Hartney exclaimed, "There goes the first one!" It was true! A tremendous flare of flame lighted up the horizon. We all glanced at our watches. It was exactly on the dot.

The intensity of our gaze toward the location of the second balloon may be imagined. It had grown too dusk to distinguish the balloon itself, but we well knew the exact point on the horizon where it hung. Not a word was spoken as we alternately glanced at the secondhands of our watches and then at the eastern skyline. Almost on the second our watching group yelled simultaneously. A small blaze first lit up the point at which we were gazing. Almost instantaneously another gigantic burst of flames announced to us that the second balloon had been destroyed!

We all stood by on the aerodrome in front of Luke's hangar for another fifteen minutes until we heard through the darkness the hum of his returning motor. His mechanics were shooting up red Very lights with their pistols to indicate to him the location of our field. With one short circle above the aerodrome he shut off his motor and made a perfect landing just in front of our group. Within a half-hour's absence from the field, Frank Luke had destroyed $100,000 worth of enemy property! He had returned absolutely unscratched.[5]

A most extraordinary incident had happened just before Luke left the ground. Lieutenant [John N.] Jeffers of my squadron had been out on patrol with the others during the afternoon and did not return with them. I was becoming somewhat anxious about him when I saw a homing aeroplane coming from the lines toward our field. It was soon revealed as a Spad and was evidently intending to land at our field, but its course appeared to be very peculiar. I watched it gliding steeply down with engine cut off. Instead of making for the field, the pilot, whoever he was, seemed bent on investigating the valley to the north of us before coming in.

Straight down at the north hillside the Spad continued its way. I ran out to see what Jeff was trying to

[5]Luke, one of the most legendary heroes of the war and the first American pursuit pilot to win the Medal of Honor (EVR did not receive it until 1930), made a specialty of shooting down balloons, scoring fourteen such wins in addition to winning four victories over German airplanes.

do. I had a premonition that everything was not right.

Just as his machine reached the skyline I saw him make a sudden effort to redress the plane. It was too late. He slid off a little on his right wing, causing his nose to turn back toward the field—and then he crashed in the fringe of bushes below the edge of the hill. I hurried over to him.

Imagine my surprise when I met him walking toward me, no bones broken, but wearing a most sheepish expression on his face. I asked him what in the world was the matter.

"Well," he replied, "I might as well admit the truth! I went to sleep coming home, and didn't wake up until I was about ten feet above the ground. I didn't have time to switch on my engine or even flatten out!"

Extraordinary as this tale seemed, it was nevertheless true. Jeffers had set his course for home at a high elevation over the lines and cutting off his engine had drifted smoothly along. The soft air and monotonous luxury of motion had lulled him to sleep. Subconsciously his hand controlled the joystick or else the splendid equilibrium of the Spad had kept it on an even keel without control. Like the true old coachhorse it was, it kept the stable door in sight and made directly for it. Jeff's awakening might have been in another world, however, if he had not miraculously opened his eyes in the very nick of time!

XXVI

Captain of the Hat-in-the-Ring Squadron

THE THREE-FINGERED LAKE is a body of water well known to the American pilots who have flown over the St. Mihiel front. It lies four or five miles northeast of Vigneulles and is quite the largest body of water to be seen in this region. The Germans had held it well within their lines ever since the beginning of the war.

At the conclusion of the American drive around St. Mihiel, which terminated victoriously twenty-two hours after it began, the lines were pushed north of Vigneulles until they actually touched the southern arm of Three-Fingered Lake. Our irresistible doughboys, pushing in from both directions, met each other in the outskirts of Vigneulles at two o'clock in the morning. Some 15,000 enemy soldiers and scores of guns were captured within the territory that had thus been pinched out.

With the lake barrier on the very edge of their line, the Germans had adroitly selected two vantage points on their end of the water from which to hoist their observation balloons. From this position their observers had a splendid view of our lines and noted every movement in our rear. They made themselves a tremendous nuisance to the operations of our officers.

Frank Luke, the star balloon strafer of our group, was, as I have said, a member of Squadron 27. On the evening of 18 September, he announced that he was going up to get those two balloons that swung above the Three-Fingered Lake. His pal, Lieutenant [Joseph Fritz] Wehner, of the same squadron accompanied Luke as usual.

There was a curious friendship between Luke and Wehner. Luke was an excitable, high-strung boy, and his impetuous courage was always getting him into trouble. He was extremely daring and perfectly blind and indifferent to the enormous risks he ran. His superior officers and his friends would plead with him to be more cautious, but he was deaf to their entreaties. He attacked like a whirlwind, with absolute coolness but with never a thought of his own safety. We all predicted that Frank Luke would be the greatest air fighter in the world if he would only learn to save himself unwise risks. Luke came from Phoenix, Arizona.

Wehner's nature, on the other hand, was quite different. He had just one passion, and that was his love for Luke. He followed him about the aerodrome constantly. When Luke went up, Wehner usually managed to go along with him. On these trips Wehner acted as an escort or guard, despite Luke's objections. On several occasions he had saved Luke's life. Luke would come back to the aerodrome and excitedly tell everyone about it, but no word would Wehner say on the subject. In fact, Wehner never spoke except in monosyllables on any subject. After a successful combat he would put in the briefest possible report and sign his name. None of us ever heard him describe how he brought the enemy machine down.[1]

Wehner hovered in the air above Luke while the latter went in for the balloon. If hostile aeroplanes came up, Wehner intercepted them and warded off the attack until Luke had finished his operations. These two pilots made an admirable pair for this work, and over a score of victories were chalked up for Squadron 27 through the activities of this team.

On the evening of 18 September, Luke and Wehner set off at five o'clock. It was just getting dark. They flew together at a medium level until they reached the lake. There they separated, Luke diving straight at the balloon that lay to the west, Wehner staying aloft to guard the sky against a surprise attack from German aeroplanes.

Luke's balloon rose out of the swampy land that borders the upper western edge of Three-Fingered Lake. Then the enemy defenses saw his approach and began a murderous fire through which Luke calmly dived as usual. Three separate times he dived and

[1]Wehner (like EVR) had been suspected of being a spy because of his Germanic name. Brooding about this situation, he was determined to clear his reputation by scoring as many victories as possible. Ultimately he became an Ace with six victories, three of which he shared jointly with Luke. The latter was also a loner who was accused by his comrades of being a braggart and coward before he vindicated himself with his achievements in shooting down balloons. The bond between the two men stemmed partly from the fact that they were both outsiders who shared a common sense of indignation.

fired, dived and fired. Constantly surrounded with a hail of bullets and shrapnel, flaming onions[2] and incendiary bullets, Luke returned to the attack the third time and finally completed his errand of destruction. The huge gasbag burst into flames. Luke zoomed up over the balloon and looked about for his friend. He was not in view at the moment, but another sight struck Luke's searching eyes, for a formation of six Fokkers was bearing down on him from out of Germany. Perhaps Wehner had fired the red signal light that had been the warning agreed on, and he had failed to see it in the midst of all that Archy fire. At any rate he was in for it now.

The German Fokkers were to the west of him. The second balloon was to the east. With characteristic foolhardiness Luke determined to withdraw by way of the other balloon and take one burst at it before the Fokkers reached him. He accordingly continued straight on east, thus permitting the pursuing formation of Fokkers to cut him off at the south.

With his first dive Luke shot down the second balloon. It burst into towering flames that were seen for miles around. Again he passed through a living stream of missiles fired at him, and escaped unhurt!

As he began his flight toward home he discovered that he was completely cut off by the six Fokkers. He must shoot his way through single-handedly. To make it worse, three more Fokkers were rapidly coming on

[2]"Flaming onions": shells that exploded with a brilliant glare.

him from the north. And then Luke saw his pal Wehner.

Wehner had all this time been patrolling the line to the north of Luke's balloons. He had seen the six Fokkers, but had supposed that Luke would keep ahead of them and abandon his attempt at the second enemy balloon. He therefore fired his signal light, which was observed by our balloon observers but not by Luke, and immediately set off to patrol a parallel course between the enemy planes and Luke's road home. When he saw Luke dart off to the second balloon, Wehner realized at once that Luke had not seen his signal and was unaware of the second flight of Fokkers coming directly on him. He quickly sheered off and went forward to meet them.

What Luke saw was the aeroplane of his devoted pal receiving a direct fire from all three of the approaching Fokker pilots. The next instant it fell over in the air and slowly began to fall. Even as it hesitated in its flight, a burst of flames issued from the Spad's tank. Wehner was shot down in flames while trying to save his comrade! It was a deliberate sacrifice of himself for his friend!

Completely consumed with fury, Luke, instead of seeking safety in flight, turned back and hurled himself on the three Fokkers. He was at a distinct disadvantage, for they had the superiority both in altitude and position, not to mention numbers. But regardless of what the chances were, Luke climbed upward at them, firing as he advanced.

Picking out the pilot on the left, Luke kept doggedly on his track, firing at him until he suddenly saw him burst into flame. The other two machines were in the meantime on Luke's tail and their tracer bullets were flashing unnoticed by his head. But as soon as he saw the end of his first enemy he made a quick *renverse-ment* on number two, and, firing as he came about, he shot down the second enemy machine with the first burst. The third *piquéd* for Germany, and Luke had to let him go.

All this fighting had consumed less time than it takes to tell it. The two Fokkers had fallen in flames within ten seconds of each other. With rage still in his heart Luke looked about him to discover where the six enemy machines had gone. They had apparently been satisfied to leave him with their three comrades, for they were now disappearing back toward the east. And just ahead of them Luke discerned fleecy white clouds of Archy smoke breaking north of Verdun. This indicated that our batteries were firing at enemy aeroplanes in that sector.

As he approached Verdun, Luke found that five French Spads were hurrying up to attack an L.V.G. machine[3] of the Germans, the same target at which our Archy had been firing. The six Fokkers had seen them coming and had gone to intercept them. Like a rocket,

---

[3] An observation plane made by the Luftverkehrsgesellschaft (LVG), a leading German aircraft manufacturer. This machine, however, is officially listed in Luke's victory record as a Halberstadt, another German reconnaissance craft.

Luke set his own Spad down at the L.V.G. It was a two-seater machine and was evidently taking photographs at a low altitude.

Our Archy ceased firing as Luke drew near. He hurled himself directly down at the German observer, firing both guns as he dove. The enemy machine fell into a *vrille* and crashed just a few hundred yards from our old Verdun aerodrome. In less than twenty minutes, Lieutenant Luke had shot down two balloons, two fighting Fokkers, and one enemy photographing machine—a feat that is almost unequaled in the history of this war!

Luke's first question when he arrived at our field was, "Has Wehner come back?"

He knew the answer before he asked the question, but he was hoping against hope that he might find himself mistaken. But Wehner had indeed been killed. The joy of Luke over his marvelous victories vanished instantly. He was told that with these five victories he had a total of eleven, thus passing me, and making Luke the American Ace of Aces. But this fact did not interest him. He said he would go to the front and see if anything had been heard from Wehner.

The following morning Major [Harold E.] Hartney, commanding officer of our group, took Luke and me on up to Verdun to make inquiries. Shortly after lunch the officer in charge of confirmations came to us and told Lieutenant Luke that not only had his five victories of yesterday been officially confirmed, but that three old victories had likewise been that morning confirmed, making Luke's total fourteen instead of eleven. And these fourteen victories had been gained by Frank Luke in *eight days!* The history of war aviation, I believe, has not a similar record. Not even the famous [Georges] Guynemer, [Rene] Fonck, [Albert] Ball, [William] Bishop, or the noted German Ace of Aces, Baron [Manfred] von Richthofen, ever won fourteen victories in a single fortnight at the front. Any aircraft, whether balloon or aeroplane, counts as one victory, and only one, with all the armies.[4]

In my estimation there has never, during the four years of war, been an aviator at the front who possessed the confidence, ability, and courage that Frank Luke had shown during those remarkable two weeks.

In order to do this boy honor and show him that every officer in the group appreciated his wonderful work, he was given a complimentary dinner that night by the squadrons. Many interesting speeches were made. When it came Luke's turn to respond he got up laughing, said he was having a bully time—and sat down! Major Hartney came over to him and presented him with a seven days' leave in Paris—which at that

[4]Guynemer, whose stature among the French public for a time rivaled that of Joan of Arc, had fifty-three confirmed victories and eleven probable ones; Fonck became the French Ace of Aces with seventy-five official wins, in addition to which he claimed fifty-two others. Ball, the first great British Ace, shot down forty-three German planes; Bishop, a Canadian, had seventy-two confirmed victories and probably won many more for which he lost credit because of his penchant for flying alone. Richthofen, the most legendary flyer of the war, had more official wins, eighty, than any pilot on either side of the conflict.

time was about the highest gift at the disposal of commanding officers at the front.[5]

The night of 24 September, Major Marr returned from Paris and announced that he had received orders to return to America. Shortly afterward Major Hartney handed me an order promoting me to the command of Squadron 94![6]

My pride and pleasure at receiving this great honor I cannot put into words. I had been with 94 since its first day at the front. I was a member of this, the very first organization to go over the lines. I had seen my old friends disappear and be replaced by other pilots whom I had learned to admire and respect. And many of these had, in turn, disappeared!

Now but three members of the original organization were left—Reed Chambers, Thorne Taylor, and I. And I had been given the honor of leading this distinguished squadron! It had Lufbery, Jimmy Hall, and Dave Peterson as members. And it led all the rest in a number of victories.

But did it? I walked over to the operations office

[5]Bored by inactivity and intent upon gaining revenge for Wehner's death, Luke returned early from his leave and died in combat soon thereafter.

[6]EVR was promoted ahead of several officers with greater seniority, including Chambers. The move was popular in the 94th but controversial higher up the chain of command, especially because of EVR's lack of formal education. The fact that EVR was not promoted to major (see Historical Introduction, p. lxi) resulted from the prejudice against him and may help explain why he preferred to be called "Captain" throughout his life despite eventually rising to the rank of Lieutenant Colonel in the reserves.

and took a look at the records. I had a suspicion that Frank Luke's wonderful run of the past few days had put Squadron 27 ahead of us.

My suspicions were quite correct. The sober fact was that this presumptuous young 27 had suddenly taken a spurt, thanks to their brilliant Luke, and now led the Hat-in-the-Ring Squadron by six victories! I hurried over to 94 quarters and called together all my pilots.

The half hour we had together that evening firmly fixed a resolve in the aspirations of 94's members. No other American squadron at the front would ever again be permitted to approach so near our margin of supremacy. From that hour every man in Squadron 94, I believe, felt that the honor of his squadron was at stake in this matter of bringing down Germans. At all events, within a week my pilots had overtaken 27's lead and never again did any American squadron even threaten to overtop our lead.

After a talk that night with the pilots, I went over and called the mechanics to a caucus. We had half-an-hour's talk together, and I outlined to them just what our pilots proposed to do with their help. And they understood that it was only by their whole-souled help that their squadron's success would be possible. How nobly these boys responded to our appeal was well proved in the weeks that followed. Rarely indeed was a dud motor found in Squadron 94 henceforward. Never did a squadron of pilots receive more faithful attendance from their helpers in the hangar than was

Rickenbacker, just after his promotion to captain

Courtesy Auburn University Archives

Rickenbacker in the cockpit of a Nieuport 28

Courtesy National Air and Space Museum, Smithsonian Institution

given us by these enthusiastic air mechanics of the Hat-in-the-Ring Squadron. I honestly believe that they felt the disgrace of being second more keenly than did we pilots.

Finally, I had a long and serious conference with myself that night. After I had gone to bed I lay awake for several hours, thinking over the situation. I was compelled to believe that I had been chosen squadron commander because, first, I had been more successful than the other pilots in bringing down enemy aeroplanes; and second, because I had the power to make a good leader over other pilots. That last proposition caused me infinite thought. Just how and wherein could I do the best by my followers?

I suppose every squadron leader has this same problem to decide, and I cannot help but believe that on his decision as to how he shall lead his pilots depends in a great measure the extent of his success— and his popularity.

To my mind there was but one procedure. I should never ask any pilot under me to go on a mission that I, myself, would not undertake. I would lead them by example as well as precept. I would accompany the new pilots, and watch their errors, and help them to feel more confidence by sharing their dangers. Above all, I would work harder than ever I did as mere pilot. My days of loafing were over!

To avoid the red-tape business at the aerodrome— the making out of reports, ordering materials, and seeing that they came in on time, looking after details of the mess, the hangars, and the comfort of the enlisted men—all this work must be put under competent men, if I expected to stay in the air and lead patrols. Accordingly, I gave this important matter my attention early next morning. And the success of my appointments was such that from that day to this I have never spent more than thirty minutes a day on ground business connected with 94's operations.

Full of this early enthusiasm, I went up on a lone patrol the very first morning of my new responsibility to see how much I had changed for the better or the worse.

Within half an hour I returned to the aerodrome with two more victories to my credit—the first double-header I had so far won!

XXVII

An Eventful "D" Day

25 SEPTEMBER 1918 was my first day as captain of Squadron 94. Early that forenoon I started for the lines alone, flew over Verdun and Fort Douaumont, then turned east toward Etain. Almost immediately I picked up a pair of L.V.G. two-seater machines below me. They were coming out of Germany and were certainly bent on an expedition over our lines. Five Fokker machines were above them and somewhat behind, acting as protection for the photographers until the lines were reached.

Climbing toward the sun for all I was worth, I soon had the satisfaction of realizing that I had escaped their notice and was now well in the rear. I shut down my motor, put down my head, and made a beeline for the nearest Fokker.

I was not observed by the enemy until it was too late for him to escape. I had him exactly in my sights when I pulled both triggers for a long burst. He made a sudden attempt to pull away, but my bullets were already ripping through his fuselage, and he must have been killed instantly. His machine fell wildly away and crashed just south of Etain.

It had been my intention to zoom violently upward and protect myself against the expected attack from the four remaining Fokkers as soon as I had finished the first man. But when I saw the effect of my attack on the four dumbfounded pilots, I instantly changed my tactics and plunged straight on through their formation to attack the photographing L.V.G.s ahead. For the Fokkers were so surprised to find a Spad in their midst and to see one of their number suddenly drop that the remaining three *viraged* to right and left. Their one idea was to escape and save their own skins. Though they did not actually *piqué* for home, they cleared a space large enough for me to slip through and continue my dive on the two-seaters before they could recover their formation.

The two-seaters had seen my attack and had already put down their heads to escape. I plunged along after them, getting the rear machine in my sights as I drew nearer to him. A glance back over my shoulder showed me that the four Fokkers had not yet reformed their line and were even now circling about with the purpose of again solidifying their formation. I had a few seconds yet before they could begin their attack.

The two L.V.G. machines began to draw apart. Both observers in the rear seats began firing at me, although the range was too long for accurate shooting. I dove more steeply, passed out of the gunner's view under the nearest machine and zoomed quickly up at him from below. But the victory was not to be easy. The pilot suddenly kicked his tail around, giving the gunner another good aim at me. I had to postpone shooting until I had more time for my own aiming.

And in the meantime, the second photographing machine had stolen up behind me and I saw tracer bullets go whizzing and streaking past my face. I zoomed up diagonally out of range, made a *renversement* and came directly back at my first target.

Several times we repeated these maneuvers, the four Fokkers still wrangling among themselves about their formation. And all the time we were getting farther back into Germany. I decided on one bold attack.

Watching my two adversaries closely, I suddenly found an opening between them. They were flying parallel to each other and not fifty yards apart. Dropping down in a sideslip until I had one machine between me and the other, I straightened out smartly and leveled my Spad. I began firing. The nearest German passed directly through my line of fire and just as I ceased firing I had the infinite satisfaction of seeing him gush forth flames.[1] The Fokker escort came tearing up to the rescue. I put on the gas and *piquéd* for my own lines.

Pleased as I was over this doubleheader, the effect it might have on my pilots was far more gratifying to me.[2]

Arriving at the aerodrome at 9:30 I immediately jumped into a motorcar, called to Lieutenant Chambers to come with me, and we set off at once to get official confirmation for this double victory. We took the main

[1] EVR was here practicing "deflection shooting," aiming ahead of an enemy so that the latter would fly into the bullet stream.

[2] EVR was awarded the Medal of Honor on 6 November 1930 for the action just described.

road to Verdun, passed through the town and gained the hills beyond the Meuse toward Etain. Taking the road up to Fort de Tavannes we passed over that bloody battlefield of 1916 where so many thousand German troops fell before French fire in the Battle for Verdun. At the crest of the hill we were halted by a French *poilu,* who told us the rest of the road was in full view of the Germans and that we must go no farther.

We asked him as to whether he had seen my combat overhead this morning. He replied in the affirmative and added that the officers in the adjacent fort also had witnessed the whole fight through their field glasses. We thanked him, and leaving our car under his care, took our way on foot to the fort.

Two or three hundred yards of shellholes sprinkled the ground between us and the fort. We made our way through them, gained admittance to the interior of the fort and in our best Pidgin French stated our errand to *M. le Commandant.* He immediately wrote out full particulars of the combat I had had with the L.V.G., signed it, and congratulated me on my victory with a warm shake of the hand. We made our adieus and hastened back to the car.

Plunging through the shallowest shellholes, we had traversed about half the distance to our car, which stood boldly out on the top of the road, when a shrill whining noise made us pause and listen. The next instant a heavy explosion announced that a shell had landed about fifty yards short of us. Simultaneously with the shower of gravel and dirt that headed our way, we dropped unceremoniously on our faces in the bottom of the deepest shellhole in our vicinity.

The Germans had spotted our car and were actually trying to get its range!

Two or three times we crawled out of our hole, only to duck back at the signal of the next coming shell. After six or eight shots, the gunners evidently considered their target too small, for they ceased firing long enough for us to make a bolt across the intervening holes and throw ourselves into the waiting automobile. I shall never forget the frightful length of time it took me to get our car backed around and headed in the right direction.

Next day was to be an important one for us and for the whole American army. Officially it was designated as "D" day, and the "zero hour," by the same code, was set for four o'clock in the morning. At that moment the artillery barrage would begin and 40,000 doughboys who were posted along the front-line trenches from the Meuse to the Argonne Forest would go over the top. It was 26 September 1918.[3]

Precisely at four o'clock I was awakened by my orderly who informed me that the weather was good. Hastily getting out of doors, I looked over the dark sky wondering as I did so how many of our boys it would claim before this day's work was done! For we had an important part in this day's operations. Headquarters had

[3]The Meuse-Argonne offensive was the last major American operation of WWI. Partly because of the difficult terrain in which it took place, it took a toll of 26,277 dead and 95,786 wounded.

sent us orders to attack all the enemy observation balloons along that entire front throughout this morning and to continue the attacks until the infantry's operations were completed. Accordingly every fighting squadron had been assigned certain of these balloons for attack, and it was our duty to see that they were destroyed. The safety of thousands of our attacking soldiers depended on our success in eliminating these all-watching eyes of the enemy. Incidentally, it was the first balloon-strafing party that Squadron 94 had been given since I had been made its leader and I desired to make a good showing on this first expedition.

Just here it may be well to point out the difficulties of balloon strafing, which make this undertaking so unattractive to the new pilot.

German "Archy" is terrifying at first acquaintance. Pilots affect a scorn for it, and indeed at high altitudes the probabilities of a hit are small. But when attacking a balloon that hangs only 1,500 feet above the guns (and this altitude is of course known precisely to the antiaircraft gunner), Archy becomes more dangerous.

So when a pilot begins his first balloon-attacking expeditions, he knows that he runs a gauntlet of fire that may be very deadly. His natural impulse is to make a nervous plunge into the zone of danger, fire his bullets, and get away. Few victories are won with this method of attack.

The experienced balloon strafers, particularly such daring airmen as Coolidge and Luke, do not consider the risks or terrors about them. They proceed in the attack as calmly as though they were sailing through a stormless sky. Regardless of flaming missiles from the ground, they pass through the defensive barrage of fire, and often return to attack the target, until it finally bursts into flame from their incendiary bullets.

The office charts informed me that the day would break this morning at six o'clock. Consequently, we must be ready to leave the ground in our machines at 5:20, permitting us thirty minutes in which to locate our individual balloons. For it is essential to strike at these well-defended targets just at the edge of dawn. As the balloons are just starting aloft, our attacking aeroplanes are but scantily visible from below.

I routed out five of my best pilots, Lieutenants [H. Weir] Cook, Chambers, Taylor, Coolidge, and [William W.] Palmer; as we gathered for an early breakfast, we went over again all the details of our prearranged plans. We had two balloons assigned to our squadron, and three of us were delegated to each balloon. Both lay along the Meuse between Brabant and Dun-sur-Meuse. Every one of us had noted down the exact location of this target on the evening before. It would be difficult perhaps to find them before daylight if they were still in their nests, but we were to hang about the vicinity until we did find them, if it took all day. With every man fully posted on his course and objective, we put on our coats and walked over to the hangars.

I was the last to leave the field, getting off the ground at exactly 5:20. It was still dark and we had to have the searchlights turned onto the field for a moment to see the ground while we took off. As soon as we lifted into the darkness, the lights were extinguished. And then I saw the most marvelous sight I have ever seen.

A terrific barrage of artillery fire was going on ahead of me. Through the darkness the whole western horizon was illumined with one mass of sudden flashes. The big guns were belching out their shells with such rapidity that there appeared to be millions of them shooting at the same time. Looking back I saw the same scene in my rear. From Lunéville on the east to Reims on the west there was not one spot of darkness along the whole front. The French were attacking along both our flanks at the same time with us in order to help demoralize the weakening enemy forces. The picture made me think of a giant switchboard that emitted thousands of electric flashes as invisible hands manipulated the plugs.[4]

So fascinated did I become over this extraordinary fireworks display that I was startled on peering over the side of my machine to discover the city of Verdun below my aeroplane's wings. Fastening my course above the dim outline of the Meuse River, I followed its windings downstream, occasionally cutting across

[4]This is one of the most admired and frequently quoted passages in the entire book. In writing it, Driggs adhered closely to the original text, which states that "there were millions of flashes from all calibres of artillery going off at once and could be seen as far as Rheims to our west and Luneville to our east . . . To me it seemed as though there was being operated a giant telephone switchboard with thousands of hands putting in the plugs all along this sector."

little peninsulas that I recognized along the way. Every inch of this route was as familiar to me as was the path around the corner of my old home. I knew exactly the point in the Meuse Valley where I would leave the river and turn left to strike the spot where my balloon lay last night. I did not know what course the other pilots had taken.

Just as these thoughts were going through my mind I saw directly ahead of me the long snaky flashes of enemy tracer bullets from the ground piercing the sky. There was the location of my balloon, and either Cook or Chambers was already attacking it. The enemy had discovered them and were putting up the usual hail of flaming projectiles around the balloon site. But even as the flaming bullets continued streaming upward, I saw a gigantic flame burst out in their midst!

Even before the glare of the first had died, I saw our second enemy balloon go up in flames. My pilots had succeeded beyond my fondest expectations. Undoubtedly the enemy would soon be swinging new balloons up in their places, but we must wait a while for that. I resolved to divert my course and fly further to the north where I knew of the nest of another German observation balloon near Damvillers.

Dawn was just breaking as I headed more to the east and tried to pick out the location of Damvillers. I was piercing the gloom with my eyes when again—straight in front of my revolving propeller I saw another gush of flame that announced the doom of another enemy balloon—the very one I had determined to attack.

While I was still celebrating over the extraordinary good luck that had attended us in this morning's expedition, I glanced off to my right and was almost startled out of my senses to discover that a German Fokker was flying alongside me not 100 yards away! Not expecting any of the enemy aeroplanes to be abroad at this early hour, I was naturally upset for the moment. The next instant I saw that he had headed for me and was coming straight at my machine. We both began firing at the same time. It was still so dark that our four streams of flaming bullets cut brilliant lines of fire through the air. For a moment it looked as though our two machines were tied together with four ropes of fire. All my ammunition was of the incendiary variety for use against gasbags. The German's ammunition was part tracer, part incendiary, and part regular chunks of lead.

As we drew nearer and nearer I began to wonder whether this was to be a collision or whether he would get out of my way. He settled the question by tipping down his head to dive under me. I instantly made a *renversement* that put me close behind him and in a most favorable position for careful aim. Training my sights into the center of his fuselage I pulled both triggers. With one long burst the fight was over. The Fokker fell over onto one wing and dropped aimlessly to earth. It was too dark to see the crash, and moreover I had all thoughts of my victory dissipated by a sudden ugly jerk to my motor that immediately developed into a violent vibration. As I turned back toward Verdun, which was the nearest point to our lines, I had recurring visions of crashing down into Germany to find myself a prisoner. This would be a nice ending to our glorious balloon expedition!

Throttling down to reduce the pounding, I was able just to maintain headway. If my motor failed completely I was most certainly doomed, for I was less than 1,000 feet above ground and could glide but a few hundred yards without power. Providence was again with me, for I cleared the lines and made our Verdun aerodrome where one flight of Squadron 27 was housed. I landed without damage, and hastily climbed out of my machine to check the cause of my trouble.

Imagine my surprise when I discovered that one blade of my propeller had been shot in two by my late adversary! He had evidently put several holes through it when he made his head-on attack. And utterly unconscious of the damage I had received, I had reversed my direction and shot him down before the weakened blade gave way! The heavy jolting of my engine was now clear—only half of the propeller caught the air.

Lieutenant Jerry Vasconcells of Denver, Colorado, was in charge of the Verdun field on which I had landed.[5] He soon came out and joined me as I was staring at my broken propeller. And then I learned that he had just landed, himself, from a balloon expedition. A few questions followed and then we shook hands spontaneously. He had shot down the Damvillers bal-

[5]Vasconcells, an Ace with six victories, had recently been placed in command of the 185th PS, a night-fighting unit.

loon himself—the same one for which I had been headed. And as he was returning, he had seen me shoot down my Fokker!

His mechanics placed a new propeller on my Spad, and none the worse for its recent rough usage, the little 'bus took me rapidly home. I landed at 8:30 on my own field. And there I heard great news. Our group had that morning shot down ten German balloons! My victory over the Fokker made it eleven victories to be credited us for this hour's work. And we had not lost a single pilot!

XXVIII

Frank Luke Strafes His Last Balloon

NEITHER SIDE could afford to leave its lines unde-
fended by observation balloons for a longer period than was necessary for replacements. Our
onslaught of the early morning had destroyed so many
Drachen, however, that it was quite impossible for
them to get new balloons up along their entire sector.

That same afternoon I flew along their lines to see
what progress they were making in replacements of
their observation posts. The only balloon I could discover in our sector was one that lifted its head just behind the town of Sivry-sur-Meuse. I made a note of its
position and decided to try to bring it down early next
morning.

Accordingly, I was up again at the same hour the following day and again found that the sky promised
clear weather. Leaving the field at 5:30, I again took a
course over Verdun in order to pick up the Meuse
River there and follow it as a guide.

On this occasion I caught a grand view of No-
Man's-Land as seen from the air by night. It was not yet
daylight when I reached the lines and there I caught a
longitudinal view of the span of ground that separated
the two opposing armies. For on both sides of this
span a horizontal line of flashes could be seen issuing

from the mouths of rival guns. The German batteries were drawn up along their front scarcely a mile back of their line. And on our side a vastly more crowded line of flashes indicated our overwhelming superiority in numbers of guns. So far as my eye could reach, this dark space lay outlined between the two lines of living fire. I followed down its course for a few miles, then turned to find the Meuse River.

After ten minutes' flight into Germany, I realized I had crossed the river before I began to turn north and that I must be some distance inside the enemy's lines. I dropped down still lower as I saw the outlines of a town in front of me, and circling above it I discovered that I had penetrated some twenty-five miles inside enemy territory and was now over the village of Stenay. I had overshot Sivry by about twenty miles.

I lost no time in heading about toward France. Opening up the throttle, I first struck west and followed this course until I had the Meuse River again under my nose. Then turning up the river, I flew just above the road that follows along its banks. It was now getting light enough to distinguish objects below.

This Meuse River highway is a lovely drive to take in the daytime, for it passes through a fertile and picturesque country. The little city of Dun-sur-Meuse stands out on a small cliff that juts into a bend of the river, making a most charming picture of what a medieval town should look like. I passed directly down Main Street over Dun-sur-Meuse and again picked up the broad highway that clung to the bank of the river.

Occasional vehicles were now abroad below me. Day had broken and the Germans were up and ready.

It occurred to me that I might as well fly a bit lower and entertain the passing vehicles with a little bullet-dodging as we met each other. My morning's work was spoiled anyway. It was becoming too late to take on a balloon now. Perhaps I might meet a general in his automobile, and it would be fun to see him jump for the ditch and throw himself down on his face at the bottom. If I were fortunate enough to get him, that would surely be helping along the war!

Ahead of me I saw a truck moving slowly in the same direction I was going. "Here goes for the first one!" I said to myself. I tipped down the nose of my machine and reached for my triggers.

As my nose went down, something appeared over my top wing that took my breath away for an instant. There directly in my path was a huge enemy observation balloon! It was swaying in the breeze, and the cable that held it to earth ran straight down until it reached the moving truck ahead of me. Then it became clear as daylight to me. They were towing a new balloon up the road to its position for observation! They had just received a replacement from the supply station of Dun-sur-Meuse, and after filling it with gas, were now getting it forward as rapidly as possible. It was just the target I had been searching for!

Forgetting the truck and crew, I flattened out instantly and began firing at the swaying monster in the air. So close to it had I come before I saw it that I had

only time to fire a burst of fifty shots when I was forced
to make a vertical *virage*, to avoid crashing through it.
I was then but 400 or 500 feet above ground.

Just as I began the *virage* I heard the rat-tat-tat-tat
of a machine gun fire from the truck on the road beneath me. And mingled with this drumfire, I heard the
sound of an explosion in the fuselage just behind my
ear! One of their explosive bullets had come very close
to my head and had exploded against a longeron or
wire in the tail of the aeroplane! There was nothing I
could do about that, however, except to fly along as
steadily as possible until I reached a place of safety and
could make an investigation of the damage received. I
cleared the side of the gasbag and then as I passed, I
turned and looked behind me.

The enemy balloon was just at the point of exploding, and the observer had already leaped from his
basket and was still dropping through air with his
parachute not yet opened. It was a very short distance
to Mother Earth, and sometimes a parachute needs
200 or 300 feet of freefall to fully open and check the
swiftness of the falling body. I wondered whether this
poor chap had any chance for his life in that short distance and just what bones he was likely to break when
he landed. And then came a great burst of fire as the
whole interior of the big balloon became suddenly ignited. I couldn't resist one shout of exultation at the
magnificent display of fireworks I had thus set off,
hoping in the meantime that its dull glare would reach
the eyes of some of our own balloon observers across

the lines who would thus be in a position to give me the confirmation of my eleventh victory.

Again I decided to pay a call at Jerry Vasconcell's field at Verdun and there get out and ascertain the extent of the damage in the tail of my Spad. Jerry welcomed me with some amusement and wanted to know whether this dropping in on him was to be a daily occurrence. Yesterday it had been a broken prop, and today a broken tail. Before answering him I got out, and together we examined my machine.

A neat row of bullet holes ran back down the tail of my machine. They were as nicely spaced as if they had been put in by careful measurement. The first hole was about four inches back of the pad on which my head rests when I am in the seat.[1] The others were directly back of it at regular intervals. One, the explosive bullet, had struck the longeron that runs the length of the fuselage, and this had made the sharp explosion I had heard at the time. The gunners on the truck had done an excellent bit of shooting!

None of the holes were in a vital part of the machine. I took off the field after a short inspection and soon covered the fifteen or sixteen miles that lay between the Verdun field and our own.

"Frank Luke, the marvelous balloon strafer of the 27th, did not return last night!"

[1] EVR had a visual defect in his right eye that caused him to aim with his left, which was contrary to usual practice. Had it not been for this circumstance the first bullet would have gone through his head.

So reads the last entry in my flight diary of 29 September 1918. Rereading that line brings back to me the common anxiety of the whole group over the extraordinary and prolonged absence of their most popular member. For Luke's very mischievousness and irresponsibility made every one of us feel that he must be cared for and nursed back into a more disciplined way of fighting—and flying—and living. His escapades were the talk of the camp and the despair of his superior officers. Fully a month after his disappearance his commanding officer, Alfred [A.] Grant told me that if Luke ever came back he would court-martial him first and then recommend him for the Legion of Honor!

In a word, Luke mingled with his disdain for bullets a very similar distaste for the orders of his superior officers. When imperative orders were given him to come immediately home after a patrol, Luke would unconcernedly land at some French aerodrome miles away, spend the night there and arrive home after dark the next night. But as he almost invariably landed with one or two more enemy balloons to his credit, which he had destroyed on the way home, he was usually let off with a reprimand and a caution not to repeat the offense.

As blandly indifferent to reprimands as to orders, Luke failed to return again the following night. This studied disobedience to orders could not be ignored, and thus Captain Grant had stated that if Luke ever did return he must be disciplined for his insubordination. The night of 27 September Luke spent with the French Cigognes at the Toul aerodrome.

The last we had heard from Luke was that at six o'clock on the night of 28 September he left the French field where he had spent the previous night, and flying low over one of the American balloon headquarters he circled over their heads until he had attracted the attention of the officers, then dropped them a brief note that he had written in his aeroplane. As may well be imagined, Luke was a prime favorite with our balloon staff. All the officers of that organization worshipped the boy for his daring and his wonderful successes against the balloon department of their foes.

Running out and picking up the streamer and sheet of paper that fell near their office, they unfolded the latter and read:

"Look out for enemy balloon at D-2 and D-4 positions.—Luke."

Already Luke's machine was disappearing in the direction of the first balloon that lay just beyond the Meuse. It was too dark to make out its dim outline at this distance, but as they all gathered about the front of their "office" they glued their eyes to the spot where they knew it hung. For Luke had notified them several times previously as to his intended victims and every time they had been rewarded for their watching.

Two minutes later a great red glow lit up the northwestern horizon and, before the last of it had died away, the second German balloon had likewise burst into flames! Their intrepid hero had again fulfilled his promise! They hastened into their headquarters and called up our operations officer and announced Frank

Luke's last two victories. Then we waited for Luke to make his dramatic appearance.

But Luke never came! That night and the next day we rather maligned him for his continued absence, supposing naturally enough that he had returned to his French friends for the night. But when no news of him came to us, when repeated inquiries elicited no information as to his movements after he had brought down his last balloon, every man in the group became aware that we had lost the greatest airman in our army. From that day to this not one word of reliable information has reached us concerning the disappearance of Luke. Not a trace of his machine was ever found! Not a single clue to his death and burial was ever obtained from the Germans! And like Guynemer, the miraculous airman of France, Frank Luke was swallowed by the skies and no mortal traces of him remain![2]

[2]Luke died in action on 29 September 1918. Seriously wounded after shooting down two German balloons, he made a forced landing near Murveau, France. His death was confirmed on 15 January 1919 by investigators of the scene. According to an affidavit made at the time, Luke was killed by machine-gun fire after refusing to surrender and drawing his revolver on German troops surrounding him. This testimony, however, was later disputed, and the incident may have been romanticized. Luke was under warrant for arrest for insubordination while performing his final mission without having authority to do so, but was awarded the Medal of Honor posthumously for completing it with extreme valor. Guynemer's body was never recovered after he was shot down by German Leutenant Kurt Wissemann on 11 September 1917 in an engagement over Poelcapelle, France.

XXIX

A Night Mission

AVIATORS are conscious of an antagonistic feeling toward them in the minds of the infantrymen in the trenches who, covered with mud and trench insects, frequently overworked and underslept, and always facing imminent death from enemy's bullets, find an ironic pleasure in contrasting their hard lot with the life of ease and excitement led by the young officers of the flying corps.

To see an aeroplane cavorting about over their heads fills them with bitterness at the thought that these well-dressed men are getting paid for that pleasant sport, while they are forced to work like beasts of burden in the rain. Infantry officers have told me that rarely have they seen an American aeroplane over them when it was needed to chase away the enemy machines.

It is not difficult to understand this bitterness under the circumstances. Much of this feeling might be cleared away, however, if the infantrymen realized that while enemy machines are strafing them, our airmen are retaliating probably twofold on the enemy troops beyond the lines. Every day our machines were engaged in this hazardous work of trench strafing. Much of the success of our infantry advances was due to the cooperation of our air forces behind the front and beyond the vision of our doughboys in the trenches. Admitting as they do the disastrous effect of aeroplane attacks on their own lines, they can easily imagine how terrified their enemy infantrymen became at the daily appearance of our fighting planes in their midst.

As to the comparative risks of injury in these two arms of warfare, I believe even the most skeptical doughboy would admit after reflection that an airman's daily duties surround him every moment with the possibilities of death. Comfort and dress, entertainments, and good food are all in our favor, of course. But I have yet to meet a pilot of any nation at war who does not try to balance this advantage with a whole-souled admiration and praise of his less fortunate brother-in-arms, who does so much more than his share of the "dirty work."

Much of this jealousy and misunderstanding is due to the fact that the man on the ground can never see and never know anything of the things the airman is doing for him. It is a pity that such must be the case, for, while rivalry between different branches of the army may be beneficial, bitterness is not.

While sitting at dinner about sundown on the evening of 30 September, discussing the latest victory claimed that afternoon by Lieutenant [Samuel] Kaye [Jr.] and Lieutenant Reed Chambers, who had destroyed a Fokker aeroplane over Romaigne, an orderly brought me a note from the C.O. of the group, requesting me to select two volunteers for a most important mission and report at headquarters with them forthwith. It was then 6:30 and quite dark.

We were naturally excited at this sudden summons, and I wondered what extraordinary necessity called for aeroplanes at this very late hour. I selected Ham Coolidge and Weir Cook out of the men who volunteered for this unknown mission, and setting off with our flying kit in our hands, we hastened over to Major Hartney's office.

There, to our great surprise, we found General Mitchell impatiently pacing the floor while awaiting our coming. He immediately welcomed us and began at once to explain the object of our hurried summons.

Our troops were at that time engaged in the attack on Montfaucon and were advancing up the ten-mile valley that runs between the edge of the Argonne Forest and the Meuse River. Montfaucon occupied the crest of the loftiest hill in this valley and was situated almost in its exact center. From this favorable spot the crown prince of Germany had viewed the battles for Verdun and the country to the south during those fierce days of 1916. Later I visited the massive headquarters of the crown prince and marveled at the extensive view of the surrounding landscape one obtained from this site.

For four days our doughboys had flung themselves courageously on the well-prepared defenses of the enemy along this valley. Costly gains were made and valuable territory was slowly yielded to our victorious troops by the Germans. Between the old line and the new line from Grandpré to the Meuse, two different American divisions named the defile through which they had separately fought "Death Valley." From their superior heights beyond the Meuse the enemy artillery swept their roads with a pitiless hail of shrapnel. An occasional rush was made by isolated regiments of our men, which gained them the shelter of intervening hills. And thus just under the crest of Montfaucon our aeroplanes had discovered a body of several thousand American doughboys who had been marooned for thirty-six hours, entirely without food or ammunition, except the small supply they had carried in with them.[1] A thick curtain of artillery fire had been placed behind them by the enemy, cutting all the roads in several places and rendering even a retreat difficult.

Major Hartney had already discussed with our group captains the advisability of carrying food to these troops by aeroplane on the morrow. The Army Headquarters expected confidently that they would be able to break through to the relief of these starving troops during the night. If this failed we should devote ourselves to their victualing by aeroplane, beginning at daybreak.

And now General Mitchell had motored over to

---

[1] This famous "Lost Battalion" consisted of 554 men, of whom 194 were rescued. Two American airmen, Erwin E. Bleckley and Harold F. Goettler, were posthumously awarded the Medal of Honor for valor in locating the trapped unit in a volunteer mission in which both men were killed. Along with Luke and EVR, they were the only American flyers to win the Medal of Honor for gallantry in WWI.

impart to us some startling news. The Army Intelligence Bureau had reported that eleven troop trains had left Metz at noon carrying to the Montfaucon front the famous Prussian Guard for an attack on our entrapped doughboys. Immediate confirmation of this fact was desired, and late as it was, aeroplanes were the only means of obtaining this confirmation, and they must be sent. Owing to the darkness, the flight would be an extremely hazardous one and only experienced pilots should be permitted to go. The searchlight would throw its beam up into the night during the entire time we were away, and we should be able to see its signal for many miles within Germany. It was imperative that the aviators should know the location of all the railway lines leading to the front from Metz and likewise necessary that they should succeed with their mission and return safely with the desired information. He would not order any individual to go, but would be pleased to have two volunteers.

I replied that every man in Squadron 94 was anxious to go. I had selected Coolidge and Cook as two of my best men and both were not only familiar with the enemy railroad lines but could find their way home if anybody could.

"Very well," said the general. "Strike the main railroad line on the Meuse, follow it up as far as Stenay and from there go to Montmédy and on to Metz. Note carefully every moving thing on that route if you have to fly as low as the treetops. Locate the time and the place of every train, how many cars it has, which way it is headed, and the nature of its load, if you can. I will wait here until you return."

Three would be better than two, I thought to myself as I accompanied Cook and Coolidge out to their machines. I saw them off and then ordered the mechanics to run out my Spad. A few minutes later I taxied down the field, turned, and headed for our row of signal lights. The motor roared as I opened up my throttle and sped swiftly back for a take-off. The tail lifted, the wheels skimmed the ground, then cleared it, and slightly elevating the controls I saw the ground lights disappearing under my lower wing.

Above all was blackness. Away to the north, fitful flashes of fire dotted the ground. Over my head our aerodrome searchlight cut a yellow slice of everwidening sky, until it lost itself among the stars. Several other searchlights were also playing about the heavens. I noted carefully the angle ours made with the horizon so I should recognize it from any distance.

"How are those boys faring tonight, I wonder?" thought I to myself as I flew at a 500-foot level over the marooned doughboys' heads. For I had left Verdun to my right and was on a route straight over Montfaucon. I must have passed over the marching thousands who were advancing under cover of the night to get a favorable position for the next day's work. On the roads below me I saw occasional lights where bridges were being stealthily repaired and shellholes refilled with earth and rock by our engineers. So congested were these roads and so badly torn by the enemy's fire that our supplies could not be brought up fast enough to keep our front line going. Our own artillery was well advanced but had no shells to fire! Even during the pauses in the enemy's barrage no food could be taken to those regiments that were cut off because the roads had been almost obliterated by the bursting shells of the enemy.

Later on I heard of the Herculean efforts made by our Engineer Corps to repair these roads by night. Enlisted men were sent up from miles behind the lines to assist in this emergency. Even one elderly colonel who happened along and discovered the situation took the post of an able-bodied military policeman and ordered the young man to work on the roads. And all through the night the German shells continued to drop in their midst, undoing their frantic construction and killing many of the workers in the process.

Against this point the Prussian Guards were coming for an attack! I wondered how headquarters got that information and how the enemy knew we were in such a bad situation in Death Valley! Aeroplanes had brought the information to both sides. I grimly assured myself that aeroplanes would prevent some of the Prussians from ever reaching their objective if we should discover their coming this night.

Turning east I soon discerned the Meuse River shining in the starlight and, following its course at 300 or 400 feet above its surface, I flew on deeper and deeper into hostile territory. Barring motor failure, I had little to fear. No enemy searchlights appeared ahead of me and so far as I know not a bullet was fired at me. There is a distinctive sound to the Hispano-Suiza motor that should have betrayed its nationality to any attentive ear familiar with aeroplane engines, but despite this fact and the low altitude at which I was compelled to fly and find my way, my passing seemed to arouse no interest. Soon I realized that I was almost forty miles behind our lines. And there between me and the next town of Stenay I saw the glare of an engine box on the tracks ahead of me. Dropping still lower down, I prepared to count the coaches as they passed under me when I discovered it was only a short freight train that was proceeding away from the front instead of toward it. Paying no further attention to its progress, I continued along over the tracks until I reached the station at Stenay. Back and forth over the sidings and switches I flew, one eye on the dusky ground and one in the direction of the enemy aerodrome that I well knew occupied the hilltop just east of the town. No unusual aggregation of railroad cars were on the tracks and no activity whatever in railroad circles appeared doing in Stenay this night. Picking up the main line to Montmédy, I cast one more glance behind me at the Fokker aerodrome and faded away into the night unpursued.

Over Montmédy ten minutes later I found one train going toward Stenay and one toward Metz, but neither was a troop train. No other coaches whatever occupied the sidings. I began to think that intelligence bureaus might sometimes be mistaken and, in spite of myself,

I felt a little disappointed. For I had an extra supply of machine-gun ammunition with me and had pictured to myself the amount of damage one small aeroplane might do to the gentlemen of the Prussian Guard inside the windows of their troop trains. All the way along the main line from Montmédy to Metz, I hoped rather than feared that I would meet the expected guests of the evening. But I was doomed to disappointment. The nearer to Metz I got, the more I realized that if their trains had left Metz at noon, as advertised, they must certainly have reached or passed Montmédy by now. I was absolutely positive that not a single coach had slipped under me unnoticed, for most of the way along I had flown scarcely high enough to clear the telegraph wires that occasionally crossed the tracks.

Glancing at my compass I swung off to the right and left the tracks. It was quite evident that the Prussian Guards scare was a false alarm. In five minutes I should be over Verdun.

Ten minutes passed and then twenty, and still no Verdun. If I had been misled by my compass and had kept too far to the west—even so, I should have crossed the Meuse long ago. I leaned over and shook the compass. It whirled a few times, then settled itself in exactly the opposite direction! Again I shook it and again it pointed to a new direction. Never have I seen a compass—except those captured from German machines—that even pretended to disclose the direction of north! Mingled with my rage was also a fear that was getting almost panicky. I searched the horizon for our searchlight but none was in sight. Thinking I might be in ground mist I rose higher, and circling about, scanned the horizon and blackness below. Not even the flash of a gun that might direct me to the battlefront was visible!

Three quarters of an hour of gasoline remained to me. And a much overrated sense of direction—and no compass. Then I thought of the North Star! Glory be! There she shines! I had been going west instead of south and would have had 200 miles or so of fast flying before striking the British lines near Ypres on my present course. Keeping the star behind my rudder I flew south for fifteen minutes, then dropping down, almost immediately found myself above a bend in a stream of water that resembled a familiar spot in the River Meuse.[2] With a sudden return of self-confidence, I followed the river until I struck Verdun—picked up our faithful searchlight, and ten minutes later I landed

---

[2]The "North Star" reference does not appear in the original text; both here and on the next page, it was added by Driggs to embellish the story. In addition, the details about the direction in which EVR thought he had been flying make sense only if one realizes that he turned back from his mission fifteen minutes after he began following the rail line from Montmedy to Metz, as his preliminary text states. The assertation that the British lines near Ypres were to the west of the area in which EVR was flying is also incorrect. Trying to create a more dramatic narrative, Driggs supplied confusing fictional details. Luis Freile, a cartographer who prepared the maps for the current edition, provided valuable advice pertaining to these points.

safely below the row of lights that marked the edge of our aerodrome.

My mechanics assured me that both Coolidge and Cook had returned. Hastening to the operations office I made my report that no German trains were coming our way, which General Mitchell received with a simple, "Thank God!" The next day our advancing troops caught up with the marooned doughboys and sent them for a much-deserved rest to the rear.

As I walked across the field to my bed I looked up and recognized my friend the North Star shining in my face. I raised my cap and waved her a salute and repeated most fervently, "Thank God!"

On the following day, which was 1 October, a large formation of our pilots crossed the lines and cruised about for nearly two hours in German lines without a fight. We scared up one covey of Fokkers but were unable to get them within range.

Changing machines, I went back alone late in the afternoon and hung about the lines until it began to grow dusk. I had spotted a German balloon down on the ground back of the Three-Fingered Lake and was convinced that it would be inadequately guarded since it was not doing duty and was supposed to be hidden from view. Sure enough, when I arrived at its hiding place I found no antiaircraft gunners there to molest me. It was too easy a job to be called a victory, for I merely poked down my nose, fired 100 rounds or so and the job was done. The balloon caught fire without any coaxing and I calmly flew homeward.

Without molestation, that is, from the enemy, I turned back across our lines at Vigneulles, and there on our own side of the trenches I met the attention of two searchlights and a furious barrage of flaming projectiles from our own guns. The latter all passed well behind my tail, as I could see them plainly leaving the ground and could trace their entire progress in my direction. The American gunners had not had the long experience of the German Archy experts, and I saw at a glance that they were all aiming directly at my machine instead of the proper distance ahead of me. Their aim was so bad that I did not even feel indignant at their overzealousness. Later I learned that this area was forbidden to our aeroplanes, and the gunners there had been ordered to shoot at everything that passed overhead after dark.

My successful expedition against the balloon was known at the aerodrome when I arrived. The glare of its fire had been seen on the field, and later telephonic reports from our observing posts duly confirmed its destruction.

XXX

A Day's Work—Six Victories

WITH THE beginning of October, Squadron 94 took on a new phase of air fighting. We were taken away from the general orders affecting the First Pursuit Wing and were delegated to patrol the lines at low altitude—not exceeding 2,000 feet. This meant serious business to us, for not only would we be under more severe Archy fire, but we would be an easy target for the higher German formations, who could *piqué* down on us at their own pleasure.

These new orders were intended to provide a means of defense against the low-flying enemy machines that came over our lines. Usually they were protected by fighting machines. Rarely did they attempt to penetrate to any considerable distance back of No-Man's-Land.

On 2 October Reed Chambers led out the first patrol under these new orders. He had five machines with him and I went along on a voluntary patrol, to see how the new scheme was going to work out. In order to act somewhat in a protective capacity, I took a higher level and followed them back and forth over their beat at 2,000 feet or more above them.

The course of this patrol was between Sivry-sur-Meuse and Romaigne. We had turned back toward the west at the end of one beat and were nearing the turning point when I observed a two-seater Hannover machine of the enemy trying to steal across our lines behind us. He was quite low and was already across the front when I first discovered him.

In order to tempt him a little more distance away from his lines, I made no sign of noticing him but throttled down to my lowest speed and continued straight ahead with some climb. The pilots in Chambers's formation were below me and had evidently not seen the intruder at all as yet.

Calculating the positions of our two machines, as we drew away from each other, I decided I could now cut off the Hannover before he reached his lines, even if he saw me the moment I turned. Accordingly I *piquéd* swiftly back, aiming at a point just behind our front, where I estimated our meeting must take place. To my surprise, however, the enemy machine did not race for home but continued ahead on his mission.

A victory seemed so easy that I feared some deep strategy lay behind it all. Closer and closer I stole up in their rear, yet the observer did not even look about him to see if his rear was safe. At 100 yards I fixed my sights upon the slothful observer in his rear cockpit and prepared to fire. He had but one gun mounted upon a *tournelle*[1] and this gun was not even pointing in my direction. After my first shot he would swing it around, I conjectured, and I would be compelled to

---

[1] "*Tournelle*": a circular track that enabled the observer to swivel his machine gun into position to fire at an attacking plane.

come in through his stream of bullets. Well, I had two guns to his one and he would have to face double the amount of bullets from my Spad. Now I was at fifty yards and could not miss. Taking deliberate aim I pulled both triggers. The observer fell limply over the side of his cockpit without firing a shot. My speed carried me swiftly over the Hannover, which had begun to bank over and turn for home as my first shots entered its fuselage.

Heading off the pilot, I braved his few shots and again I obtained a position in his rear and had him at my mercy. At that critical moment my guns jammed!

Infuriated at this piece of bad luck, I still had the thought to realize that the enemy pilot did not know I could not shoot, so I again came up and forced him to make a turn to the east to avoid what he considered a fatal position. And at that moment I saw Reed Chambers flying directly toward me, the rest of his patrol streaming in along behind him. Reed was firing as he flew. His first bursts finished the pilot, and the Hannover settled with a gradual glide down among the shellholes that covered the ground just north of Montfaucon—a good two miles within our lines.

It was the first machine that I had brought down behind our lines—or assisted to bring down, for Reed Chambers shared this victory with me—in such condition that we were able to fly it again.[2]

[2]This aircraft was a Hannover CL-3, a two-seat observation plane. The episode becomes important later in the book when the captured machine is used in making a film.

The next day, 3 October, a carefully planned attack on an enemy balloon back of Doulcon was carried out in the middle of the afternoon by our squadron. Montfaucon was still the center of operations for the American army. The country was extremely difficult owing to the hills and forests along the Meuse River, all of which the Germans had amply prepared for stubborn defense. The presence of their observation balloons added one source of benefit to them that we knew could be destroyed. So we were sent out in full daylight to accomplish this end.

Thorne Taylor led our formation. Practically our whole squadron left the aerodrome at three o'clock. Ham Coolidge and [Charles I.] Crocker, who were selected as the two balloon strafers for the day, flying with us on the patrol. At 3:30 precisely we were to find ourselves over the enemy balloon at Doulcon, and there these two pilots were to make a sudden dash down at the balloon, one behind the other. It was a new daylight dodge we would try to put over the Germans before they suspected the object of our mission.

We expected to find enemy planes about guarding this important observation post of the enemy, and it was necessary to take along enough machines of our own to sweep them away from the path that our two strafers must take to get to their balloon. Therefore, I had all the pilots set their watches exactly with mine and gave them all instructions to cross the lines precisely at 3:45 and fly between Coolidge and Crocker and any hostile aircraft that might intercept them. With every man fully schooled in his part of the game, we all took off.

Walter [L.] Avery of Squadron 95 accompanied us. Avery was the pilot who had forced down the celebrated German Ace [Carl] Menckoff early in August on the Château-Thierry front. Menckoff then had a string of thirty-seven[3] victories to his credit and, strange as it may seem, this was Avery's first air combat. Avery disabled Menckoff's motor with one of his bullets, and the German pilot decided it wiser to drop down on our side of the lines to surrender himself rather than take the chance of being killed trying to glide home on a crippled machine. Great was his disgust, when he landed, to discover that his conqueror was a green American pilot.

As the formation continued its patrol some distance this side of our lines, Coolidge and Crocker left the rest and placed themselves a good distance the other side of Montfaucon. We found no enemy machines in our vicinity, but were not sure that they would not appear as soon as we approached the Doulcon balloon.

As my watch neared the hour I crept a little nearer the point of attack. Looking over the situation ahead of me some four or five miles, I suddenly saw two Spads streaking it ahead with all their speed in the direction of the balloon. I looked at my watch. It was but 3:40. Coolidge and Crocker were each afraid that the other would steal a march on him and were both so anxious to get the balloon that they disobeyed orders

[3]Actually thirty-nine.

and had gone in several minutes ahead of the stated time. Looking around I saw that my formation of Spads was just coming up in implicit obedience to orders. But now, instead of protecting our two picked men, we would arrive there too late.

As we all opened up in pursuit of the two pilots, I saw, advancing to cut them off from the balloon, a formation of six Fokkers. Then one lone Spad seemed to appear from somewhere in the clouds and flew in to engage the Fokkers. During the brief melee that followed many things happened at the same time. The lone Spad fell to earth and crashed back in Germany. The balloon burst into flames, indicating that either Coolidge or Crocker had succeeded in reaching the mark despite the Fokkers. And at the same moment the clouds behind me seemed to be emitting swarms of Fokker fighting aeroplanes that hurtled themselves on our Spads.

They were behind me, for I had distanced the others somewhat and had altered my direction to go to the rescue of the unknown Spad that had just fallen. But as I had started too late to be of any assistance, I again diverted my course to attack two German biplane machines that I could distinguish coming in to the fight from the direction of Dun-sur-Meuse. I wondered whether it was Coolidge or Crocker or some other who had fallen. Whoever it was, he had made a gallant fight, although if they had obeyed orders and waited for the agreed time of attack, he would not have had such odds against him.

One of the biplane machines saw me coming and cravenly turned back without notifying his companion. I surprised the latter and after a very brief bit of maneuvering shot him down completely out of control. Knowing it would be extremely difficult to gain a confirmation of this victory so far behind the German lines I waited about for a few moments until I saw him crash violently into the ground. I was satisfied I had destroyed him, whether anybody else ever knew it or not. In fact, this victory of mine never was confirmed.

Many twisting combats were in progress as I gained again the part of the heavens above Doulcon. Several machines had fallen, but whether friend or foe, I could not distinguish from this distance. The Spads were scattered all over the sky and our formation was hopelessly destroyed. I determined to call them together and take them back to our lines. Our balloon was in flames, our mission ended, and we were taking unwise risks fighting ten miles within the German lines where a mishap would drop some luckless pilots prisoners in their territory.

The enemy pilots were only too willing to let us go. As I collected my pilots about me and headed for home, the Fokkers lost no time in widening the distance between us. I dropped back and saw that the last of the Spads had crossed the lines and were well on their way. Then, noticing something going on east of me, I made a detour to investigate it.

It was a combat between two machines that was going on just south of our front. Hastening ahead with all possible speed, I arrived there at a most fortunate moment to find that Ted Curtis of 95 had just been forced to abandon an attack on a German L.V.G. by reason of a gun jam. The opposing pilot was endeavoring to make his escape as I reached him from one side, and a Spad that I later recognized as belonging to Ham Coolidge came in on the other.

Diving down with terrific speed, I began firing at 100 yards. With my first burst I noticed the gas tank of the enemy machine catch on fire. Ham began firing as he approached on the other side, but already the two unfortunate occupants of the observing machine knew their coming doom. The L.V.G. descended rapidly, the wind fanning the flames into a fiery furnace. The two unfortunate aviators must have been burned to a crisp long before the ground was reached. When the crash did come, there was a great explosion, and all that remained of the aeroplane was a black cloud of smoke and dust that ascended a few yards and was scattered to the four winds.

Adjusting matters that night, I found that Ham Coolidge was the hero of the day with the balloon and one Fokker to his credit besides one-half the vanquishing of the L.V.G. Thorne Taylor, Will Palmer, and Crafty [Wiley B.] Sparks had each brought down a Fokker, making a total of five besides the two-seater that I had crashed back of Dun-sur-Meuse. Our lead was now safely beyond that of our next rival— Squadron 27. And from that day it increased and has never been lessened.

XXXI

"Seeing the War"[1]

IT WAS NOT until the morning of 5 October that I learned that the Hannover machine that Reed Chambers and I had shot down on 2 October was still lying under guard of our doughboys only a mile or so north of Montfaucon. It seemed to be in good condition and the officers there had telephoned to us to send out and bring it in to our hangars. I might say in passing that it is extremely rare to find an enemy machine within our lines that has not been cut to pieces for souvenirs by 1,001 passersby before it has been on the ground a single hour. It is marvelous how quickly a crowd gathers at the site of a crashed machine. Motor drivers leave their trucks on the road and dash across the fields to examine the curiosity and to see if they cannot find a suitable souvenir straight from Germany to carry away with them. From every direction soldiers and French peasants come running to the wreck. By the time the pilot gets safely landed and makes his way to the scene, little of the enemy machine remains.

[1]This chapter is firmly based on the original text, which is, however, much shorter. The skill with which Driggs made a vivid and convincing account of the material makes the chapter a good example of the excellent work he did in transforming the original text into a fine piece of writing.

Up to this time, the American air force had never captured one of these two-seater Hannover machines. We were, all of us, anxious to fly different types of German aeroplanes, so as to compare them with our own and to examine what new devices they employed, to test their engine and to see toward what improvements their designers were tending. So as soon as we heard that our victim of 2 October had landed without crashing and was being cared for near Montfaucon, we lost no time in getting into an automobile and making our way to the front lines.

It was raining the morning we set off, and no flying was likely to be possible until after midday at best. We ran west and north until we struck the eastern edge of the famous Argonne Forest at Varennes, and there we began to get graphic pictures of the results of the gigantic artillery duel that had been going on for the last fortnight between the American forces and the Germans. The roads from Varennes to Montfaucon were almost entirely remade. Along both sides of the road for as far as the eye could reach, the shellholes covered the landscape as thickly as in almost any part of No-Man's-Land. The soil was the familiar yellow clay. Since the rainfall, the country through which we were passing resembled a desolate fever-stricken swamp.

Trees were sheared of their branches, and even the trunks of large trees themselves were cut jaggedly in two by the enemy's shells. Occasionally the ugly base of a dud shell could be seen protruding six or eight inches from the tree's trunk. The nose had buried itself squarely in the tree, but for some reason the shell had failed to explode.

And along the whole way numberless strings of motor trucks were passing and repassing, some laden with ammunition, food, medical, and other supplies hurrying to the front lines, dodging as they splashed through the slimy mud the slower-going processions of heavy guns. Long lines of "empties" were coming against this stream, many of them not empty it is true, but filled with the wounded who were being carried back to a field hospital for amputations or other surgical operations.

Occasionally we would find ourselves blocked as the whole procession came to a halt. Somewhere up the line a big twelve-inch gun had slithered around across the road and had completely blocked all traffic. On several occasions we waited half an hour before the road was cleared and the procession again was resumed.[2]

Finally, we left the main road and struck a slightly less congested, but far more disreputable road, which led us up to the crest of the hill on which stood Montfaucon. Guns of the Americans were sounding behind us now, and ahead we heard the enemy guns steadfastly replying. The town itself was nevertheless occupied by some of our troops, and a Y.M.C.A. hut had been opened within the ruins of a little shop on Main

[2]On the previous day, 4 October, American forces had begun to attack the Hindenburg Line, the most heavily defended part of the German front in the Argonne Forest.

Street at about the center of the winding settlement.
Here we stopped and left our car at the side of the
street. A long queue of doughboys stood in line waiting to get to the rude shop window where chocolate
and cigarettes were being sold as fast as the two
Y.M.C.A. officers could pass them out. We entered the
side door and warmed our muddy boots before a small
open fire burning in the center of the floor of what had
once been the kitchen. Here we ate a lunch of biscuits
and chocolate while we questioned the men as to the
exact location of the aeroplane we had brought down.

The machine was lying quite unhurt, we were informed, a mile or so nearer the enemy trenches to the
north of the town. We again took our car and made our
way slowly through the narrow and desolate streets.
On both sides the stone and mortar buildings had
been leveled almost flat. The streets had been completely filled with the debris of bricks, beams, and rub-
ble but enough space had been cleared through the
center to permit one vehicle to pass at a time. As we
reached the edge of the town we saw one substantial
building on the very top of the hill which, though
badly battered, remained the most conspicuous and
most pretentious object in Montfaucon. We instantly
recognized it from our numerous observations from
the air. It was the residence of the crown prince
through those early campaigns against Verdun of
1915–1916. More recently it had been occupied by the
general commanding the German armies. And now it
was in our hands!

Leaving the car, we walked up to make an inspection of this celebrated headquarters. It stood on a ledge of rock that hung over the hillside from its very peak. Around its base was a huge mountain of reinforced concrete from six to eight feet in thickness. From within, one caught a wonderful view of the whole surrounding country.

The German Hannover machine we found just beyond the town. It was indeed in remarkably good condition. It had glided down under the control of the pilot and had made a fairly good landing, considering the rough nature of the ground. The nose had gone over at the last moment and the machine had struck its propeller on the ground, breaking it. The tail stood erect in air, resting against the upper half of a German telegraph pole. A few ribs in the wings were broken, but these could easily be repaired.

A newly dug grave a few yards away indicated the last resting place of the observer that my bullets had killed in air. The pilot had been sent back to one of our hospitals for treatment. A bullet had pierced his face, shattering his jaw.

While the mechanics were taking the Hannover apart for loading, we proceeded on to one of our observation posts facing the German lines, where we got a close-up view of the regular war. It was a spectacle never to be forgotten!

Through the periscopes I saw the German trenches just opposite me, behind which our shells were dropping with a marvelous accuracy. They were passing over my head with a continuous whine, and the noise and jarring "crump" of their explosions so near our post made it necessary to shout our conversation into one another's ears. Enemy shells were passing overhead—mostly directed at our artillery to our rear.

Our shells were creeping back nearer and nearer to the open ditches in which the German troops were crouching. I watched the gradual approach of this deadly storm in complete fascination. Some gigantic hand seemed to be tearing up the earth in huge handfuls, forming ugly yellow holes from which sprang a whirling mass of dirt, sticks, and dust. And nearer and nearer to the line of trenches this devastating annihilation was coming. To know that human beings were lying there without a possible means of escape—waiting there while the pitiless hailstorm of shrapnel drew slowly closer to their hiding places—seemed such a diabolical method of torture that I wondered why men in the trenches did not go utterly mad with terror.

Suddenly I noticed that our gunners had drawn back their range to the exact line of the trenches. A first shell fell directly into the trench in front of me, tearing it open and gutting it completely for a space of thirty feet. The next instant a German soldier sprang out of the trench alongside this point, and flinging down his rifle proceeded to run for all he was worth back to a safer zone in the rear trenches. Hardly had he gone ten yards when a high explosive shell lit in front of him. Before I saw the burst of the shell I saw him stop with his arms flung up over his head. Next instant he was simply swept away in dust and disappeared, as the explosion took effect. Not a vestige of him remained when the dust had settled and the smoke had cleared away.

At five o'clock, the men had our Hannover loaded on their trailer and we were ready to depart for home. Passing down the Montfaucon hill by another road, we came upon a row of concrete dugouts built into the side of the hill by the Germans, but now occupied by America troops. Doubtless, the Germans had expected this occupation by their enemies and had waited for a few days to make certain that the little huts would be well filled with our troops before springing their surprise. Just as we approached this group of buildings the first German shell fell full into the middle of them! They had gotten the exact range the first shot!

Lieutenant Chambers and I were cut off from our road and for a few minutes we had the panic of our lives. A motor truck a short way ahead of us, which was likewise standing still waiting for this storm to pass, got a direct hit and was blown into fragments. Reed and I waited for no more, but made a bolt for the nearest shelter we could find.

Flat on our faces at the bottom of a nearby trench, we listened to the shells bursting about our ears. While not wishing any ill luck to any other poor chaps, we did most fervently hope that the Germans had not miscalculated their range by 200 yards in our direction. A bold glance over the top of our parapet showed that the concrete buildings were already a mass of dust. Just then one shell landed not fifteen feet in front of my nose, and I threw up my feet and struck the water in the bottom of my ditch as hard as possible.

As suddenly as it had started the bombardment ceased. Frugal souls, these Germans are! Not a shell too few, not one too many, is their very efficient motto. But we did not trust to this motto for several more minutes; and when we did cautiously emerge from our hole, we spent several more minutes washing the clay mud from our uniforms.

One more extraordinary spectacle Reed Chambers and I witnessed on that memorable day. Not two miles further on we espied a formation of nine Fokkers pass overhead, proceeding at a very low level in the direction of our rear. The sky was still cloudy and threatening but no rain was falling. We stopped the car, to avoid being mistaken for a general and thus attracting Fokker bullets through our car. Both of us jumped out and ran to an open space where we could see in what direction the pilots were directing their course. As we looked up through the trees we saw over our heads two darting Spads coming down straight at the tail of the Fokker procession from a high altitude. Although we could not distinguish whether they were American or French, we knew even at that distance that the two pursuing machines were Spads.

It was probably the most exciting moment Reed or I had ever experienced. We both shouted for joy to see the clever stalking of such a superior force by the two brave Spads. Moreover, this was the first air battle that either of us had ever seen from the ground, and it afforded us a panorama of the whole that is impossible to get from the center of a fight.

The two *piquéing* Spads opened fire on their downward course when at only 3,000 feet above ground. Their aim was not good, however, and neither of the attacked machines received a vital hit. Then the scene of action became one churning mass of revolving and looping aeroplanes. The leading Fokkers had reversed directions and were attacking the Spads. These latter did not keep together, but each was carrying on a separate freelance type of combat, occasionally pouring out streams of flaming bullets at any enemy machine that crossed its path.

For a good five minutes or longer the aerial tumult continued, without any further results than giving us spectators below a most beautiful exhibition of contortions and airmanship. I was full of admiration for the two aviators who, I was now almost certain, must be Americans and must belong to our group. At any rate, they were brave fellows to stick so long against such odds. Then we saw two machines coming our way out of control. They were some distance away, but since they were headed toward Germany and were not being pursued, it was very evident that they were Fokkers. The two brave Spads had been victorious.

Soon both wounded Fokkers were passing directly above us. Motors cut off and steadily losing height, one was absolutely certain to crash near us, while the other seemed still to be under the control of its pilot. They were Fokkers, sure enough! As we looked back to the scene of the recent combat, we saw the Spads streaking it homeward with the balance of the Fokkers strung out behind them in a useless pursuit. No Fokker can overtake a good Spad unless he has sufficient advantage in elevation to increase his speed by diving. The victorious Spads lost themselves in the distant clouds; and the Fokkers, after reforming their depleted numbers, returned to their lines some distance to the east of us.

The last we saw of the two victims, one had crashed nose down at less than a mile from where we stood. The other had succeeded in gliding almost two miles further, finally crashing, as we ascertained next day, in No-Man's-Land just north of Montfaucon.

The day was getting late and our progress home would be slow owing to the enormous traffic on the roads, so we did not take time to visit the spot of the nearest Fokker's fall. Thus we returned joyfully homeward after a most exciting and successful day, with our captured two-seater Hannover safely following along behind. And at mess that night, to crown our satisfaction, we learned that the two victorious Spad operators who had that afternoon added two more victories to the score of Squadron 94 were sitting opposite us, grinning with complacency. They were Lieutenant Jeffers and Lieutenant Kaye.

XXXII

A Regular Dogfight

On the afternoon of 10 October, Squadron 94 received orders to destroy two very bothersome enemy balloons, one of which was located at Dun-sur-Meuse, the other at Aincreville. The time for this attack was fixed for us at 3:50 p.m. sharp. A formation of defending planes from Squadron 147 was directed to cover our left wing while a similar formation from Squadron 27 was given the same position on our right. I was placed in command of the expedition and was to arrange all minor details.

Selecting Lieutenants Coolidge and Chambers to act as the balloon executioners, I sent orders to all the pilots who were to accompany our secret raid to assemble their formation at 3,000 feet above Montfaucon at precisely 3:40. Then, with Coolidge and Chambers ahead of us, the united force would proceed first to the Dun balloon, where we would protect the two strafers against enemy aeroplanes while they went in to attack their objective. Then, after destroying the first, if circumstances permitted, we should proceed on to Aincreville, destroy that balloon, and beat a retreat straight for home. If Coolidge and Chambers encountered any hostile aircraft they were instructed to avoid fighting, but retire immediately to our formation.

A clear afternoon made it certain that the German machines would be thick about us. According to our secret intelligence reports, the enemy had here concentrated the heaviest air force against the Americans that had ever been gathered together since the war began. Both the von Richthofen Circus and the Loerzer Circus[1] were now opposed to us, and we had almost daily seen the well-known red noses of the one and the yellow-bellied fuselages of the other. Also, we had distinguished the checkerboard design of the Jagdstaffel No. 3 and the new scout machines that had lately been sent to the front—the Siemens-Schuckert, which was driven by a four-bladed propeller and which had a much faster climb than had the Spad.[2]

This heavy consolidation of enemy aircraft along our front was necessary to the Germans for two reasons. Their retreating infantry must hold the Meuse front until they had time to withdraw their troops from Belgium and the north, or the latter would be cut off; secondly, the allied bombing squadrons that were now terrifying the Rhine towns were all located along this front and must be prevented from destroying those

[1]One of the greatest German Aces, Bruno Loerzer, was a close friend of Hermann Goering. Loerzer later became a high-ranking officer in the Luftwaffe during WWII.

[2]The Siemens-Schuckert D-IV, an excellent one-seat fighter plane introduced by the Germans in August 1918. Powered by a new, improved rotary engine, it was highly maneuverable and had outstanding climbing ability. Jasta 3, mentioned here, typified the caliber of the German flyers now facing the Americans, being an elite unit with eighty-three confirmed victories.

Prussian cities so dear to the German heart. General Trenchard of the British Independent Air Force proved he was right when he demonstrated that his bombing of enemy cities would necessarily withdraw from the battlefront much of the enemy's air strength to defend those helpless cities against such attacks.

So it is not necessarily to be believed that Germany was actually in such fright over the appearance of the American airmen that she straightway sent all her best aviators to the Verdun region to oppose us. She really had quite other objects in view. But such a move nevertheless resulted in filling the skies opposite us with the best fighting airmen in the German service. It promised to be a busy month for us.

Fourteen of my Spads then left the ground on 10 October at 3:30 in the afternoon, with eight of 147's machines and seven of those from Squadron 27 taking their places on the right and left of us as arranged. I pushed my Spad No. 1 up several thousand feet above the flotilla to watch their progress over the lines from a superior altitude. The enormous formation below me resembled a huge crawling beetle, Coolidge and Chambers flying in exact position ahead of them to form the stingers.

We arrived over the lines to be welcomed by an outlandish exhibition of Archy's fury, but despite the large target we made, no damage was received, and none of our Spads turned back. Reaching a quieter region inside German territory, I looked about me. There, indeed, was our Dun balloon floating tranquilly in the sunshine. It was 3:40 by my watch. We had but ten minutes to maneuver for position and reach our objective. I looked down at my convoy and found that 147's formation at the left had separated themselves somewhat widely from the others. Then studying the distant horizon I detected a number of specks in the sky, which soon resolved themselves into a group of eleven Fokkers flying in beautiful formation and evidently just risen from their aerodrome at Stenay, a dozen miles beyond Dun. They were approaching from the west and must reach the detached formation of 147's pilots before the rest of my flight could reach them, unless they immediately closed up. I dived down to dip them a signal.

On my way down I glanced around me and saw, approaching us from Metz in quite the opposite direction, another formation of eight Fokkers. Certainly the Germans had wonderful methods of information that enabled them to bring to a threatened point this speedy relief. While I debated an instant as to which danger was the most pressing, I looked below and discovered that the enemy balloon men were engaged in pulling down their observation balloon, which was the object of our attack back of Dun-sur-Meuse. So, they suspected the purpose of our little expedition! It lacked yet a minute or two of the time set for our dash at the balloon, and as I viewed the situation it would not be wise for Coolidge and Chambers to take their departure from our formation until we had disposed of the advancing Fokkers from the west. Accordingly,

I kept my altitude and set my machine toward the rear of the Stenay Fokkers, which I immediately observed wore the red noses of the von Richthofen Circus. They were heading in at the 147 formation that was still separated almost a mile away from our other Spads. Lieutenant Wilbur White of New York was leading 147's pilots. He would have to bear the brunt of the Fokker attack.

Evidently, the Fokker leader scorned to take notice of me as his scouts passed under me and plunged ahead toward White's formation. I let them pass, dipped over sharply, and with accumulated speed bore down on the tail of the last man in the Fokker formation. It was an easy shot and I could not have missed. I was agreeably surprised, however, to see that my first shots had set fire to the fuel tank and that the machine was doomed. I was almost equally gratified the next second to see the German pilot level off his blazing machine and with a sudden leap overboard into space let the Fokker slide safely away without him. Attached to his back and sides was a rope that immediately pulled a dainty parachute from the bottom of his seat. The umbrella opened within a fifty-foot drop and settled him to earth within his own lines.

I was sorry I had no time to watch his spectacular descent. I truly wished him all the luck in the world. It is not a pleasure to see a burning aeroplane descending to earth bearing with it a human being who is being tortured to death. Not unmixed with my relief in witnessing his safe jump was the wonder as to why the Germans had all these humane contrivances and why our own country could not at least copy them to save American pilots from being burned to a crisp!

I turned from this extraordinary spectacle in midair to witness another that in all my life at the front I have never seen equaled in horror and awfulness. The picture of it has haunted my dreams during many nights since.

Upon seeing that my man was hit I immediately turned up to retain my superiority in height over the other Germans. Now as I came about and saw the German pilot leap overboard with his parachute, I saw that a general fight was on between the remaining ten Fokkers and the eight Spads of Squadron 147. The Fokker leader had taken on the rear Spad in White's formation when White zoomed up into a half-turn, executed a *renversement* and came back at the leader to protect his pilot from a certain death. White was one of the finest pilots and best air fighters in our group. He had won seven victories in combat. His pilots loved him and considered him a great leader, which he most assuredly was. White's maneuver occupied but an instant. He came out of his swoop and made a direct plunge for the enemy machine, which was just getting in line on the rear Spad's tail. Without firing a shot, the heroic White rammed the Fokker head on while the two machines were approaching each other at the [combined] rate of 250 miles per hour!

It was a horrible yet thrilling sight. The two machines actually telescoped each other, so violent was the impact. Wings went through wings and at first glance both the Fokker and Spad seemed to disintegrate. Fragments filled the air for a moment, then the two broken fuselages, bound together by the terrific collision, fell swiftly down and landed in one heap on the bank of the Meuse!

For sheer nerve and bravery, I believe this heroic feat was never surpassed. No national honor too great could compensate the family of Lieutenant White for this sacrifice for his comrade pilot and his unparalleled example of heroism to his squadron. For the most pitiable feature of Lieutenant White's self-sacrifice was the fact that this was his last flight over the lines before he was to leave for the United States on a visit to his wife and two small children. Not many pilots enter the service with loved ones so close to them![3]

This extraordinary disaster ended the day's fighting for the German airmen. No doubt they valued their own leader as much as we did Lieutenant White, or perhaps they got a severe attack of "windup" at witnessing the new method of American attack. At any rate, they withdrew and we immediately turned our attention to the fight that was now in progress between the Spads of Squadron 27 at our right and the enemy formation from Metz. It looked like a famous dogfight.

[3]This paragraph contains a veiled but mordant commentary on the fact that White, who was recommended for the Medal of Honor for his valor in this action, received only an Oak Leaf Cluster citation added to a Distinguished Service Cross he had already won. Remarkably, the German pilot bailed out and survived.

As I came about and headed for the mix-up, I glanced below me at Dun and was amazed to see one of our Spads *piquéing* on the nested balloon through a hurricane of flaming projectiles. A "flaming onion" had pierced his wings and they were now ablaze. To add to his predicament, a German machine was behind his tail, firing as he dived. I diverted my course and started down to his rescue, but it was too late. The fire in his wings was fanned by the wind and made such progress that he was compelled to land in German territory, not far from the site of the balloon. In the meantime other things were happening so rapidly that I had little opportunity to look about me. For even as I started down to help this balloon strafer, I saw another Spad passing me with two Fokkers on his tail, filling his fuselage with tracer bullets as the procession went by. A first glance had identified the occupant of the Spad as my old protégé—the famous Jimmy Meissner! For the third time since we had been flying together, Providence had sent me along just in the nick of time to get Jimmy out of trouble. Twice before on the old Nieuports Jimmy had torn off his wings in too sudden a flip and his unscrupulous antagonists had been about to murder him as he wobbled along, when I happened by. Now, after a four-month interlude, Jimmy comes sailing by again, smiling and good-natured as ever, with two ugly brutes on his tail trying their best to execute him.

I quickly tacked onto the procession, settling my sights into the rear machine and letting go a long burst as I came within range. The one opponent fell off and dropped down out of control, the other Fokker immediately pulling away and diving steeply for home and safety.

Two other Fokkers fell in that dogfight, neither of which I happened to see. Both Coolidge and Chambers, though they had been cheated of their balloon, brought down a Fokker apiece, which victories were later confirmed. The Spad that had dropped down into German hands after being set afire by the flaming onions belonged to Lieutenant [William E.] Brotherton, like White and Meissner, a member of Squadron 147.

Four more victories were thus added to 94's score by this afternoon's work. We did not get the balloons but we had done the best we could. I was never in favor of attacking observation balloons in full daylight and this day's experience—the aroused suspicions of the observers, the pulling down of the balloon as strong aeroplane assistance arrived at the same time, and the fate of Lieutenant Brotherton, who tried unsuccessfully to pass through the defensive barrage—is a fair illustration, I believe, of the difficulties attending such daylight strafings. Just at dawn or just at dusk is the ideal time for surprising the *Drachen*.

Our captured Hannover machine, it will be recalled, had been brought back to our aerodrome and by now was in good condition to fly. We left the Maltese Cross and all their markings exactly as we found them and after telephoning about to various American aerodromes in our vicinity that they must not practice target shooting at a certain Hannover aeroplane that they might encounter while wandering over our part of the country, we took the machine up to see how it flew. The Hannover was a staunch heavy craft and had a speed of about 100 miles an hour when two men (a pilot and an observer) were carried. She handled well and was able to slow down to a very comfortable speed at landing.

Then it became a popular custom to let some pilot get aloft in her and as he began to clear the ground, half a dozen of us in Spads would rise after him and practice *piquéing* down as if in an attack. The Hannover pilot would twist and turn and endeavor to do his best to outmaneuver the encircling Spads. Of course, the lighter fighting machines always had the best of these mock battles, but the experience was good for all of us, both in estimating the extent of the maneuverability of the enemy two-seaters and in the testing of our relative speeds and climbings.

While engaged in one of these mock combats over our field one afternoon we came down to find Captain [Merian ?] Cooper,[4] the official movie picture expert,

[4]It has been assumed that this person was Merian C. Cooper, an adventurer, explorer, journalist, and cinematic pioneer who later became famous for producing such films as *King Kong, Stagecoach,* and *The Quiet Man.* Further research, however, casts doubt on this assumption. Merian Cooper, a member of the 20th Bombardment Squadron, was wounded in action on 26 September 1918 and became a prisoner of war. He was apparently still a captive when the mock battle was filmed. It is therefore unclear who "Captain Cooper" was. For advice on this matter, the editor is grateful to Col. David T. Zabecki.

standing below watching us. He had his camera with him and had been attempting to grind out some movie films while we were flying overhead. He spent the night with us and after some planning of the scenario, we decided to take him up in the rear seat of a Liberty aeroplane and let him catch with his camera a real movie of an aeroplane combat in midair. All the details carefully arranged, we gathered next morning on the field, put him in the rear seat of the Liberty, and helped him strap in his camera so that the pressure of the wind would not carry it overboard. Jimmy Meissner was to be his pilot. Jimmy climbed in the front seat, warmed up his motor and when everything was ready and we other "actors" were sitting in our seats waiting for him to get away, Jimmy gave the signal, opened up his motor, and began to taxi over the grass. Several hundred feet down the field he turned back, facing the wind, which was blowing from the west. Here he prepared for his real takeoff. His machine rushed along with ever-quickening speed until the tail lifted, the wheels next skimmed the ground, and the Liberty rose gradually into the air. Just as they approached the road that skirts the west side of the aerodrome, the Liberty's engine stopped. A line of wires ran along the roadside some fifteen feet above ground. Jimmy saw them and attempted to zoom over them—but in vain. The Liberty crashed full in the middle of the highway, bounded up a dozen feet, and after a half-somersault stuck her nose in the ground the other side of the road and came to a rest.

We hurried over, expecting to find the occupants badly injured, as the Liberty herself appeared to be a total wreck. But out stepped Jimmy and Captain Cooper, neither of them the worse for this experience. And to complete our surprise, the camera, although covered with the debris of the machine, was quite unhurt!

That ended our little movie show for this day. We had no other two-seater machine on hand. But we were delighted to find that Captain Cooper, in spite of his narrow escape, was quite determined to go through with the show. So we went to the supply station for another machine and again put the captain up for the night while awaiting its coming.

XXXIII

An Aeroplane Movie Show

THE NEW LIBERTY duly arrived and, after a brief rehearsal of our parts in the coming show, we again had our machines run out on the field on the morning of 21 October and took our stations in the line. Captain Cooper was again placed in the rear seat of the Liberty, with Jimmy Meissner in the front seat acting as his pilot. Jimmy was to keep his machine as near the actors as possible, always flying to the left side, so that the photographer might face the show and keep his handle turning with the least possible difficulty.

Reed Chambers sat in the front seat of the captured Hannover and piloted it. He carried two guns that would fire only tracer and flaming bullets.

In the rear seat of the Hannover sat Thorne Taylor, the villain of the play. He too had a gun, one that swung on a *tournelle* and which would emit a most fearsome amount of smoky and fiery projectiles when the climax of the action was reached. As a clever *pièce de résistance,* Thorne carried with him, down out of sight of the camera until the proper time came, a dummy German pilot stuffed with straw. At the height of the tragedy, Thorne was supposed to duck himself down out of sight behind his cockpit and heave overboard the stuffed figure, which would fall with outstretched arms and legs, head over heels to earth. This would portray the very acme of despair of the German aviators, who, it would be seen, preferred to hurl themselves out to deliberate death rather than longer face the furious assaults of the dashing young American air fighters.

As to the latter—I was supposed to be *it*. In my old Spad No. 1, with the Hat-in-the-Ring insignia plainly inscribed on the sides of the fuselage and the red, white, and blue markings along and tail sufficiently glaring to prove to the most skeptical movie fan that this was indeed a genuine United States aeroplane— I was to be Jack, the Giant Killer, with an abundance of smoky and fiery stuff pouring from all of my guns every time the monstrous hostile machine hove in sight. Films of a distant formation passing through the sky had been taken early in the game so as to delude the innocent public into the belief that I was going up to demolish the whole caravan with my one resistless machine. A series of falls and *vrilles* would put the one Hannover out of the fighting enough times to account for a whole formation of them. Then as the last desperate encounter took place, Thorne Taylor, after shooting all his spectacular ammunition well over my head, would force the dummy to commit suicide rather than longer endure the suspense of waiting.

It was a clever plot. The whole aerodrome was in raptures over the idea and everybody left off work to gather on the field to witness the contest. I doubt if the later performances will ever have a more expectant, more interested, or so large an audience.

Rickenbacker with the captured Hannover

Jimmy and his camera operator got away safely this time, and right behind them the comedian and tragedians of the show winged their way. Arriving at 2,000 feet above the field we pulled up our belts and began the performance. It was necessary to keep an eye on the camera, so as not to get out of its beam while pulling off our most priceless stunts, and at the same time we had to be a little careful as to the direction in which our bullets were going. Captain Cooper was thrusting his head out into the windstream, manfully trying to keep my swifter-moving machine always within the eye of his camera. As I came up under the Hannover aeroplane's tail I would let off a terrific stream of flaming projectiles that are perfectly visible to the naked eye and certainly ought to be caught by a camera even in the daytime. Thorne shot as lustily under me and over me as I approached and even Reed's front guns were spitting death in a continuous stream at the imaginary enemy planes ahead of him.

Over and over we repeated the performance, the Hannover dying a dozen deaths in as many minutes. Our movie ammunition nearing exhaustion, it became necessary to stage a big hit that denoted the climax of the play. Coming about above the Hannover, while Captain Cooper was grinding industriously away not over twenty feet from its side, I came down in a swift *piqué,* made a zoom and a *renversement* on the opposite side of the Hannover, and kicking my rudder over came back directly at the enemy, full into the gaping lens of the camera. Firing my last rounds of ammuni-

tion as I approached, I saw them go safely over the tops
of both machines. As I drew in to the closest possible
distance that remained safe for such a maneuver,
I threw my Spad up into a zoom, passed over the
vanquished German and came back in a loop somewhere near my original position. As I glanced at the
Hannover I saw that she was doomed! A quantity of
lampblack, released by the crafty Taylor, was drifting
windward, indicating that something seriously wrong
had occurred with the enemy machine. Such a dense
cloud of smoke would satisfy the dullest intellect that
he must soon begin to suspect fire. Ah, ha! There she
comes! I knew she was afire! Sure enough, several
bright landing flares suddenly ignited under the Hannover's wings throwing a bright gleam earthward but
prevented from injuring the wings themselves by the
tin surfaces above them. Finding longer existence on
such a burning deck utterly unendurable, the poor
dummy gathered himself together in the arms of the
stalwart Taylor and with one tremendous leap he departed the blazing furnace forever!

While Taylor kept himself resolutely hidden below
decks, Chambers, throwing out the last of his sack of
lampblack, lifted over onto the side the doomed machine and gave a good exhibition of the falling leaf.[1]
Down—down it drifted, the daring photographer lean-
ing far out of his cage to catch the last expiring gasps
of the stricken Hannover—the last of the wicked formation of hostile machines that had dared to cross

[1]"Falling leaf": a maneuver designed to trick an opponent into

our frontiers early in the picture. And then—just then—the real climax of the play did appear.

We had necessarily wandered some little distance away from the vicinity of our aerodrome while firing genuine flaming bullets over each other, so that the falling missiles would not cause any injuries to property or persons below. Paying little attention as to just where we were flying so long as open country was below us, we had not noticed that we were some miles south and west of our starting place and almost immediately over the edge of a French aerodrome. Suddenly a puff of real Archy smoke in the vicinity of the Hannover told me that some enthusiastic outsider was volunteering his services in behalf of our little entertainment. Another and another shell burst before I could reverse my direction and get started to place my Spad close to the black machine wearing the Iron Cross of the Kaiser. Reed Chambers took in the situation at a glance. He pointed down the Hannover's nose and began at once to descend for a landing on the French aerodrome. At the same moment, several French aircraft left the field and began climbing up to assist me in my task of demolishing the Hannover.

Diving down to intervene between them before any more shooting was done, I succeeded in satisfying the Frenchmen that I had the affair well in hand and that the Hannover was coming down to surrender. Without

---

believing that one's plane had been disabled and was falling out of control.

further incident we all landed and got out of our machines. The French pilots, their mechanics, and *poilus* gathered about in a curious body while I laughingly hurried over to the side of Reed's machine and explained to the assembly the meaning of this strange performance. They all laughed heartily over their mistake—all except Reed and Thorne Taylor of the Hannover crew who, from the expressions seen on their faces, seemed to admit that the joke was on them.

Getting away again, the Hannover flew home under my protection. After it had landed, I climbed up through the clouds where Jimmy and the movie man were still waiting for me. There I stunted for a while in front of the camera, giving some excellent views of an aeroplane bursting through the clouds and some close-up views of all the aerial tumbling that a Spad is capable of performing.

Next day, Captain Cooper departed with his films for Paris, where he expected to turn them over to the American authorities, and if permitted, take a copy of them for public exhibition in Paris and the United States. A day or two after Christmas, on my way through Paris to New York, I learned that these pictures had turned out very well and would soon be shown in the movie palaces of the cities of America.

The captured Hannover was flown into the American Station at Orly, near Paris, a few days after the Armistice was signed, and from there was shipped to America to be placed on exhibition. Major Hartney and Laurence L. Driggs, of New York, who were visiting us at that time, flew in it from Verdun to Paris in a little less than an hour and a half. One captured Fokker machine and an escort of two Sopwith Camels and one Spad accompanied them, for the enemy machines still carried the war markings of the German Air Service, and inquisitive Frenchmen along the way might be tempted to try to capture them a second time. So far as I know, these were the only two enemy aeroplanes captured by the American forces during the war. The Fokker came down upon our field at Verdun just a day or two before the end of hostilities, and was turned over to Squadron 95 as their capture, since they operated this field. The pilot had given himself up, saying he thought he was landing on his own aerodrome at Metz. He had become lost in the fog, and as the two aerodromes are similarly situated along the edge of a river's course, his mistake was probable.

The following afternoon I escaped assassination by four red-nosed Fokkers by the narrowest margin ever vouchsafed to a pilot, and at the end of the combat flew safely home with my twenty-first and twenty-second victories to my credit. Curiously enough, I had gone out over the lines alone that day with a craving desire to get a thrill. I had become "fed up" with a continuation of eventless flights. Saying nothing to any of my fellows at the aerodrome, I went off alone with an idea of shooting down a balloon that I thought might be hanging just north of Montfaucon. While I did not get a shot at the balloon, I got the thrill I needed for several days to come.

It was about 5:30 in the afternoon when I ordered out my machine and set off for Montfaucon. As I neared the Meuse valley, I found the whole vicinity was covered with a thick haze—so thick, in fact, that the Germans had hauled down all their observation balloons. There was nothing a mile away that could be observed until another day dawned. Over to the south the sky was clearer. Our own balloons were still up. But no enemy aeroplanes would be likely to come over our front again so late in the evening.

While I was reflecting thus sadly, a bright blaze struck my eye from the direction of our nearest balloon. I headed around toward this spot in the shortest possible space of time. There could be but one explanation for such a blaze. A late-roving German must have just crossed the lines and had made a successful attack on our balloon over Exermont! He ought to be an easy victim, I told myself, as soon as he should start to cross back into Germany since I was on his direct road to the nearest point in his lines. He was now coming my way. Though I could not see him, I did see the bursting Archy shells following his course northward. He must pass considerably under me, and no doubt would be quite alone.

Just then a series of zipping streams of fire flashed by my face and through my fuselage and wings! I divined, rather than saw, what this was without looking around. Two or perhaps more than two enemy machines were *piquéing* on me from above. Utterly absorbed in planning what I should do to catch the other fellow, I had been perfectly blind to my own surroundings. The balloon strafer had a protective formation waiting for him. They had seen me come over and doubtless been stalking me for many minutes without my knowing it.

These thoughts flashed through my mind as I almost automatically zoomed up and did a climbing *chandelle* to escape the tracer bullets. I did not even stop to look at the position of my assailants. Knowing they were above, I concluded instantly that they had prepared for my diving away from them, and therefore that would be the best thing for me to avoid. I fortunately had reasoned correctly. As I sped upward, two red-nosed Fokkers, my old friends of the von Richthofen Circus, sped down and passed me. But even before I had time enough to congratulate myself on my sagacity, I discovered that only half of them had passed me. Two more Fokkers had remained above on the chance that I might refuse to adopt the plan they had determined for me.

One glimpse of the skillful contortions of these two upper Fokkers showed me that I was in for the fight of my life. I lost all interest in the progress or existence of the balloon strafer that had destroyed one of our balloons under my very nose. My one dearest desire was to get away off by myself, where thrills were never mentioned and were impossible to get. The masterly way in which the Fokkers met and even anticipated every movement that I made assured me that I had four very experienced pilots with whom to deal.

Zigzagging and sideslipping helped me not one whit and I felt that I was getting a wind up that would only sap my coolness and soon make me the easy prey of these four extremely confident aviators. The two machines that had first attacked me impudently remained below me in such a position that they invited my attack, while also preventing my escape in their direction. I made up my mind to start something before it was too late. Even though it meant getting into trouble, I decided that would be better than waiting around for them to operate on me as they had no doubt been practicing in so many rehearsals. Noting a favorable opening for an attack on the nearest man below me, I suddenly tipped over at him and went hurtling down with all my speed, shooting from both guns.

I had aimed ahead of him, instead of directly at him, to compel him either to pass ahead through the path of my bullets or else dip down his nose or fall over onto his wing—in either case providing me with a fair target before he could get far away. He either preferred the former course or else did not see my bullets until it was too late. He ran straight through my line of fire and he left it with a gush of flame issuing from his fuel tank. I fully believe that several bullets passed through the pilot's body as well.

Considerably bucked up with this success I did not seize this opportunity to escape, but executed blindly a sudden loop and *renversement,* under the strongest impression that my two enemies above would certainly be close on my tail and preparing to shoot. Again

I had guessed correctly, for not only were they in just the position I expected to find them, and just where I, myself, would have been were I in their places, but they were also startled out of their senses over my sudden and unexpected assault on their comrade. It is never an encouraging sight to see a comrade's machine falling in flames. It is sufficient to make the stoutest heart quail unless one is hemmed in and is fighting for his very life. But however that may be, my three neighbors did not turn to continue the combat with me, nor did they even pause for an instant to threaten my pursuit. All three continued their headlong dive for Germany with a faster and heavier Spad machine following them and gaining on them every second.[2] My blood was up and I considered that I had been badly treated by the red-nosed Germans. I was three miles inside their lines, other enemy machines might very easily be about—I had no time to look about to see—and I had just escaped from the very worst trap into which I had ever fallen. Yet I could not resist the mad impulse of paying back the three Germans for the scare they had so recently given me.

Though the Spad is faster than even the Fokker, the fleeing planes had a slight start over me and I did not immediately overtake them. One of the three gradually fell back behind the others. The ground was getting nearer and nearer and it was growing very much

[2]Because Rickenbacker's identity was well known to the Germans, the large numeral 1 on his Spad may have helped induce their hasty retreat.

darker as we approached the earth's surface. At about 1,000 feet above ground I decided the nearest Fokker was within my range. I opened fire, following his gyrations as he maneuvered to avoid my ever-nearing stream of lead. After letting go at him some 200 bullets, his machine dropped out of control and I ceased firing. His two companions had never slackened their pace and were now well out of sight in the shadows. I watched my latest antagonist flutter down and finally crash, and then awoke to the fact that I was being fired at by hundreds of guns from the ground. The gunners and riflemen were so near to me that I could distinctly see their guns pointed in my direction. I had dropped down to within 100 yards of earth.

All the way back to the lines I was followed by machine-gun bullets and some Archy. Absolutely untouched, I continued on to my field, where I put in my claim for two enemy Fokkers, and after seeing to the wounds of my faithful Spad, walked over to the 94 for supper.

XXXIV

An Overzealous Ally

W AR FLYING is much like other business—one gets
accustomed to all the incidents that attend its
daily routine, its risks, its thrills, its dangers, its good
and bad fortune. A strange sort of fatalism fastens to
the mind of an aviator who continues to run the gauntlet of Archy. He flies through bursting shells without
trying to dodge them, with indeed little thought of
their menace. If a bullet or shell has his name written
on it there is no use trying to avoid contact with it. If
it has not—why worry?

On Sunday, 27 October, only a fortnight before the
end of the war, Hamilton Coolidge, one of the best pilots and most respected men in the American air service, met an annihilating death from a direct hit by an
Archy shell in full flight. The shell had not yet burst
when it struck the Spad in which Coolidge was sitting.
The aeroplane was moving forward at its usual fast
speed when the mounting shell, probably traveling at
the speed of 3,000 feet per second, struck squarely
under the center of the aeroplane's engine. Poor
Coolidge must have been killed instantly. The Spad
flew into fragments and the unfortunate pilot dropped
like a stone to the ground.

Coolidge was one of the very top-score Aces of

Squadron 94 and one of the most popular men in the service. A graduate of Groton and later of Harvard, he possessed all the qualifications of leadership and a brilliant career in any profession he might have chosen to adopt. In his work at the front he never shirked and never complained. The loss of Lieutenant Hamilton Coolidge was one of the severest that we had been called on to suffer.

It was beginning to be a matter of constant conjecture among us as to just what day Germany would cave in and surrender. The collapse of Austria and the constant and obvious weakening of the German troops opposite our sector were well known to us. Hence it seemed doubly bitter that Ham Coolidge would meet death now, just as the end of the war was at hand. Especially tragic was it to all of us who knew Coolidge's fighting ability that he should be the one airman who should meet his end in this incredible manner. More than one pilot bitterly remarked that no German airman could down Ham Coolidge, so they had to kill him by a miracle!

And miracle it was, for no other American pilot, and only one or two other aviators during the whole course of the war were shot down from on high by an Archy in full flight. The shell had Hamilton's name written on it and there was no escape!

Coolidge, with his usual intrepidity, was hurrying in to the assistance of a formation of American Liberty bombing machines which, after dropping their eggs on the enemy town of Grandpré, as they started home, were in turn attacked by a large number of swifter-flying Fokker machines. The Archy shells were directed at the bombers and not at the Spad of Ham Coolidge! After having scornfully passed through hundreds of barrages that were aimed at him, our unlucky Ace had collided with a shell not intended for him!

Although I did not see this ghastly accident to poor Coolidge, I was in the midst of the same barrage of Archy on the other side of Grandpré at the same time. During the combats that followed, I again succeeded in bringing down two of the red-nosed Fokkers. The first victim was on my tail when I first noticed him. With one backward loop I had reversed our positions and had my nose on *his* tail. One short burst from both my guns and he tumbled down through space to crash a few miles within the German lines.

The second combat occurred just a few minutes later. The last of the Liberty bombing machines had passed over the lines or had crashed in flames and I thought the day's work was over when I noticed something going on to the east of me in the region of Bantheville. I began climbing and speeding forward to get a look at this performance when, to my surprise, I discerned that one of the Liberty machines had been left behind and was in very evident distress. Fortunately there was but a single enemy Fokker on his tail. The Yankee pilot was kicking his machine about, and the gunner at the rear was managing to keep his enemy at bay when, at a favorable elevation above them both, I found an opportunity to *piqué* down and catch the

Fokker unaware of my approach. The Liberty motor, I discovered, was almost dud. It had either been struck by a bullet or had developed some interior trouble of its own. The pilot had all he could do to maintain headway and avoid the maneuvers of his enemy. Each time he banked the Liberty, it fell downward 200 or 300 feet. The Fokker had only to worry him enough and the American machine must drop into German territory, a captive.

As I began firing, the German pilot, who had been so intent on the capture of his prize that he had forgotten to watch his rear, zoomed suddenly up to let me pass under him. But that was too old a dodge to entrap me. I began a similar zoom just a fraction of a second before he started his and I was the first to come out—on top. As I again prepared to open fire I saw a curious sight. The Fokker with a red nose had not been able to complete his loop. He had stalled just at the moment he was upright on his tail, and in this position he was now hanging. And more extraordinary still, his engine had stalled and his propeller was standing absolutely still. I could see the color and laminations of the wood, so close had I approached to my helpless victim.

On 10 March 1918, there is the following entry in my flight diary: "Resolved today that hereafter I will never shoot a Hun who is at a disadvantage, regardless of what he would do if he were in my position."

Just what episode influenced me to adopt that principle and even to enter it into my diary I have forgotten. That was very early in my fighting days and I had then had but few combats in air. But with American flyers, the war has always been more or less a sporting proposition and the desire for fair play—the anger it always arouses in a true American to see any violation of fair play—prevents a sportsman from looking at the matter in any other light, even though it be a case of life or death. However that may be, I do not recall a single violation of this principle by any American aviator that I should care to call my friend.[1]

My Fokker enemy was now in a very ludicrous position. Of course he could not continue hanging on there forever with his nose pointing upward, his tail to the ground and his propeller dead.[2] He began falling with a tailslip. He was wondering why I didn't finish him or at least didn't begin some attack so that he might know which way to head his last dive. We were more than 10,000 feet above ground, and looking down I saw that we were still two or three miles within German lines. Naturally enough, the pilot will turn his nose homeward when he falls far enough to get headway for a glide. Accordingly I kept control of

[1]This paragraph has no counterpart in the original text, and was added by Driggs to increase the book's appeal to the American readers.

[2]One of the most remarkable features of the Fokker D-VII was its ability to hang on its whirling propeller in a near-vertical position while spraying an opponent with bullets from underneath. As the original text indicates, however, the plane immediately began falling when its engine stopped. Through skillful writing, Driggs gives the impression that the Fokker hung momentarily in the air.

the situation by heading him off and firing a few shots to show him that I did not mean to let him escape.

Now the tables are turned. Instead of my Fokker friend nursing homeward to Germany a captured and crippled American machine, I am endeavoring to impress upon him that an American is desirous of escorting back to the American lines a slightly crippled but very famous Fokker with a red nose. What a triumphant entry I will make with one of Baron von Richthofen's celebrated fighting planes! I picture the flights over our field I will make with my prize tomorrow. The pilot was satisfied that I had the upper hand and he was gliding along in the proper direction with admirable docility. We should clear the lines by at least five miles. I could steer him from behind by firing a few bursts ahead, which had the effect of pushing him over in the direction I wanted him to go. It was as simple as driving a tame horse to the creek.

Over the lines we passed with the Fokker gliding steadily along ahead of me, no other aeroplanes in the sky. Under the impression that I knew this country better than my companion might know it, I compelled him to steer for the Exermont field, which lay just about four miles behind our front-line trench. He willingly complied, immediately heading in the desired direction and apparently quite content to play fair with me and spare me his Fokker, since I had spared him his life. Of course, I was fully aware that he might attempt to set fire to his machine as soon as he touched the ground. I should have done the same had I been in his place. But I did not intend that he should have this opportunity. With his dead engine he could not change his course once he began to settle to the ground. I would put myself immediately behind him and if he attempted to do any injury to his aeroplane I would shoot him on the spot. With this plan in mind I left him a moment when he was making his last circle over the field at about 300 feet altitude and withdrew so that I might turn and land my machine in such a position that he must come to a stop just ahead of me. And then I received one of the worst disappointments of my whole life.

A Spad aeroplane suddenly appeared from out of the sky just as I turned away from my convoy. The unknown idiot in the Spad began firing a long burst into my helpless captive. I did not suspect his presence until I heard him firing. Whipping madly back, I *piquéd* down and intervened between the malignant Spad and my protégé, even firing a short burst to warn the intruder away. The latter understood me well enough, for he left us and did not return. The marks on his machine were not familiar to me and to this day I do not know whether this interfering person was an American or a Frenchman. But whichever he was, he had absolutely ruined all my chances of a capture.

The Fokker pilot had been at the outside of his turn when this unexpected attack was received. The Spad had headed him off, compelling him to turn to the right instead of to the left in the direction of the field. Now he was so low that it would be suicide to attempt to make the field. Trees and rough ground were beneath him and the only safe course would be to pancake as flatly as possible in the rough open ground directly ahead of him. All my hopes vanished as I saw the nature of his landing place. I circled above him until after the crash. He had overshot his mark a little and ended up against the edge of the opposite bit of woods.

I saw the pilot disentangle himself from the wreckage and walk out on the ground. An officer on horseback and some of our doughboys were advancing on the run to make him a prisoner. He waved his thanks to me as I passed overhead and I waved back in the most friendly manner. Returning home I was somewhat mollified to learn that my belated commission as captain had just arrived. I had been acting captain for several weeks and had been told that my commission was on its way, but these rumors often proved unfounded. But it had arrived at last and I would this night add an extra bar to each shoulder. And then I was told of the awful loss of poor Hamilton Coolidge. Surviving six months of very active flying over enemy's lines, fighting nearly 100 combats and escaping without a single wound while he brought down confirmed eight enemy aeroplanes, our gallant comrade had been suddenly swept away by a catastrophe that appalled us to contemplate!

Early next morning I secured a staff car and proceeded up to the front to find the spot where lay the last remains of my dear friend. We reached Montfaucon and turned northwest around the edge of the Argonne Forest, passing on the way the wreckage of my red-nosed Fokker just outside the town of Exermont. Arrived to within a mile of our front line, sheltered all along the road by hanging curtains of burlap and moss, part of which had been left by the Germans and partly our own concoction of camouflage, we were halted by an officer who told me we could move no farther without coming under shellfire from the enemy guns.

Abandoning the car at the roadside, we skirted the edge of some woods that adjoined the road and made our way on foot to the flat lands just across the Aire River from the opposite town of Grandpré. And here, in the bend of the Aire, almost in full sight of the enemy, we came upon the body of Captain Coolidge. A lieutenant in infantry who had seen the whole spectacle and had marked down the spot where Ham's body had fallen, accompanied us and it was through his very kind offices that we reached the exact spot without much searching. The chaplain of his regiment likewise accompanied us. And there, not sixty yards behind our front lines, we watched the men dig a grave. The chaplain administered the last sad rites. Amid the continuous whines of passing shells we laid the poor mangled body of Hamilton Coolidge in its last resting place. Over the grave was placed a cross suitably engraved with his name, rank, and the date of his tragic death. A wreath of flowers was laid at the foot of the cross. And with uncovered head, I then took a photograph of the grave, which later was sent "back home" to the family who mourned for one of the most gallant gentlemen who ever fought in France.

XXXV

The End Draws Near

OCTOBER was a month of glorious successes for Squadron 94, having brought us thirty-nine victories with but five losses. For, besides Coolidge and Lieutenant [Alan] Nutt, the squadron had also lost Lieutenant [Raymond J.] Saunders of Billings, Montana, shot down on 22 October, when out after balloons with Cook and Jeffers. Cook on this occasion succeeded in setting fire to the balloon he was attacking, and Jeffers, turning on the Fokker that had just sunk Saunders, shot him down in flames some sixty seconds later.

On 29 October, Lieutenant [Edward G.] Garnsey of Grand Haven, Michigan, fell in our lines near Exermont, after having fought a brilliant combat against greatly superior numbers. Reed Chambers, after bringing down an enemy machine on 22 October, which he attacked at the tail of a Fokker formation containing five aeroplanes, returned to the aerodrome in considerable pain from a sudden seizure of appendicitis and next day was sent to the hospital, where he had the appendix removed.

The squadron had developed eight Aces, including Lufbery, Campbell, Coolidge, Meissner, and Chambers, all of whom were now absent, and Cook, Taylor, and me, who were left to carry on to the end of the war. Meissner was absent only in the sense that he was now in command of Squadron 147, and his victories were going to swell the score for his new squadron instead of our own.

Many others were "going strong" at the end of October, and needed but the opportunity to fight their way up into the leading scores of the group. Rain and dud weather kept us on the ground much of the time, and when we did get away for brief patrols, we found the enemy machines were even more particular about flying in bad weather than we were. None put in an appearance and we were forced to return empty-handed so far as fighting laurels were concerned.

Our first Night-Flying Squadron had been formed early in October, under command of Captain Seth Low of New York,[1] and had its hangars on our group aerodrome. This was not a squadron of bomb-carrying aeroplanes, but one with which to attack bombing machines of the enemy and prevent their reaching their intended targets over our lines. The night-flying aeroplanes were the English Sopwith Camels, a light single-seater capable of extraordinary evolutions in the air and able to land on the ground in

[1]Organized as a day-fighting unit in mid-August 1918, the 185th became operational on 18 October 1918. Low was in charge until 7 November when Jerry C. Vasconcells replaced him. Due to the hazards involved and unfamiliarity with the Camels, the results of the night fighting were unimpressive, as the following account indicates, and the unit returned unofficially to daytime operations under Vasconcells.

the darkness at a very low speed. The British had in-augurated this special defense against the German bombers in their raids on London. Later the same sys-tem was tried at the British front with such success that a score of German bombers were brought down in a month by one squadron of Night-Flying Camels.

Of course, such a defense must have the coopera-tion both of signaling and listening squads, to notify the Night Flyers as to just when and where an attack is threatened, and also the timely cooperation of the searchlight squads is essential to enable the airmen to pick up the enemy machines in the darkness while at the same time blinding with the glare the eyes of the enemy pilots. Principally by reason of the lack of this cooperation, our Camel Squadron, though it made several sorties along the lines during the month of Oc-tober, did not meet any enemy bombers and had no combats. Time and study of this problem would doubtless have made of the Squadron 185 a valuable defense to our sector of the front, including the cities of Nancy, Toul, and Columbey-les-Belles, which were repeatedly visited at night by German Gothas.[2]

Bombs were getting heavier and more destructive. More and more machines were being devoted to this

---

[2]After Zeppelins proved generally ineffective in strategic bomb-ing, Germany developed a series of large twin-engine bombers, some of which, particularly the famous G-IV, were known as Gothas because they were made by the Gothaer Waggonfabrik AG. Although not all heavy German bombers were Gothas, the name became generic among Allied forces for any German plane of this type.

branch of aviation. But now instead of the German monopolizing this terror-spreading game, the tables were turned, and the Allies dropped ten times the amount of bombs into German cities. Even the oldest residents were moving out of the beautiful Rhine cities.

On the next to the last day of October, I won my twenty-fifth and twenty-sixth victories, which were the last that I saw added to my score. Two others that I had previously brought down were never confirmed. After the deplorable death of Frank Luke, who had won eighteen victories in less than six weeks of active flying at the front, there were no other American air fighters who were rivaling me in my number of victories. But ever since I had been captain of Squadron 94 the spur of rivalry had been entirely supplanted in me by the necessity of illustrating to the pilots under my orders that I would ask them to do nothing that I, myself, would not do. So covetously did I guard this understanding with myself that I took my machine out frequently after the day's patrol was finished and spent another hour or two over the lines. The obligations that must attend leadership were a constant thought to me. Never did I permit any pilot in my squadron to exceed the number of hours flying over the lines that was credited to me in the flight sheets. At the close of the war only Reed Chambers's record approached my own in number of hours spent in the air.[3]

[3]By the end of the war EVR had flown fifty sorties. Chambers, who ranked second among squadron members, had twenty-seven.

I allude to this fact because I am convinced after my six weeks' experience as squadron commander that my obedience to this principle did much to account for the wholehearted and enthusiastic support the pilots of my squadron gave me. And only by their loyalty and enthusiasm was their squadron to lead all the others at the front in number of victories and number of hours over enemy lines.

With Reed Chambers's forced absence at the hospital, the leadership of our First Flight was put in charge of Lieutenant Kaye. On 30 October I had been out on two patrols in the forenoon, both of which had been without unusual incident or result. When Kaye left the field with his flight at three o'clock in the afternoon I decided to accompany him to observe his tactics as flight leader. This formation, composed of only four machines, two of which were piloted by new men, was to fly at only 2,000 feet elevation and was to patrol to enemy lines between Grandpré and Brieulles. I took my place considerably in their rear and perhaps 1,000 feet above them. In this position we reached Brieulles and made two round trips with them between our two towns without discovering any hostile aeroplanes.

As we turned west for the third trip, however, I noticed two lone Fokkers coming out of Germany at a low elevation. From their maneuvers I decided that they were stalking Lieutenant Kaye's flight and were only waiting until they had placed themselves in a favorable position before beginning their attack. I accordingly turned my own machine into Germany to get behind them, keeping my altitude and trusting they would be too intent on the larger quarry to notice me.

I had hardly begun to turn back when I saw that they had set their machines in motion for their attack. Opening up myself I put down my nose and tried to overtake them, but they had too great a start. I saw that Kaye had not seen them, and in spite of the odds in our favor I feared for the two new men who were at the end of the formation and who must assuredly bear the first diving assault of the Fokkers. Fortunately, Kaye saw them coming before they had reached firing range and he immediately turned his formation south in the direction of home. "Cook is with Kaye and those two will be able to defend the two youngsters if the Fokkers really get to close quarters," I thought to myself. I could not hope to overtake them myself, anyway, if they continued back into France. So, after a little reflection I stayed where I was, witnessing a daring attempt of the Fokkers to break up Kaye's formation which, nevertheless, was unsuccessful. Both Fokkers attacked the rear Spad, which was piloted by Lieutenant [Raymond W.] Evitt, one of our new men. Instead of trying to maneuver them off, he continued to fly straight ahead, affording them every opportunity in the world of correcting their aim and getting their bullets home. Evitt discovered on landing that one of his right struts was severed by their bullets!

After this one attack the Fokkers turned back. I was, in the meantime, flying deeper into Germany, keeping one eye on the two enemy machines to discover in which direction they would cross the lines to reach their own side. They seemed in no hurry to get back, but continued westward, heading toward Grandpré. Very well! This suited me perfectly. I would make a great detour, coming back out of Germany immediately over Grandpré with the hope that if they saw me they might believe me to be one of their own until we got to close quarters.

But before I reached Grandpré I noticed them coming toward me. I was then almost over the town of Amenencourt and quite a little distance within their lines. They were very low, and not more than 1,000 feet above the ground at most. I was quite twice this height. Like lambs to the slaughter they came unsuspectingly on, not half a mile to the east of me. Letting them pass, I immediately dipped over, swung around as I fell, and opening up my motor, *piquéd* with all speed on the tail of the nearest Fokker. With less than twenty rounds, all of which poured full into the center of the fuselage, I ceased firing and watched the Fokker drop helplessly to earth. As it began to revolve slowly, I noticed for the first time that again I had outwitted a member of the von Richthofen crowd. The dying Fokker wore a brilliant nosepiece of bright red!

As my first tracer bullets began to streak past the Fokker, his companion put down his nose and dived for the ground. As he was well within his own territory, I did not venture to follow him at this low altitude, but at once began climbing to avoid the coming storm of

Archy and machine-gun fire. Little or none of this came my way, however, and I continued homeward, passing en route over the little village of St. George, which was then about two miles inside the enemy lines. And there, directly under my right wing, lay in its bed a German observation balloon just at the edge of the village. On a sudden impulse I kicked over my rudder, pointed my nose at the huge target, and pulled the triggers. Both guns worked perfectly. I continued my sloping dive to within 100 feet of the sleeping *drachen*, firing up and down its whole length by slightly shifting the course of my aeroplane. Not a human being was in sight! Evidently the Germans thought they were quite safe in this spot, since this balloon had not yet been run up and its location could not be known to our side. I zoomed up and climbed a few hundred feet for another attack if it should be necessary. But as I balanced my machine and looked behind me I saw the fire take effect. These flaming bullets sometimes require a long time to ignite the balloon fabric. Doubtless they traveled too fast to ignite the gas, unmixed with air.

The towering flames soon lit up the sky with a vivid glare and, keeping it behind me, I speeded homeward, with many self-satisfied chuckles at my good fortune. But too much self-satisfaction always receives a jolt. I had not gone ten miles before I received the worst kind of a scare.

It had become quite dark and I was very near to the ground. Still some distance inside the German lines, for I had kept east in the hope that another balloon might be left for my last rounds of ammunition, I thought of looking at my watch to see how late it really was. I had fuel for only two hours and ten minutes. A vague sort of premonition warned me that I had been overlooking something of importance in the past few minutes. One glance at my watch and I realized exactly what had been weighing in the back of my mind. The time indicated that I had now been out exactly two hours and ten minutes.

A real terror seized me for a moment. I was not up far enough above earth to glide for any distance when my motor stopped. Even as I banked over and turned southward I wondered whether my motor would gasp and expire in the turning. I feared to climb and I feared to stay low. I gazed over the sides of my office and tried to make out the nature of the landing ground below. Throttling down to the slowest possible speed to save fuel I crept toward the lines. It was dark enough to see that suspicious soldiers below were shooting at me on the chance that I might be an enemy. Glad I was to see those flashes receding farther and farther to my rear. I had passed the lines somewhere west of Verdun and now must chance any open field I came to when the engine gave its last cough. Why didn't it stop? I wondered. It was now five or six minutes overdue. In miserable anticipation of the lot Fate had in store for me I struggled on, noting with additional gloom that the searchlight that should long ago be pointing out the way to my aerodrome had not been lighted. I could not be more than ten miles from home. Why couldn't those men attend to their business when pilots were known to be out? I took out my Very pistol and fitted in a red light. That would notify them at home that I was in trouble and in a hurry to land.

Just as I fired the second Very light I heard the motor begin its final sputtering. And then just as I felt cold chills running up my back, the blessed landing lights flashed out and I saw I was almost over the field. Forgetting all my recent joy I made myself as wretched as possible the following few seconds in concluding that I could not by any possibility reach the smooth field. It seemed to work—the treatment. I had expatiated my sins of overconfidence and appeased the Goddess of Luck, for I cleared the road, landed with the wind and struck the ground with a quiet thud less than 100 feet from the entrance to 94's hangar—right side up! But I walked over to mess with a chastened spirit.

The following morning was rainy, and all the afternoon it continued to pour. Just before dusk we received orders to have our whole force over the lines at daybreak to protect an infantry advance from Grandpré to Buzancy. We all felt that we were to witness the last great attack of the war. And we were right.

A heavy fog of the genuine Meuse-Valley variety prevented our planes leaving the ground until the middle of the forenoon. All the morning we heard the tremendous artillery duel at the north of us and very impatiently waited for a clearing of the weather. That dull morning was somewhat relieved by our receipt of

newspapers stating that Turkey had surrendered un-
conditionally and that Austria was expected to follow
suit the following day. Placing about 100 of these jour-
nals in my plane, I set out for the lines with our patrol
at 9:30.

Arriving over the front lines I flew at an altitude of
only 100 feet from the ground. And there I saw our
doughboys after their victorious advance of the morning crouching in every available shellhole and lying
several deep in every depression while looking forward for a snipe shot at any enemy's head that came
into view. Others were posted behind woods and
buildings with bayonets fixed, waiting for the word to
go forward. As I passed overhead I threw overboard
handfuls of morning papers to them and was amused
to see how eagerly the doughboys ran out of their
holes to pick them up. With utter disdain for the
nearby snipers, they exposed themselves gladly for
the opportunity of getting the latest news from an aeroplane. I knew the news they would get would repay
them for the momentary risk they ran.

Dropping half my load there I flew on over the
Moselle valley where I distributed the remainder of the
papers among the men in the front-line trenches along
that sector. Returning then to the region of Buzancy I
first caught sight of a huge supply depot burning. A
closer view disclosed the fact that it was German, and
German soldiers were still on the premises. They were
destroying materials that they knew they couldn't save.
They were contemplating a fast retreat.

A few dashes up and down the highways leading to the north quickly confirmed this impression. Every road was filled with lorries and with retreating artillery. All were hurrying toward Longuyon and the German border.

All the way up the Meuse as far as Stenay I found the same rush for the rear. Every road was filled with retreating Germans. They were going while the "going was good" and their very gestures seemed to indicate that for them it was indeed the *"finis de la guerre."* I hurried home to make my report which I felt certain would be welcome to those in authority.

The following day I obtained permission to visit Paris on a three-days' leave. For the first time since I had been in France I found the streets of Paris illuminated at night and unrestrained gaiety possessing the boulevards and cafés. With the Place de la Concorde and the Champs-Elysées crammed with captured German guns and German aeroplanes, with flags and bunting everywhere, it looked here, too, that people thought it was the *"finis de la guerre."* Personally, I am glad that I was with my squadron instead of in Paris on the night the war ended. For great as were the sights there, none of them could have expressed to an aviator such a view of the sentiment and feeling of aviation over the termination of this game of killing as was exhibited at our own aerodrome on the night the official order "Cease Firing!" came to us.

XXXVI

Last Victory of the Great War

Rᴇᴛᴜʀɴɪɴɢ from Paris on 5 November I found it still raining. Almost no flying had been possible along this sector since my departure. In fact, no patrol left our field until 8 November, the same day on which we caught by wireless the information that the German delegates had crossed the lines to sign the Armistice. Peace was actually in sight.

For weeks there had been a feeling in the air that the end of the war was near. Such a certainty of victory should have operated to produce a desire to live and let live among men who were desirous of "seeing the end of the war," that is, men who preferred to survive rather than run the risks of combat fighting now that the war was fairly over.

But it was at this very period of my leadership of Squadron 94 that I found my pilots most infatuated with fighting. They importuned me for permission to go out at times when a single glance at the fog and rain showed the foolishness of such a request.

On 9 November Lieutenant [John] Dewitt and Captain [Cedric G.] Fauntleroy came to me after lunch and begged me to go to the door of my hut and look at the weather with them. I laughed at them but did as they requested. It was dark and windy outside, heavy, low clouds driving across the sky, though for the moment no rain was falling. I took a good look around the heavens and came back to my room, the two officers following me. Here they cornered me and talked volubly for ten minutes, urging my permission to let them go over the lines and attack one last balloon that they had heard was still swinging back of the Meuse. They overcame every objection of mine with such earnestness that finally, against my best judgment, I acquiesced and permitted them to go. At this moment Major [Maxwell] Kirby, who had just joined Squadron 94 for a little experience in air fighting before taking command of a new group of squadrons that was being formed, and who as yet had never flown over the lines, stepped into the room and requested permission to join Dewitt and Fauntleroy in their expedition. Lieutenant Cook would go along with him, he said, and they would hunt in pairs.

Full of misgivings at my own weakness, I walked out to the field and watched the four pilots get away. I noted the time on my watch, noted that a heavy wind was blowing them away and would increase their difficulties in returning, blamed myself that I had permitted them to influence me against my judgment.

The weather grew steadily worse, rain fell, and the wind grew stronger. When darkness fell, shortly after four o'clock, I ordered all the lights turned on the field, and taking my seat at the mouth of our hangar I anxiously waited for a glimpse of the homecoming Spads. It was nearing the limit of their fuel supply.

Night fell and no aeroplanes appeared. The search-lights continued to throw their long fingers into the clouds, pointing the way home to any wandering scouts who might be lost in the storm. Foolish as it was to longer expect them, I could not order the lights extinguished and they shone on all through the night.

The next day was Sunday and another Decorations Ceremony was scheduled to take place at our field at eleven o'clock. A number of pilots from other aerodromes were coming over to receive the Distinguished Service Cross from the hands of General [Hunter] Liggett[1] for bravery and heroic exploits over enemy's lines. Several of our own group, including myself, were to be among the recipients.

The band played, generals addressed us, and all the men stood at attention in front of our line of fighting planes while the dignified ceremony was performed. Two more palms were presented to me to be attached to my decoration. The army orders were read aloud praising me for shooting down enemy aeroplanes. How bitter such compliments were to me that morning nobody ever suspected. Not a word had come from any of my four pilots.

In fact, a message had come in the night before that a Spad had collided in air with a French two-seater near Beaumont late that afternoon. A hurried investigation by telephone disclosed the fact that no other Spads were missing but our own.

---

[1] Liggett, an outstanding tactician, had by this time been promoted to command of the American First Army.

At the conclusion of the presentation of decorations I walked back to the hangar and put on my coat, for it was a freezing day and we had been forced to stand for half an hour without movement in dress tunic and breeches. The field was so thick with fog that the photographers present could scarcely get light enough to snap the group of officers standing in line. No aeroplanes could possibly be out today or I should have flown over to Beaumont at daybreak to ascertain which of my pilots had been killed there.

I fairly ran the rest of the way to my hangar where I demanded of the mechanics what news they had heard about Captain Fauntleroy. I was informed that he had just landed and had reported that Lieutenant Dewitt had crashed last night inside our lines but would be back during the course of the day. And to cap this joyful climax to a day's misery, I was told five minutes later at group headquarters that Major Kirby had just telephoned in that he had shot down an enemy aeroplane across the Meuse this morning at ten o'clock, after which he had landed at an aerodrome near the front and would return to us when the fog lifted!

Major Kirby's victory was quickly confirmed, later inquiries disclosing the wonderful fact that this first remarkable victory of his was in truth the last aeroplane shot down in the Great War! Our old Squadron 94 had won the first American victory over enemy aeroplanes when Alan Winslow and Douglas Campbell had dropped two biplane machines on the Toul aerodrome. Squadron 94 had been first to fly over the lines and had completed more hours flying at the front than any other American organization. It had won more victories than any other—and now, for the last word, it had the credit of bringing down the last enemy aeroplane of the war!

The story of Major Kirby's sensational victory can be told in a paragraph. He had become lost the night before and had landed on the first field he saw. Not realizing the importance of telephoning us of his safety, he took off early next morning to come home. This time he got lost in the fog that surrounded our district. When he again emerged into clear air he found he was over Etain, a small town just north of Verdun. And there flying almost alongside his Spad was another aeroplane which a second glance informed him was an enemy Fokker! Both pilots were so surprised for a moment that they simply gazed at each other. The Fokker pilot recovered his senses first and began a dive toward earth. Major Kirby immediately *piquéd* on his tail, followed him down to within fifty feet of the ground firing all the way. The Fokker crashed head on, and Kirby zoomed up just in time to avoid the same fate. With his usual modesty, Major Kirby insisted he had scared the pilot to his death. Thus ended the War in the Air on the American Front.

While listening to these details that evening after mess, our spirits bubbling over with excitement and happiness, the telephone sounded and I stepped over and took it up, waving the room to silence. It was a message to bring my husky braves over across to the

Squadron 95 mess to celebrate the beginning of a new era. I demanded of the speaker, (it was Jack [John L.] Mitchell, captain of Squadron 95) what he was talking about.

"Peace has been declared! No more fighting!" he shouted. *"C'est le finis de la guerre."*

Without reply, I dropped the phone and turned around and faced the pilots of Squadron 94. Not a sound was heard; every eye was on me but no one made a movement or drew a breath. It was one of those peculiar psychological moments when instinct tells everyone that something big is impending.

In the midst of this uncanny silence a sudden BOOM-BOOM of our Archy battery outside was heard. And then pandemonium broke loose. Shouting like mad, tumbling over one another in their excitement the daring young pilots of the Hat-in-the-Ring Squadron sensing the truth darted into trunks and kitbags, drew out revolvers, German lugers that some of them had found or bought as souvenirs from French *poilus,* Very pistols, and shooting tools of all descriptions, and burst out of doors. There the sky over our old aerodrome was aglow and shivering with bursts of fire. Searchlights were madly cavorting across the heavens, paling to dimness the thousands of colored lights that shot up from every conceivable direction. Shrill yells pierced the darkness around us, punctuated with the fierce rat-tat-tat of machine guns that now added their noise to the clamor. Roars of laughter and hysterical whoopings came to us from the men's quarters beside the hangars. Pistol shots were fired in salvos, filled and emptied again and again until the weapon became too hot to hold.

At the corner of our hangar I encountered a group of my pilots rolling out tanks of gasoline. Instead of attempting the impossible task of trying to stop them, I helped them get it through the mud and struck the match myself and lighted it. A dancing ring of crazy lunatics joined hands and circled around the blazing pyre, similar howling and revolving circuses surrounding several other burning tanks of good United States gasoline that would never more carry fighting aeroplanes over enemy lines. The stars were shining brightly overhead and the day's mist was gone. But at times even the stars were hidden by the thousands of rockets that darted up over our heads and exploded with their soft plonks, releasing varicolored lights that floated softly through this epochal night until they withered away and died. Star shells, parachute flares, and streams of Very lights continued to light our way through an aerodrome seemingly thronged with madmen. Everybody was laughing—drunk with the outgushing of their long pent-up emotions.

Another pilot, this one an Ace of Squadron 27, grasped me securely by the arm and shouted almost incredulously, *"We won't get shot at any more!"* Without waiting for a reply he hastened to another friend and repeated this important bit of information as though he were doubtful of a complete understanding on this trivial point. What sort of a new world will this be without the excitement of danger in it? How queer it will be in the future to fly over the dead line of the silent Meuse—that significant boundary line that was marked by Archy shells to warn the pilot of his entrance into danger.

How can one enjoy life without this highly spiced sauce of danger? What else is there left to living now that the zest and excitement of fighting aeroplanes are gone? Thoughts such as these held me entranced for the moment and were afterward recalled to illustrate how tightly strung were the nerves of these boys of twenty who had for continuous months been living on the very peaks of mental excitement.

In the mess hall of Mitchell's squadron we found gathered the entire officer personnel of the group. Orderlies were running back and forth with cups brimming with hastily concocted punch with which to drink to the success and personal appearance of every pilot in aviation. Songs were bellowed forth accompanied by crashing sounds from the piano—the proudest of 95's souvenirs, selected from an officer's mess of an abandoned German camp. Chairs and benches were pushed back to the walls and soon the whole roomful was dancing, struggling, and whooping for joy, to the imminent peril of the rather temporary walls and floor. Some unfortunate pilot fell, and in a trice everybody in the room was forming a pyramid on top of him. The appearance of the C.O. of the group brought the living mass to its feet in a score of rousing cheers to the best C.O. in France. Major Hartney was hoisted up on the piano, while a hundred voices shouted, "SPEECH—SPEECH!" No sooner did he open his lips than a whirlwind of sound from outside made him pause and reduced the room to quiet. But only for an instant.

"It's the Jazz Band from old 147!" yelled the pilots and like a tumultuous waterfall they poured *en masse* through a doorway that was only wide enough for one at a time.

Whooping, shrieking, and singing, the victors of some 400-odd combats with enemy airmen encircled the musicians from the enlisted men of Squadron 147. The clinging clay mud of France lay ankle deep around them. Within a minute the dancing throng had, with their hopping and skipping, plowed it into an almost bottomless bog. Someone went down, dragging down with him the portly bass drummer. Upon this foundation, human forms in the spotless uniforms of the American Air Service piled themselves until the entire group lay prostrate in one huge pyramid of joyous aviators. It was later bitterly disputed as to who was and who was not at the very bottom of this historic monument erected that night under the starry skies of France to celebrate the extraordinary fact that we had lived through the war and were not to be shot at to-morrow.

It was the *"finis de la guerre!"* It was the *finis d'aviation.* It was to us, perhaps unconsciously, the end of that intimate relationship that since the beginning of the war had cemented together brothers-in-arms to a closer fraternity than is known to any other friend-ship in the whole world. When again will that pyra-mid of entwined comrades—interlacing together in one mass boys from every State in our Union—when again will it be formed and bound together in mutual devotion?[2]

---

[2]While some of the foregoing description of the pandemonium that took place comes from the original text, Driggs wrote most of it based on his own memories of the occasion. The original lacks the panache of Driggs's vivid prose, showing once more the great role he played in making *Fighting the Flying Circus* the literary achievement that it is.

EPILOGUE

How can one enjoy life without
this highly spiced sauce of danger?
What else is left to living
now that the zest and excitement of
fighting airplanes are gone?

THESE POIGNANT WORDS, from the final chapter of *Fighting the Flying Circus,* provide a suitable introduction to the experiences awaiting Rickenbacker after he returned to America from the war. The rest of his life was a disappointing search for the fulfillment he had found in the perilous skies over the Western Front.

Rickenbacker received a frenzied welcome in 1919 that became steadily less rewarding as multitudes showered him with adulation. He was unprepared for the media pressure that came with being a celebrity and had nightmares as he crossed the country in Pullman cars. Waving to crowds in Los Angeles "in a mock-up of an airplane covered completely with flowers" made him feel "like an idiot." At one point he went back to Columbus after suffering a reported "nervous breakdown." He "wondered which was worse, combat or the onslaught of well-wishers, hero-worshippers, and fast-buck operators."[1]

What Rickenbacker wanted most was to become an

[1]Rickenbacker, *Autobiography*, 141-142; newspaper clippings, Scrapbook I, AUA.

aircraft manufacturer. But the rational side of him persuaded him that the time was not ripe. Postwar markets were too glutted with surplus planes to make his dream practicable.

Seeking solitude in a remote area in New Mexico, Rickenbacker pondered what to do. Reluctantly, he went back to the familiar world of the automobile industry. The magic of his fame attracted financial backing, and he poured his energy into making a car whose alluring style and innovative features showed his artistic flair and love of machinery. The fact that the vehicle bore his name only compounded his dismay when the Rickenbacker Motor Company failed in 1927, leaving him deeply in debt.

Rickenbacker could have avoided the burden of his obligations by taking advantage of bankruptcy, but honorably chose not to do so, using every means of turning an honest dollar until his debts were retired. His frustration intensified when Florida Airways, a mail-carrying venture with his wartime comrade, Reed Chambers, met the same fate as his automotive firm.

Rickenbacker believed too deeply in free enterprise to concede defeat. Backed by bankers in Detroit, he bought the Indianapolis Speedway. Meanwhile, he pursued one aeronautical enterprise after another, but none worked out as he had hoped. In 1935, he took charge of Eastern Air Transport, a General Motors subsidiary whose airplanes were obsolete and whose prospects were dubious.

In three years Rickenbacker transformed Eastern

A joyful Rickenbacker after sea rescue, 1942

Rickenbacker during his tenure at Eastern Airlines

Courtesy National Air and Space Museum, Smithsonian Institution

413

into a highly profitable firm only to learn, in 1938, that General Motors planned to sell it to rental car magnate John Hertz. Eastern could not possibly have fetched what Hertz offered for it—$3 million—had Rickenbacker not built it into a flourishing enterprise.

Furious, Rickenbacker persuaded GM's chief executive, Alfred Sloan, to give him time to find backing to counter Hertz's offer with one of his own. He foiled Hertz by raising $3.5 million among investors, including Laurance Rockefeller. Thus Rickenbacker became president of a new business entity, Eastern Air Lines. By 1941 its routes stretched from the Mississippi River to the Atlantic Ocean. It had an argosy of aircraft that he proudly called "The Great Silver Fleet." Its profits were the envy of the industry.

Then came a succession of adversities that would have tried the spirit of even the most resolute warrior.

Rickenbacker had not suffered a scratch in World War I. In 1941, however, he almost died when an airliner in which he was flying crashed near Atlanta, Georgia. Despite receiving multiple injuries, he made a remarkable recovery. While Rickenbacker was convalescing, the Japanese attacked Pearl Harbor and America entered World War II. Despite his battered condition, he wanted to do his part.

During the war he performed special missions. In October 1942, while Rickenbacker was crossing the Pacific with a secret message to General Douglas MacArthur, the plane in which he was flying became lost between Hawaii and Canton Island and had to be ditched in the ocean. Rickenbacker and seven companions, one of whom died, drifted on rubber rafts for almost twenty-four days and endured harrowing privations until they were rescued. Despite dehydration and severe weight loss, Rickenbacker delivered his message to MacArthur and came home to a hero's deserved welcome.

Rickenbacker was physically impaired when he returned to Eastern Air Lines after the war. No matter how many liquids he drank, he was always thirsty. As a result of the Atlanta crash, one of his legs was shorter than the other, and he walked with a limp. He was in constant pain and needed frequent osteopathic treatments.

For a few years Eastern remained extremely profitable. But Rickenbacker made critical mistakes in judgment that gradually undermined its fortunes. During the 1930s he had become a bitter critic of Franklin D. Roosevelt and the New Deal. After the war, he became embroiled in strife with the Civil Aeronautics Board (CAB), a federal agency that closely regulated the airline industry. Beginning in 1945, the CAB awarded new routes to smaller airlines, particularly Delta, that competed with Eastern in markets it had formerly had to itself. Rickenbacker was a frugal manager. He was indignant that airlines with higher costs than Eastern got subsidies that it did not.

Rickenbacker was partly to blame for his troubles. He was openly contemptuous of federal bureaucrats, which did not endear him to the CAB when important route cases were decided. His penny-pinching habits resulted in poor service to the traveling public. He let himself be guided by emotion and loyalty to friends instead of exercising hard-headed business judgment. By placing members of two unions in the same cockpit crews, he caused jurisdictional strikes that shut down Eastern while competitors continued to fly. He guessed wrong in making the transition to the jet era and chose a turboprop, the Lockheed Electra, that federal regulators saddled with speed restrictions after it crashed while being used by other airlines. Delta, which made wiser choices, benefited greatly from Eastern's misfortunes.[2]

Trying to solve Eastern's problems without humiliating a beloved leader, the directors made Rickenbacker chairman of the board and appointed a new chief executive. But the company was plagued by factional disputes. A much-desired merger with American Airlines was vetoed by the Justice Department. In 1963 Rickenbacker was forced to retire. He did so with dignity, warmly welcoming Eastern's new head, Floyd D. Hall.[3] Inwardly, however, he was devastated by what had happened.

After retiring, Rickenbacker traveled widely with his wife, Adelaide. He expressed his ultra-conservative

2. W. David Lewis and Wesley Phillips Newton, *Delta: The History of an Airline* (Athens: University of Georgia Press, 1979), 271.

3. Robert J. Serling, *From the Captain to the Colonel: An Informal History of Eastern Airlines* (New York: Dial Press, 1980), 374-385.

political and economic views vigorously. In 1967 he published his autobiography, which was ghostwritten by a Virginia newspaperman, Booten Herndon. It became a best-seller.

During the final years of his life, Rickenbacker wrote and spoke about international affairs and traveled widely. On one of his trips he went to East Germany and had lunch with two surviving veterans of the Flying Circus, against which he had fought so many years before. Government officials gave him permission to visit the Hero Veteran Graveyard in East Berlin, where he paid homage at the graves of Germany's greatest World War I aces: Oswald Boelcke, Ernst Udet, and Manfred von Richthofen.

But Rickenbacker's life became increasingly barren, and his health deteriorated. In 1972, just before his eighty-second birthday, he had a stroke. Rallying, he took Adelaide to Switzerland, but soon after then arrived, he was breathing with difficulty. Taken to a hospital in Zürich, he died of pneumonia in the land of his ancestors on 23 July 1973. News of his death brought an outpouring of tributes from all over the world. His ashes were interred in Columbus while jet interceptors from his old unit, now known as the 94th Fighter Squadron, roared overhead in a final tribute to America's Ace of Aces.

ADDITIONAL READING

In addition to the sources cited in the text, the following books contain additional information about World War I and the airplanes, aviators, and aerial battles of the Great War.

Angelucci, Enzo. *The Rand McNally Encyclopedia of Military Aircraft 1914-1980.* New York: Military Press, 1983.

Bingham, Hiram. *An Explorer in the Air Service.* New Haven: Yale University Press, 1920.

Bowen, Ezra, et al. *Knights of the Air.* Alexandria, Va.: Time-Life Books, 1980.

Chandler, Charles Def., and Frank P. Laum. *How Our Army Got Wings.* New York: Ronald Press, 1943.

Coffman, Edward M. *The War to End All Wars.* Madison, Wis.: University of Wisconsin Press, 1986.

Cooke, James J. *The U.S. Air Service in the Great War, 1917-1919.* Westport, Conn.: Praeger, 1996

Flammer, Philip M. *The Vivid Air: The Lafayette Escadrille.* Athens: University of Georgia Press, 1981.

Franks, Norman L. R., Frank W. Bailey, and Russell Guest. *Above the Lines: The Aces and Fighter Units of the German Air Service.* London: Grub Street, 1993.

Gilbert, Martin. *The First World War.* New York: Henry Holt and Company, 1994.

Hall, Norman S. *The Balloon Buster: Frank Luke of Arizona.* Garden City, N.Y.: Doubleday, Doran & Company, Inc., 1928.

Hudson, James J. *Hostile Skies: A Combat History of the American Air Service in World War I.* Syracuse: Syracuse University Press, 1968.

Kennett, Lee. *The First Air War, 1914-1918.* New York: Free Press, 1991.

Lawson, Eric, and Jane Lawson. *The First Air Campaign, August 1914-November 1918.* Conshohocken, Pa.: Combined Books, 1996.

Mason, Herbert M., Jr. *The Lafayette Escadrille.* New York: Smithmark Publishers, Inc., 1995.

Maurer, Maurer, ed. *The U.S. Air Service in World War I.* 4 volumes. Washington, D.C.: Office of Air Force History. 1978-1979.

Meijering, Piet Hein. *Signed with Their Honor: Air Chivalry During Two World Wars.* New York: Paragon House, 1988.

Mitchell, William. *Memories of World War I.* New York: Random House, 1960.

Morrow, John H., Jr. *The Great War in the Air.* Washington: Smithsonian Institution Press, 1992.

Rawlings, John D. R. *The History of the Royal Air Force.* New York: Crescent Books, 1984.

Spick, Mike. *The Ace Factor: Air Combat & the Role of Situational Awareness.* Shrewsbury, U.K.: Airlife Publishing, 1988.

Stallings, Laurence. *The Doughboys.* New York: Harper & Row, 1963.

Sweetser, Arthur. *The American Air Service.* New York: D. Appleton and Co., 1919.

Index

INDEX

Albatros C-X, C-XII, 73, 114n, 115–116, 118

Albatros D-III, l, 56n

Albatros D-Va, l, 21, 51, 64, 67, 84, 97–99, 106, 124–126, 133–136

Atkinson, Bert M., 190–191, 195, 198, 205, 217

Avery, Walter L., 339

Baer, Paul F., 275, 281

Ball, Albert, 296

Baylies, Frank L., 144, 275, 282

Bishop, William, 296

Bleckley, Erwin E., 326n

Boelcke, Oswald, liv–lv, 418

Bonnell, Geoffrey H., 215

Breguet aircraft, 371

Bristol aircraft, l

Brooklands Motor Speedway, xxxix

Brotherton, William E., 361

Bruce, Alexander B., 254

Buddy, Harold, 258

Buford, Edward Jr., 216, 229n, 232

Campbell, Douglas, lix, lxx–lxxi, 9, 12, 15–21, 27, 38, 41, 44–45, 58, 121–128, 144, 147–148, 150–154, 172–178, 233, 281n, 389, 404

Casgrain, Wilfrid V., 138, 141–142

Caudron aircraft, xlv, 147n

Cazeau, gunnery school at, xlvi, 33, 71, 143n

Chambers, Reed M., 37–38, 41–47, 83–84, 91, 95, 104, 105n, 107, 110, 205, 214, 233, 260, 263–264, 275, 285, 297, 305, 309, 311, 324, 334, 336, 343, 349–350, 353, 355–356, 361, 365, 369–372, 389, 392–393, 414

Chapman, Charles, 70, 87

Chapman, Victor, 35

Cignones (Storks), French elite unit, 282, 320

Coatalen, Louis, xxxvi, xxxix

Cook, H. Weir, 309, 311, 325, 327–328, 332, 339–340, 389, 394, 402

Coolidge, Hamilton, 188–190, 308–309, 325, 327–328, 332, 338–340, 342, 353, 355–356, 361, 379–381, 386–389

Cooper, Captain, 362–365, 369, 372

Coppens, Willy, 206–207, 212

Crocker, Charles I., 338

Croix de Guerre, 60, 87–89

Curtis, Edward P., 242, 258, 342

Curtiss JN-4, 147

Davis, Philip W., 64, 67

DeHavilland DH-4, xlvii, 276n

DeHavilland DH-9, 121, 122n

Dewitt, John, 401–402, 404

Dodd, Townsend F., xl–xliii

Driggs, Laurence La Tourette, xxiii, lxiii-lxiv, lxvii-lxxii, 6on, 310n, 332n, 343n, 372, 383, 410n

Duesenberg, August & Frederick, xxxiii, xxxv

8th (French) Army, 59–60, 86, 120

Evitt, Raymond W., 394

Fauntleroy, Cedric G., 401–402, 404

5th (American) Army Corps, 260

1st (American) Army Corps, 260, 403n

1st (American) Pursuit Group , lx, 186n, 191n, 217

1st (American) Pursuit Wing, 191n, 334

Foch, Marshal Ferdinand, 234

Fokker D-VII, li, 30, 134, 218, 227, 231, 245–249, 254, 275, 277–282, 284, 292–295, 303–305, 312, 314, 324, 333, 340–342, 350–352, 356–360, 373, 377–378, 381–385, 387, 389, 393–395, 405

Fokker E-III Eindecker, xlix

Fonck, Rene, 89, 282n, 296

Foulois, Benjamin D., 185

4th (American) Army Corps, 260

Frayer, Lee, xxviii, xxx, xxxiv, lv

Garnsey, Edward G., 389

Garros, Roland, xlix

Gerard, French General, 59d, 86, 88–89, 120

Gnome monosoupape engine, lii-liii, lix, 104

Goettler, Harold F., 326n

Grant, Alfred A., 258, 320

Green, M. Edwin, 71–72, 74, 76–79

Guynemer, Georges, 282n, 296, 322

Halberstadt reconnaissance plane, 294n

Hall, Floyd D., 417

Hall, James Norman, 31–32, 53–60, 71–81, 85, 87, 100, 118, 126–127, 136, 297

Hallion, Richard P., 250n

Handley-Page bombers, 198–199

Hannover CL-3, 185–186, 336, 343–344, 347, 349, 352, 361–362, 365–366, 369–372

Harmon, Millard F., 28

Hartney, Harold E., lx-lxi, 215, 222, 258, 286, 295–297, 325–326, 372, 408–409

Hat-in-the-Ring emblem, origin of, 35–36

Herndon, Booten, 418

Hispano-Suiza engine, liii, lix-lxi, 185, 330

Holden, Lansing C., 258

Huffer, Jean W. F. M., lix, 35–36, 47, 63, 83n, 85, 181

Independent Air Force (British), 121, 198, 355

Indianapolis Speedway, xxxvi, 414

Issoudun, American training base at, xliii-xlv, 147

Jeffers, John N., 287-288, 352, 389
Johnson, Davenport, 28-29

Kaye, Samuel, 324, 352, 393-394
Kirby, Maxwell, 143, 402, 404-405
Kurtz, Paul B., 103-107, 110-112

Lafayette Escadrille, xl, xliv-xlv, lix, 11, 31, 80, 83n, 118, 281
Lafayette Flying Corps, 35n, 143n
Legion of Honor, 89n, 320
Libby, Frederick, 144
Liberty engine, 121, 122n, 276n, 363-365, 380-382
Liggett, Hunter, 120, 403
Loerzer, Bruno, 227, 354
Loomis, William F., 189-190, 205
Low, Seth, 390
Lufbery, Raoul, xxiii, lv, lix, lxiii, 11, 15-21, 27, 51, 61-64, 70n, 80, 92, 95, 117-120, 127, 144, 255, 275, 281-282, 297, 389
Luke, Frank, 258, 285-287, 290-298, 308, 319-322, 326n, 392
L.V.G., German reconnaissance plane, 294-295, 303-304, 306, 342

MacArthur, Douglas, 415-416
McArthur, John, 237-239

Magoun, Francis P., 144
Marr, Kenneth, lix, 83, 181-182, 218, 254, 297
Medal of Honor, lxii, 287n, 305n, 322n, 326n, 359n
Meissner, James A., lxx-lxxi, 64, 67-69, 78, 87-88, 100, 131, 136-138, 173-178, 185, 191-192, 197, 205, 214, 233, 258, 360-361, 363-365, 369, 389-390
Miller, James, xliv, 27-29, 127, 147
Miller, Zenos R., 234-236
Mitchell, John A., 127
Mitchell, John L., 131, 137-138, 258, 406, 408
Mitchell, William ("Billy"), xlii-xliv, lxi, lxvii, lxix, 85-86, 88, 120, 122n, 185n, 255n, 325-327, 333
Morane-Saulnier aircraft, xlv

91st (American) Observation Squadron, 189
94th (American) Pursuit Squadron, xlvi, lix-lxi, lxx, 8-10, 31, 33, 37, 69, 71, 103, 127, 131, 138, 143,148, 154, 164, 181n, 186n, 187, 191n, 215-217, 221, 228, 239, 256, 259, 281n, 297-298, 301-303, 308, 327, 334, 352-353, 392, 398, 401, 404, 406
95th (American) Pursuit Squadron, 28, 33, 71,132, 137-138, 141, 143n, 188, 191n, 215-216, 228-231, 256, 258 , 276, 285, 342, 373, 406, 408
Nieuport 17, l, 147n

Nieuport 23, 147n

Nieuport 28, l-liv, lix, 12, 17, 20, 31–33, 47–49, 57, 62, 64, 67, 69, 72, 76–78, 81, 82n, 87, 90, 98–100, 102, 104, 110, 114n, 115, 117, 126–127, 130–131, 133–136, 138, 142, 150–152, 160, 164–165, 169, 171, 174–175, 179–182, 185, 189, 208n, 209n, 232, 360

Nutt, Alan, 389

103rd (American) Pursuit Squadron, 281

139th (American) Pursuit Squadron, 282

147th (American) Pursuit Squadron, 191n, 215–216, 228, 256, 258, 353, 356–358, 361, 390, 409

185th (American) Pursuit Squadron, 313n, 390–391

Ordre Pour le Mérite ("Blue Max"), 89n

Palmer, William W., 309, 342

Pershing, John J., xli, lx–lxi, lxx, 7, 28n, 198n, 257n

Peterson, David McK., 31, 37, 41, 43, 69–70, 87–88, 258, 297

Pfalz D-III, 56–58, 74–75, 79, 122–126

Putnam, David E., 144, 275, 282

Reinhard, Wilhelm, 227

Rembercourt, aerodrome at, lxi, 77, 256

Richthofen, Manfred von, xix, 227n, 250n, 296, 384, 418

Rickenbacher, Elizabeth, xxiii

Rickenbacher, Wilhelm, xxiii

Rickenbacker, Adelaide, 417

Rickenbacker, Edward V., parentage and youth, xxiii–xxiv, xxvii; automotive and racing career, xxviii–xxx, xxxiii–xxxvi; enlists as driver on General Pershing's staff, xli–xlii; becomes combat pilot, xliv–xlvi; takes command of 94th PS, lix–lxii; conducts sortie that ultimately wins him Medal of Honor in 1930, lxii; has first patrol, 11–12, 15–22; wins first victory, 53–60; as flight commander, 81–82; receives *Croix de Guerre,* 86–90; escapes death in wing-shredding episode, 97–102; pays tribute to Campbell as first official American ace, 143–144, 147–154; discusses importance of aerial observation, 157–158; visits Paris and learns he has become an ace, 183–185; is hospitalized, 215–218; returns to duty with Spad XIII, 218, 221–222; has ear surgery in Paris 233; visits younger brother at nearby camp, 251–253; discusses failure to supply American pilots with parachutes, 255; becomes American Ace of Aces, 279–285; takes command of 94th Pursuit Squadron, 297–298, 301–302; secures official confirmation of victories, 305–307; emergency landing with damaged propeller, 312–314; takes part in Meuse-Argonne offensive, 353–361; is frustrated in attempt to capture Fokker D-VII intact, 381–386; discusses record of 94th Pursuit Squadron, 389–392; wins final victories, 392–400; returns home, 411, 414; as chief executive of Eastern Air Lines, 414–415; survives plane crash, 415–416; encounters business reverses, 416–417

Rickenbacker, Louis E., 251n

Rickenbacker Motor Company, 414

Rockefeller, Laurance S., 415

Roosevelt, Edith Carow, 229n

Roosevelt, Franklin D., 416

Roosevelt, Quentin, xxiii, 228–232

Roosevelt, Theodore, xxvii, lxvii, 229n

Ross, Cleo, 213n

Royal Air Service, xxxix, lxvii

Rumpler observation plane, 113–114, 148–151, 153, 159–163, 166–170, 173–176, 178–181, 199, 222

Salmson 2A2, 189, 245, 248–249

Saunders, Raymond J., 389

2nd (American) Pursuit Group, 280

Sewell, Sumner, 258, 276

Siemens-Schuckert D-IV, 354

Sloan, Alfred, 415

Smythe, Walter, 113–114, 117, 128–130, 159–160, 162, 165, 171, 254

Sopwith Camel, 373, 390–391

Sopwith Pup, 1

Spaatz (Spatz), Carl, xlvi

Spad VII, 1

Spad XIII, li–liv, lix–lxi, 21, 48, 185, 218, 221, 232–233, 237, 241, 245–249, 279–280, 288, 293–294, 304, 314, 328, 336, 339–341, 350–351, 355, 358–362, 370–371, 377–379, 381, 385, 402, 405

Sparks, Wiley B., 342

Taylor, Frank J., 197–200

Taylor, William H., 258

Taylor, Thorne, 185, 205, 233, 297, 309, 338, 342, 365–366, 370, 372, 389

Thaw, William, 35, 89, 281

3rd (American) Balloon Company, 284

3rd (American) Pursuit Group, 282

Thom, Karl, 232

Three-Fingered Lake, 277, 289–291, 333

Tobin, Edgar G., 282

Trenchard, Hugh, 121, 122n, 355

26th (American) Division, 87

27th (American) Pursuit Squadron, 191n, 216–217, 228, 234, 237, 256, 259, 285, 290–291, 298, 313, 342, 353, 355, 359, 407

Udet, Ernst, 418

United Press Association, 197

U.S. Army
    Air Service, xliii-xliv, 12, 80,
        110, 409
    Signal Corps, xl-xlii, xlv-
        xlvii, lxviii, 251
U.S. War Department, lxviii

Vasconcells, Jerry, 313, 319, 390
Vickers machine gun, 150, 162,
    179
Villeneuve-les-Vertus ,
    aerodrome at, xlvi, lv, lix,12,
    24, 28-29

Walters, Gary, 36
Wanamaker, Walter B.,
    217-218
Wehner, Joseph F., 290-293,
    295, 297n
Wentworth, John, 36
White, Wilbur, 357-359,
    361
Wilson, Woodrow, lxviii
Winslow, Alan, 38, 41, 44-45,
    185, 233, 239-240, 404
Winslow, Paul, 240
Wood, Leonard, lxvii

List of The Lakeside Classics

The Lakeside Classics

Number	Title	Year
1.	The Autobiography of Benjamin Franklin . . .	1903
2.	Inaugural Addresses of the Presidents of the United States from Washington to Lincoln . .	1904
3.	Inaugural Addresses of the Presidents of the United States from A. Johnson to T. Roosevelt .	1905
4.	Fruits of Solitude by William Penn	1906
5.	Memorable American Speeches I. The Colonial Period	1907
6.	Memorable American Speeches II. Democracy and Nationality	1908
7.	Memorable American Speeches III. Slavery	1909
8.	Memorable American Speeches IV. Secession, War, Reconstruction	1910
9.	The Autobiography of Gurdon Saltonstall Hubbard	1911
10.	Reminiscences of Early Chicago	1912
11.	Reminiscences of Chicago During the Forties and Fifties.	1913
12.	Reminiscences of Chicago During the Civil War .	1914
13.	Reminiscences of Chicago During the Great Fire.	1915
14.	Life of Black Hawk	1916
15.	The Indian Captivity of O. M. Spencer	1917
16.	Pictures of Illinois One Hundred Years Ago . .	1918
17.	A Woman's Story of Pioneer Illinois by Christiana Holmes Tillson	1919

Number	*Title*	*Year*
18.	The Conquest of the Illinois by George Rogers Clark	1920
19.	Alexander Henry's Travels and Adventures in the Years 1760-1776	1921
20.	John Long's Voyages and Travels in the Years 1768-1788	1922
21.	Adventures of the First Settlers on the Oregon or Columbia River by Alexander Ross	1923
22.	The Fur Hunters of the Far West by Alexander Ross	1924
23.	The Southwestern Expedition of Zebulon M. Pike	1925
24.	Commerce of the Prairies by Josiah Gregg . . .	1926
25.	Death Valley in '49 by William L. Manly	1927
26.	Bidwell's Echoes of the Past—Steele's In Camp and Cabin.	1928
27.	Kendall's Texan Santa Fe Expedition	1929
28.	Pattie's Personal Narrative	1930
29.	Alexander Mackenzie's Voyage to the Pacific Ocean in 1793	1931
30.	Wau-Bun, The "Early Day" in the North-West by Mrs. John H. Kinzie.	1932
31.	Forty Years a Fur Trader by Charles Larpenteur .	1933
32.	Narrative of the Adventures of Zenas Leonard. .	1934
33.	Kit Carson's Autobiography	1935
34.	A True Picture of Emigration by Rebecca Burlend	1936
35.	The Bark Covered House by William Nowlin . .	1937
36.	The Border and the Buffalo by John R. Cook . .	1938
37.	Vanished Arizona by Martha Summerhayes . .	1939

Number	*Title*	*Year*
38.	War on the Detroit by Thomas Verchères de Boucherville and James Foster	1940
39.	Army Life in Dakota by Philippe de Trobriand .	1941
40.	The Early Day of Rock Island and Davenport by J. W. Spencer and J. M. D. Burrows	1942
41.	Six Years with the Texas Rangers by James B. Gillett	1943
42.	Growing Up with Southern Illinois by Daniel Harmon Brush	1944
43.	A History of Illinois, I, by Gov. Thomas Ford . .	1945
44.	A History of Illinois, II, by Gov. Thomas Ford .	1946
45.	The Western Country in the 17th Century by Lamothe Cadillac and Pierre Liette	1947
46.	Across the Plains in Forty-nine by Reuben Cole Shaw	1948
47.	Pictures of Gold Rush California.	1949
48.	Absaraka, Home of the Crows by Mrs. Margaret I. Carrington.	1950
49.	The Truth about Geronimo by Britton Davis . .	1951
50.	My Life on the Plains by General George A. Custer	1952
51.	Three Years Among the Indians and Mexicans by General Thomas James	1953
52.	A Voyage to the Northwest Coast of America by Gabriel Franchère	1954
53.	War-Path and Bivouac by John F. Finerty . . .	1955
54.	Milford's Memoir by Louis Leclerc de Milford .	1956
55.	Uncle Dick Wootton by Howard Louis Conard .	1957
56.	The Siege of Detroit in 1763	1958

Number	Title	Year
57.	Among the Indians by Henry A. Boller	1959
58.	Hardtack and Coffee by John D. Billings	1960
59.	Outlines from the Outpost by John Esten Cooke	1961
60.	Colorado Volunteers in New Mexico, 1862 by Ovando J. Hollister	1962
61.	Private Smith's Journal	1963
62.	Two Views of Gettysburg by Sir. A. J. L. Fremantle and Frank Haskell	1964
63.	Dakota War Whoop by Harriet E. Bishop McConkey	1965
64.	Honolulu by Laura Fish Judd	1966
65.	Three Years in the Klondike by Jeremiah Lynch	1967
66.	Two Years' Residence on the English Prairie of Illinois by John Woods	1968
67.	John D. Young and the Colorado Gold Rush	1969
68.	My Experiences in the West by John S. Collins	1970
69.	Narratives of Colonial America, 1704-1765	1971
70.	Pioneers by Noah Harris Letts and Thomas Allen Banning, 1825-1865	1972
71.	Excursion Through America by Nicolaus Mohr	1973
72.	A Frenchman in Lincoln's America, Volume I, by Ernest Duvergier de Hauranne	1974
73.	A Frenchman in Lincoln's America, Volume II, by Ernest Duvergier de Hauranne	1975
74.	Narratives of the American Revolution	1976
75.	Advocates and Adversaries by Robert R. Rose	1977
76.	Hell among the Yearlings by Edmund Randolph	1978
77.	A Frontier Doctor by Henry F. Hoyt	1979

The Lakeside Classics

435

Number	Title	Year
78.	Mrs. Hill's Journal—Civil War Reminiscences by Sarah Jane Full Hill	1980
79.	Skyward by Rear Admiral Richard E. Byrd	1981
80.	Helldorado by William M. Breakenridge	1982
81.	Mark Twain's West	1983
82.	Frontier Fighter by George W. Coe	1984
83.	Buckskin and Blanket Days by Thomas Henry Tibbles	1985
84.	Autobiography of an English Soldier in the United States Army by George Ballentine	1986
85.	Life of Tom Horn	1987
86.	Children of Ol' Man River by Billy Bryant	1988
87.	Westward Journeys by Jesse A. Applegate and Lavinia Honeyman Porter	1989
88.	Narrative of My Captivity among the Sioux Indians by Fanny Kelly	1990
89.	We Pointed Them North by E. C. "Teddy Blue" Abbott and Helena Huntington Smith	1991
90.	A Texas Ranger by N. A. Jennings	1992
91.	From Mexican Days to the Gold Rush by James W. Marshall and E. Gould Buffum	1993
92.	My Life East and West by William S. Hart	1994
93.	The Logbook of the Captain's Clerk by John S. Sewell	1995
94.	Arctic Explorations by Elisha Kent Kane, M. D., U. S. N.	1996
95.	Fighting the Flying Circus by Capt. Edward V. Rickenbacker	1997

Designed, typeset, printed, and bound by
R.R. Donnelley & Sons Company.
Text was set and pages output by ComCom,
the R.R. Donnelley composition facility
located in Allentown, Pennsylvania.
The body typeface is 11/12 pt. Bulmer.
Images were scanned and proofed
on state-of-the-art equipment in the
Crawfordsville, Indiana,
Book Manufacturing Division
electronic prepress center.
Maps were created by GeoSystems of
Lancaster, Pennsylvania.
Electronic information was converted into
press-ready plates using computer-to-plate technology.
The book was printed and bound
in the Crawfordsville Book Manufacturing Division.
Paper stock is 50-pound
White Lakeside Classics Opaque,
a 50-percent recycled sheet manufactured by Glatfelter.
Cloth for the one-piece case binding is
Roxite C Vellum Chocolate Brown,
manufactured by Holliston Mills, Inc.